B&T
$10.00

THE DEVELOPMENT OF
MODERN ITALY

THE DEVELOPMENT OF
MODERN ITALY

BY

CECIL J. S. SPRIGGE

NEW YORK

Howard Fertig

1969

First published in 1943 by Gerald Duckworth & Co., Ltd.
Copyright 1944 by Yale University Press

HOWARD FERTIG, INC. EDITION 1969
Published by arrangement with Gerald Duckworth & Co., Ltd.

Library of Congress Catalog Card Number: 68-9633

PRINTED IN THE UNITED STATES OF AMERICA
BY NOBLE OFFSET PRINTERS, INC.

TO THE
MEMORY OF MY FATHER
S. S. S.

'Nil me poeniteat . . . patris hujus'

CONTENTS

INTRODUCTION: BRITAIN AND THE ITALIAN PROSPECT . 7

I. THE TRIUMPH OF PIEDMONT 19

II. THE DOMINION OF DRYASDUST 47

III. GOVERNMENT BY MAN OF DESTINY 62

IV. POWER WITHOUT GLORY: GIOLITTI 72

V. NATIONAL SOUL-SEARCHING 89

VI. WAR AND REVOLUTION: A REHEARSAL . . . 98

VII. WAR AND REVOLUTION: THE GREAT TEST . . . 112

VIII. EXIT GIOLITTI 123

IX. WAR; BUT WHAT FOR? 135

X. DEFEAT BY VICTORY 153

XI. STILLBIRTH OF A DEMOCRACY 168

XII. MUSSOLINI FINDS HIS WAY 193

TABLEAU OF FASCISM'S CAREER IN POWER . . . 204

POSTSCRIPT 206

NOTES ON SOURCES AND LITERATURE 207

INDEX 213

INTRODUCTION

BRITAIN AND THE ITALIAN PROSPECT

1. *Britain and Europe.* Even among the problems of Britain's new relations to the European continent, that of making contact with a mortified and depressed Italy may appear outstandingly baffling and repellent, and many pretexts may be found for neglecting it. Difficult as it is to strike the right line of a British policy towards Italy, is it even wise to try to do so? Does not British membership of the United Nations mean that a world policy has already been agreed upon in principle? Has any nation in regard to any detailed problem, even one so big as that of its whole relation to an ex-enemy, either the need or the duty to go beyond applying in detail the principles of the Atlantic Charter?

There can be no such exemption from politics in the name of high principles.

Some guidance these principles do indeed give us. But they are affirmations of a desire to solve problems fairly and decently, not a prescription of how to solve them. Concrete solutions mean the reaching of agreement on defined issues by the representatives of contrasting interests—in the present state of mind of mankind national interests. The unity of the United Nations tempers their single policies: it does not, and cannot, supersede them.

Many, however, may think that a British policy towards Italy is part of a complex programme which can well be left for consideration until our great Allies have spoken and acted—and set new limits upon our own freedom of action. Some of the Allies agree with them. Candid friends to an overstrained veteran, they recommend the reduction of British world commitments to a minimum. British victory will in their view have served its best purpose by facilitating the world leadership of more resolute, consequential and ruthless powers.

Among ourselves many refuse to look beyond the prime aim of procuring a peace of iron strength to ensure our property and our security against future wars. What more 'policy' is needed than the permanent disarmament and disablement of formidable

7

enemies, and the denial of opportunities of mischief to the others? they ask. Even these people will, of course, agree that there must be territorial and other terms in the peace settlement between Britain and Italy as between all participants in the war. 'Policy' in this introduction means something more fundamental. By a British policy towards Italy is meant an effort on the part of Britain to profit by the existence of Italy, to bear Italy in mind as a factor worth influencing and capable of conferring benefit, both in the handling of the peace settlement and in the working out of a post-war relationship.

The question here at issue is whether on a broad view of the future the issues arising between the two nations should be dealt with on the British side as a matter of detail and routine, or in a consciously purposive manner as a distinct and important feature of a national policy towards the states of Europe.

The idea of a natural intercourse and cohabitation between each of the nations of Europe and the British nation standing among them as a courageous and generous pioneer is to many people a frightening one. It evokes images of baffling entanglements. Wearied minds yearn for *dis*entanglement from alien problems which would tax British strength. But since Britain and the British Empire cannot, it is recognized, isolate themselves in the world, as the next best course it is hoped at least to limit sustained contacts to an association with a few great powers, perhaps only two, for the maintenance of external world order.

The psychology of the war itself overclouds the thought of our future relations with Europe, impeding a bold computation of the advantages to our safety, our wealth and our higher well-being which might accrue from them. Even our European allies are sometimes, to speak frankly, felt to be encumbered with problems which render their friendship burdensome. In its first phase as a series of campaigns fought by Continental allies with British support, the war was a tale of gallant failures. Only when two vast powers from the West and the East were dragged by our enemies into the war did the United Nations become a formidable world coalition. The task of learning to view Poland, Norway, Greece, Holland and Belgium, the Czech nation, the Serbs and Southern Slavs as not latent but actual creative forces will not be easy for Englishmen who for years have perforce thought of these as martyred nations.

Loyalty and experience demand in any case that these allied nations which have suffered in the common cause shall receive the first attention of Britain while they engage upon the reconstruction of their national lives. The fragmentation of their energies into national units too small to weigh in the counsels and contests of the world, unless marshalled by some leadership which in 1939 did not exist, now masks their importance. The leader to which these nations look is England. For all of them England had represented a hope or a guarantee of the consolidation of victories over tyranny, thanks to the spectacle which Britain so long exemplified of a concilation of order and freedom, tradition and progress. On this high plane as well as on humbler and more popular planes a European task awaits Britain and cannot be shirked unless what we took up arms for in 1939 is forsworn.

2. *The Anglo-Italian Future.* Our first thought in regard to Europe must be for our European allies. But what of our enemy in the Mediterranean? Must we take an aftermath of stifled vengefulness for the punishments meted out to the Italians by the United Nations to be Fate's own prescription for the Anglo-Italian relations of the next generation? Or does Fate at best prescribe a sullen distance between two nations which after trying out amity and enmity will have no more to say to each other? Such will be the consequences of the Anglo-Italian war unless a clear and resolute will is at work to correct them.

It will seem to many in Britain that strategic safeguards secured against Italy may close the chapter of our reciprocal intimacy as friends and enemies (enmity, too, being a sort of intimacy) who were unsatisfactory friends and unequal enemies.

To many in Italy it will in that case seem opportune to await sullenly a chance of taking revenge or at least of making good bitter losses by assisting in the humiliation of that particular victorious power which will appear to have principally compassed Italy's defeat.

To this end will be turned the energies of a diplomacy served by some of the best brains in Europe eager to subvert our understandings with other nations and responsive to every blandishment of others more radically desirous of revenge. Is all this inevitable?

3. *The Problem of Fascism.* The question is raised here not because any direct answer is to be offered. The future of Anglo-Italian relations cannot here be discussed in detail nor is this book concerned directly even with their past. Its concern is chiefly with the forms of Italian political life during a period when

a close association with Great Britain was taken for granted; and with the breakdown of those forms which ushered in the era of antagonism. Anxiety about Anglo-Italian relations does, however, underlie this book and can alone justify the examination of a relatively out-of-date situation by one who is not a professional historian, nor a writer of reminiscences, but a newspaper correspondent concerned with the present and the future. This book, a pre-history of Italian Fascism, is offered as a contribution to problems of the present moment.

The overwhelmingly important aspect of Italian politics for Britain is that of the nemesis which overtook Mussolini's Fascism. The popular doctrine and sentiment about this process is simple. Fascism was identified first and foremost with the subordination of Italian policy to Germany, secondly with a pitiless police and factional rule holding down the Italian people alike in peace and in war.

The identification of Mussolini with Italy's recent subordination to Germany needs no illustration, and his command of the enormous organization of Fascismo, uniting in his hands the whole educational journalistic and athletic activity of the country besides all the traditional powers of Government, was indisputably the means by which between 1935 and 1943 Mussolini performed the feat of making his country the instrument of its traditional enemy for injury against its traditional friend. British denunciation of Mussolini's Fascism on these grounds is universal and sincere.

The other connotation given to Italian Fascism as a system of reactionary repression gains much present convincingness in the mind of the British public from the fact that Britain's greatest military Ally has by its prowess equated the 'anti-Fascist' ideals of the proletariat and of Communism with those of efficiency and valour. There are difficulties, however, about accepting this second connotation of Fascism as an adequate account of what happened to Italy between the wars. An entire generation of Italians grew up accepting the Fascist discipline with a very large measure of acquiescence. Upon this fact, partly, was based the large measure of British applause for Fascism, challenged only, until 1935, by a minority of writers and speakers in this country.

There was later an abrupt change, not always traceable to a conscientious re-examination of the Fascist question in the light of new facts, by former keen pro-Fascists.

A policy towards Italy safe for Britain must be based upon a conscientious diagnosis of Italy and not upon the feelings of the moment, however enthralling the moment and however strong in consequence the appeal of a uniform attitude among the Allies and in our nation may be. Only an active British policy can make of the future Italy a partner at peace instead of a puppet in hands working for revenge. But what a disaster if an active British policy started by mistaking the location of the Italian national will with which it sought to come to grips! Policy must be preceded step by step by vision. First, it must be seen what men, what forces, what interests and what ideas susceptible of harmonizing with British purposes have a chance of flourishing in the future Italy. Then, and then only, is it safe to promote that chance and to enter into close associations.

The inspection of Italian men and forces cannot be made in the field of present events without a survey of the past out of which they grew. Present events are viewed necessarily under a strong emotion blinding the eye to the complexity of the objects. But by tracing these objects to roots lying outside the range at all events of our most agitating emotions we may gain the requisite correctness of vision.

4. *Cause and Nature of Fascism.* The need for such a research into the forces of Italian politics, projected backwards into time, presented itself to the writer long before this war in the course of some twenty years of concern with the affairs of Italy; and in this manner.

How was Mussolini's dictatorship to be interpreted to the readers of the Rome Correspondence of *The Manchester Guardian* at a time when no direct question of Anglo-Italian relations was involved, or likely to be involved in the triumph of the dictatorship?

The great Editor of that newspaper, Mr C. P. Scott, allowed his Rome Correspondent (the Author) to think out for himself which were the creative and progressive and which were the negative and destructive forces in Italy. It did not enter the mind either of the Editor or of his Correspondent that the good health of Italy could fail to be a British interest.

The materials for forming his judgement lay to some extent in the Author's previous direct experience of Italy as a student in pre-Fascist Rome. This had familiarized him with the crisis in Italian parliamentarism while Fascism was still a local phenomenon in Milan. The journalist's privilege of approach to all men gave him opportunities for discussing Italian history at length with some of the best minds in the Italian schools and with all sorts and conditions of ordinary Italians. On these experiences, supported by such literary research as the working journalist can afford, the present book is based.

A reference to the very earliest of these direct impressions may usefully precede the main narrative.

The sensation of political Rome in the middle of 1920 was the return to office of the almost octogenarian Giovanni Giolitti, whose figure bulks so largely in this book. The return of Lord North to power in joint harness with Charles James Fox who had just denounced him as 'void of honour and honesty, the most infamous of mankind,' scandalized England in 1783, but that was an event on the surface of a settled nation. Giolitti had been hounded out of Italian political life in 1915 in a moment of stirring national crisis with all the publicity that Press and the agitation of the streets could afford. The history of Italy at war from 1915 to 1918 had been, in the minds of many of the guides of Italian public opinion, the history of the emancipation of Italy from the toils of that politician who represented an intolerable falsity and stuffiness in her life. Yet in 1920 the same Giolitti, aged but unchanged in outlook and in intentions, had resumed the supreme power at the almost universal entreaty of the responsible men of Italy.

It was a baffling frustration for those who during the war had directed Italy's hopes and desires upon a more genuine freedom, a more honest and open political life, interpreting Italy's war at the side of the democratic powers as a rediscovery of the soul of the Risorgimento.

The return to power in 1920 of this master figure of the Italian administration of 1900–15 was accomplished, like Giolitti's other acts, with a skilful avoidance of unnecessary controversy. But nothing could cancel the significance which the ordinary Italian put on it: it meant that the war had in every sense been a colossal error. Already the Italians had become convinced that their allies had outwitted and cheated them in the apportionment of spoils. Now the return of Giolitti showed that even in the most intimate domestic field the war had been a misadventure ending in an attempt to get back, greatly the worse for wear, to the *status quo ante*—unless the return of Giolitti was an irrelevant episode by the wayside pending a harmonization of Italy's policy with the mood of her sufferings and achievements in the late war. That prospect, however, if it had been glimpsed for a moment in 1919 was felt by 1920 to have been lost.

Disappointment, rancour and frustration coursed through the country.

The Fascist 'revolution,' to give to the events of 1922 a description really more applicable to Mussolini's overthrow of traditional internal and external policy in 1924 and 1938, found its entry into Italian history in a vacuum set up by the disappearance of aspirations which in an elusive variety of forms ran through the history of Italy from the period of the wars of unification to that of the post-war crisis in 1919.

The main part of this book attempts to trace in the story of Modern Italy the progress of these aspirations, which found their tragic culminating expression in the sacrifice of some 600,000 Italian lives in the war of Italy's alliance with Great Britain. The records of Italy from 1900 to 1915 show strong evidence that many young officers and soldiers of the martyred generation faced the war in a conscious fervour of high ideals. The Italy of 1919 was a country still groping for some political transformation to correspond with these aspirations. The Italy of 1920—though not, of course, all Italians or the finest of Italians—had sunk into a mood of frustration which sought only a minimum of safety in a return to a past which it had already condemned as unworthy to survive. It was the triumph of the mood of the comfortably established and of the timid. But aspirations which have stirred the life of peoples without attaining their ends do not vanish away leaving them in comfortable possession of former imperfect satisfactions. They leave a trail of rancour and resentment. The Italy of 1921 was shot through with spasms of disappointment for the failure of those elusive hopes, and with vengefulness for the disturbances set in motion by them.

It was the collapse of the expectation of a signal progress to be achieved by Italy following her war and victory which set up the tide by which Mussolini profited to bring off his extraordinary achievement. He relied in no small measure upon the explosive force which had been generated among the fighters of the war of 1915 in the service of purposes of which he became famed as the negator—purposes of creative co-operation between the classes and the nations, purposes of self-government for all and of the curbing of privilege and arbitrary power by a true representation of the people. It was an essential part of Mussolini's own career to have been himself the spokesman of these objects of popular zeal while hopes were still set upon them. Then, in an utterly changed condition of the national mood, it fell to him to tap the forces of reaction against those disturbing Utopian enthusiasms. It is part of the purpose of this book to bring out the complexity of his rôle.

The acceptance of Mussolini as head of the Government in October 1922 was, if not universal in Italy, at all events widespread through many contrasting groups and antagonistic classes.

The reader who follows the argument of the concluding chapters will be deprived of any easy assurance that the Fascist 'revolution' either saved Italy, or (what is now a much more popular doctrine) violently interposed to prevent a desirable and progressive evolution. He will see in the installation of the Fascists in Rome the consequence of an ambition pursued by Mussolini simultaneously along two routes. One was the route of insurrectionary action for which the way had been prepared by the generation-old insurrectionary theories and threats of one school of socialists, and notably by Mussolini himself; though in the final trial of strength those whom he led were the avowed enemies of socialism. The other and at least an equally important route was that of parliamentary haggling and compromise, a game which Mussolini played with all the zest of one who has an illicit trump up his sleeve—the trump of readiness for insurrection if the normal methods of gaining the power failed.

The consideration how Mussolini achieved power will show that the elements of the public and official world of Italy which in 1922 did not actively or with passive acquiescence contribute to the Fascist solution were few indeed. The humane and liberal aspirations of the Italians had by that time fallen out of the purview of practical politicians for whom the significant sentiments are always those which offer a way to power.

There are times when moral fervour can fuse itself with the practical urge of politics, but Italy in 1922 was too weakened by disappointment to attempt a solution of her political affairs on the moral plane. It was a moment when quick and ruthless decision answered the needs of the nation. This book tells the story of the precedent disappointment. The Fascists have always acknowledged the fact of this disappointment, but have attempted to trace it entirely to the misdeeds of their former allies. It is the endeavour of this book to trace the disappointment to roots native in the internal situation of Italy herself.

5. *Post-Fascist Italy*. The sacrifice of moral considerations has

in course of time brought its train of agonizing problems, of which the Italian people by 1943 were at last forced to take the measure.

By that date they had come, under Fascism, to an impasse as grave as that from which Fascism at the beginning offered a quick release. By 1943 the call for a new phase rang out even among the baffled and embarrassed spokesmen of the despotism which the Fascist solution had engendered.

This does not, however, do away with the fact that the official and public world of Italy once fully accepted and for long fully identified itself with Fascism. It shows only that Fascism failed to fulfil their expectations. The hard fact with which a realistic British policy must come to grips is that Fascism had its origin in the logic of events. Fascism was not a senseless per-version of a state of contentment, but a desperate method of replacing a state reckoned to be intolerable when other methods had failed. If Fascism then itself become intolerable that does not justify the remoter past, but calls for a new attempt to solve the old discontent.

What sort of an attempt can that be if it is to satisfy the exig-encies of England and of the United Nations for the elimination of those responsible for Italy's aggression against us?

The discovery of forces in Italy ready, on the plane of politics, to initiate and take responsibility for a new era in the country's external relations and internal stewardship is an inscrutable enterprise. Abandonment of the word 'Fascism,' removal of certain outstanding personages and the lopping away of certain highly offensive manifestations, such as those directed against the Jews, will not constitute a truly radical change as long as a governing class of State and Party functionaries, so long closely intermingled, represent an authority springing from the same roots as the Fascist régime. There is every reason to hold that a close British intimacy with an Italian régime which had only nominally changed its nature would set in motion once again the cycle of events which has culminated in this war.

On the other hand, a sudden attempt to produce a practical political system from different roots may engender confusion and bring disrepute upon all those, including in our hypothesis of an active British policy the British Government itself, who have promoted or befriended it. It is exceedingly hard to see how such a newly invented régime could be other than a resuscitation of what, in 1922, the Italians decisively interred and would hasten to inter again.

Fascism was essentially, according to the doctrine of this book, a phenomenon which acquired life from the failure of the liberals of Italy to dispossess the small class of intriguers and traffickers who loomed intolerably large in the governmental system prior to 1915. It represented the absence, from the leadership offered by Italian liberalism, of men of firm principle, capacity for sincere utterance and contact with the everyday problems of the country. It represented the breakdown of the positions of authority held in part before the last war by such superior men, of whom as individuals Italy has never been and never is in want. The breakdown was procured first by an insurrectionary socialism of poor quality, which immolated the ideas of freedom and of the nation to a hasty appetite for popular triumph: and secondly by Fascism, that connubium between the small class of outworn politicians whom the Socialists enraged, and the counter-insurrectionary forces set in motion throughout the country — among the 'small men' as among the rich — by the long exasperation of an unfulfilled social-revolutionary threat.

6. *The Lesson for Britain.* The short-term practical lesson for British policy to be derived from understanding the nature of the Fascist régime may appear negative rather than positive. It is to keep the first contacts with Italy upon an empirical level. No radiant New Italy will rise suddenly from the ashes. A great gulf has been fixed, and fixed for a long time, between the world of Italian practical politics and the natural and healthy soil of Italian human nature from which a development of Italy on lines of orderly progress may be hoped for. An attempt to overlook this gulf, to force the appearance of what purported to be a 'New' Italy would earn contempt if the changes were made on the surface only in order to fulfil the letter of an anti-Fascist obligation. It would breed confusion and catastrophe if a real disturbance of equilibrium were attempted in a premature effort to fulfil its spirit.

The justification for any immediate internal changes in Italy to be required by the United Nations should lie in their own need for security, not in the appetite for an emotionally desired change.

Such a cautious approach to the re-establishment of contact must not be confounded with the refusal of all vital contact between Britain and the future Italy which, it was previously argued, would have in it the seeds of new wars. On the contrary, the maintenance of a courteous 'distance' in the first years of peace may be the best contribution to a future restoration of a close co-operation between the two countries as an element of British strength and moral authority in the world.

Moreover, it should be made clear that a non-committal attitude towards a provisional régime in Italy does not in any way require the muffling of the voice of British policy in its enunciation of permanent British desires in regard to Italy. On the contrary, the extension of support for, Italy's territorial integrity and for the restoration of Italy's economy in collaboration with Britain may be all the more impressively timed if it assists the Italian nation while its leadership is still unsettled. An active British policy must discover such accents of approach to the Italian people as soon as possible, and must proclaim its intentions as clearly and firmly as possible. It will thus, amid inevitable confusion, gain prestige and influence for Britain in the further and more settled future.

In due time a genuine rebirth is to be expected in Italy of the liberal method of politics (which alone reconciles progress with order) consecrated to the cause of social efficiency and justice. One limiting factor in the changes to be expected in the basic structure of Italy lies in the special position of that country as the centre of the organization of Catholic Christianity. The other lies in the consideration that the very idea of the 'nation' as elaborated by the European thinkers of the nineteenth century was bound up in the spectacle of Italy travailing to throw off alien and effete dominations. The friendly approval with which the emergence of the Italian nation was viewed in this country presupposed that the force of this new nation built up from such ancient and precious elements would be thrown on the side of the idea of orderly political progress, which is not so much a British doctrine as the soul of Britain. What otherwise could justify in the eyes of British friends of orderly progress that breach of continuity which dispossessed Austria and the Bourbons of their legitimate Italian domains?

If Italy was to disclaim the theory of the nation as the vehicle of human nature in its aspiration to freedom and order, if Italy was to embrace conceptions of order without freedom in the name of a mystical Empire of Europe, why should she not have served those concepts as incarnated in Hapsburg Vienna and Papal Rome?

If, on the other hand, the life of the Italians was to be based upon historical materialism, why introduce the meaningless interlude of national independence between the State system of the Congress of Vienna and the 'withering away of the State' predicted by Karl Marx?

The present book is offered to fellow-journalists and to others upon whom may depend our future relations with Italy, in the conviction that 'there will always be an Italy' for reasons closely bound up with our own assurance that 'there will always be an England'; and in the hope and prayer that temperate use of victory and a tough sense of the realities with which we have to deal may convert the co-existence of these nations from a chapter of blood and tears, toil and sweat to one of mutual benefit and enrichment.

There is a long and honourable history behind the association of England with Italy which is not immediately obvious if attention is paid solely to its political and economic aspects, important though (to take two examples) the enjoyment of the support of the power which lies across the centre of the Mediterranean must always be to a power which has made that sea its pathway; and the enjoyment of a friendly economic relation with a community requiring our own chief surplus product— coal.

A full sense of the possible value of the association can be gained only by assessing the mutual influences which have passed and still, despite everything, are passing between two peoples one of which shines in the aesthetic and speculative and the other in the ethical and practical sphere of our single European civilization.

CECIL J. S. SPRIGGE.

LONDON, 1943.

CHAPTER ONE

THE TRIUMPH OF PIEDMONT

THE first chapter is a miniature history of the Unification of Italy. The stirrings of later Italian politics cannot be understood without entering into the drama of the creation of the Italian State in the nineteenth century not by a unanimous national movement, but by the concurrence of several movements bitterly hostile to each other.

These are briefly described, and the characteristic thoughts of their leaders are compared and contrasted, in the following five sections:

I. THE DYNASTY OF SAVOY.—This dynasty ruled over a small and somewhat obscure kingdom in the north-west corner of Italy. How came it to play a leading part in the unification of the country, and to mount ultimately the throne of all Italy?

II. THE GIOBERTIAN EPISODE.—Gioberti was a priest-philosopher who dreamed of uniting all Italy under the presidency of the Pope. He failed, but his tradition lived on.

III. MAZZINI AND CAVOUR.—These were the greatest minds of their generation, the twin founders, if any deserve this title, of United Italy. Few men have ever regarded each other with greater disapproval and hatred. Alone, neither could have brought Italy into being.

IV. CAVOUR, GARIBALDI AND VICTOR EMMANUEL.—A tale of shifting alliances and recrudescent embitterments.

V. THE UNIFICATION OF ITALY.

I. THE DYNASTY OF SAVOY

Italy's natural frontier of sea and Alpine ranges is too clearly defined to leave much doubt about what is meant by 'Italy': such doubts as remain concern the propriety of including in this single geographical expression the great adjacent islands, Sicily, Sardinia and Corsica, and the proper location of the Alpine limit, which some would carry round the northern end of the Adriatic down the Dalmatian coast, on the line of the so-called Dinaric Alps, making the Adriatic an Italian lake.

Though so well marked off from the outer world Italy is a country of great internal distances, stretching six hundred miles long from the Alps to the Ionian Sea, and four hundred from the

Alpine frontier towards France, to the range west of Fiume.
Moreover, the Apennine ranges abruptly sever the north and
north-eastern plains from the centre and the south. As the crow
or the aviator flies, Turin is nearer to London than to Brindisi
and Brindisi is nearer to Constantinople than to Turin. Between
A.D. 400 and almost 1800 Italy was never an administrative unity
and there was small reason for any extensive travel from one end
of it to another, except on the part of friars and artists in certain
centuries. Only a few generations ago the inhabitants of Milan
and Turin were as ignorant of the aspect and customs of southern
Italy as of northern Africa. As for eastern Italy, Venice (the
English traveller Arthur Young remarked in 1789) was 'at the
very extremity of civilized Europe'. There were, however,
certain centres which by the time of the French Revolution had
for centuries been the capital cities of republics or monarchies,
and which, having adopted the Tuscan dialect as their Court
language, keeping their own local languages for colloquial use,
were regarded as the seats of an Italian civilization. Rome, of
course, had a unique prestige, but Venice, Florence, Milan,
Genoa and Naples were proud rivals. It should be noticed that
the part of Italy which lay nearest towards the busy heart of
eighteenth-century Europe, that is, towards the Anglo-French-
Dutch regions where men's minds were swept up in the enthusiasm
of material progress and liberal institutions, was not the domain of
any one of these historic Italian centres, like Tuscany, or Venetia,
or the Roman plain, or even the Neapolitan Kingdom. It was
the far from typically Italian, largely French-speaking mountain
state of Piedmont, with its capital in Turin. Turin was Italy's
north-western outpost. French and English revolutions seemed
very distant events to the Tuscans, prospering quietly under
Hapsburg heirs of the Medici dynasty, or to citizens of the
Venetian republic, mouldering on the accumulated wealth of a
decadent commerce and a lost colonial empire, or to the ragged
populace of Rome augustly immobile under the rule of the priests.
But Turin, a city not often mentioned in Italian itineraries, had
for two centuries before the great Revolution been involved in
the affairs of France. The Ducal House of Savoy fought from
generation to generation to avoid being absorbed in France, or
being forced to make over to France its Alpine frontiers in return
for precarious compensation in the plains. Thus Piedmont
became closely concerned with France, yet by the same token a
bulwark of Italy against France. In alliance with Austria, the

House of Savoy moreover added to its domains the previous Spanish fief of Sardinia, and with it the title of King.

Turin was the capital now of an Italian kingdom. Yet the prevailing Court language was French. So was the outward aspect of the town. The 'bloody Piedmontese' of Milton's sonnet (Duke Charles Emmanuel II, a grandson of Louis XIII of France) had begun the rebuilding of Turin on a geometrical plan. Addison, in the diary of his Italian journey in the year 1700, could report that the Court of Turin was reckoned 'the most splendid and polite in Italy'. He adds a significant detail: 'There is one convenience in this city [Turin] that I never observed in any other. . . . By the help of a river . . . they can convey a little stream of water through all the more considerable streets, which serves to cleanse the gutters. . . . The manager opens his sluice every night and distributes the water into what quarter of the town he pleases.' The eighteenth-century kings of Piedmont-Sardinia thus gave an enlightened attention to town-planning and street-lighting, but they did not omit to further the wider interests of their domain by the ordering of their State finances, the codification of the laws, and a new system of army training, for which Victor Amadeus III took his model from Prussia.

The kings, who worked hard to give their little state conveniences and discipline, watched over their subjects with paternal solicitude and severity. Unsubmissive temperaments were jealously watched. Count Vittorio Alfieri, the one Piedmontese of high genius in the eighteenth century, lived out his long life significantly enough in France, England, Tuscany—anywhere to get away from the curious prying of the King and his ministers into the daily life of a great nobleman. One other subject of the King of Piedmont became a figure of European importance in the age of revolution—he was Count Joseph de Maistre, whose gospel of reaction has even now not ceased to radiate hostility to liberty. It is notable that even de Maistre was viewed with disapproval by the Court of the Savoys for his too agile intellect, and was kept for ten years on mission in Russia as the best means of ensuring his absence. For all their practical competence, the kings of Piedmont were obstinate despots.

As the great revolution welled up in France, the Court of Turin was foremost in denouncing and suppressing the new subversive ideas, and later in welcoming Royalist *émigrés* and in looking to Austria to set a topsy-turvy world in balance again. But the revolutionary French overran Piedmont in one of their first campaigns, and for sixteen years the royal Savoys were in exile. When Napoleon's fall permitted their return they immediately promulgated an edict revoking all that had been done in their domains since 1798. The State offices were restored to holders named in the Court year-book for 1798. Not only Great Britain, but even Russia, in vain advised Victor Emmanuel I to grant a Constitution in his restored dominions which now included also the resentful ex-sovereign state of Genoa. The Piedmontese king would not temper his legitimist absolutism with any concessions. Henceforth the dynasty lived encircled by the impatience and ridicule of the modern-minded and above all of the Genoese. It was, on the other hand, a dynasty pleasing to that Austrian power which Napoleon's fall had left predominant in Italy.

What made this antiquated dynasty peculiarly uninspiring was that the inner royal family consisted solely of three elderly and childless brothers, the youngest of them fifty years old at the restoration. Naturally there was great interest in their distant cousin who stood next in the order of succession, young Carlo Alberto, of the junior line of the house, the line of Carignano. He was the heir of a different policy and attitude from that of the Court, for when his distant cousins of the senior royal line fled into exile, Carlo Alberto's father had stayed in Turin and had demonstratively welcomed France and the French reforms. On his death his widow had taken her children to Paris, where Carlo Alberto, at sixteen years of age, became a lieutenant of Napoleon's imperial dragoons. As soon as Victor Emmanuel was again in possession of his capital the young man was called back to Turin by his royal and indignant cousin, to be forcibly re-educated into legitimist and orthodox ways. Carlo Alberto was torn in twain. The Court needed him as a pillar of conservatism and suspected that he remained ever a revolutionary: the agitators and conspirators needed him to lead Piedmont forward into the new century of science and progress, but they found to their cost that he had learned to put dynasty before modernity. Thus Carlo Alberto was first the hope of the reformers: next he was execrated by them as a traitor. It was not until 1848, the year of political eruptions throughout Italy and Europe, that from doubts and contradictions Carlo Alberto issued forth to a clear discernment of a policy which was both flattering to his own dynastic ambitions, and also agreeable to revolutionaries and conspirators against legitimism. 1848, of course, was a year of immense upheavals.

Amid revolutions and insurrections throughout Europe, Lombardy and Venetia—Austria's Italian spoil from the vast estate of Napoleon—rose in that year in rebellion against Vienna; and Carlo Alberto, now King of Piedmont, marched from his neighbouring capital to support Milan against the Austrians, negotiating, as he passed through, for the union of the Lombard provinces with his own kingdom. Disastrously defeated, he abdicated in favour of his young son Victor Emmanuel II, and died soon afterwards in exile. It was, however, Carlo Alberto who placed the Kingdom of Piedmont in the forefront of the problems of the Italian peninsula. Piedmont was, from now on, unmistakably the enemy of Austria and of all that since Napoleon's downfall Austria's domination in the Italian peninsula had come to signify. Under Carlo Alberto Piedmont became the direct enemy of Austria as ruler of Lombardy and Venice: and by reflection the indirect enemy of a dynasty in the Kingdom of Naples which submitted to threats and accepted assistance from Austria: enemy also of the minor Austrianized rulers of Parma and Modena, and even in some degree of the mild, benevolent, but conservative Grand Ducal House of Tuscany: enemy also of that great Italian institution the Papacy, as long as it continued to rely on the secular arm of Vienna. Piedmont was pitted against all these powers which based themselves on the principle of Legitimism and was counted among those powers in Europe which by contrast rejected the pattern of perpetual peace as laid down by the Vienna Treaty of 1815 and the Holy Alliance.

The attainment of this conspicuous position by Piedmont and its Savoy dynasty must now be placed in its setting among the movements which were coursing through the Italian states a generation after the fall of Napoleon.

During the French invasion and occupation of Italy the entire peninsula had been for a few years under the rule of a single master, Napoleon. This was not the sort of Italian national unity that had for centuries been vaguely dreamed of, especially as Napoleon had held Italy firmly sundered into three main parts. Still, Napoleon had given a taste of unity, and his enemies, in 1815, had insisted upon restoring the old divisions, chiefly for the advantage of Austria. With the war of 1848—preceded by the proclaiming of a Constitution—Carlo Alberto staked out for the monarchy of Piedmont a claim for leadership in Italian rebelliousness against that settlement. This could not but amount to a claim to lead Italy towards unity. But in Italy the notion of a leadership from the far north-west was still novel and un-palatable. The consciousness of an Italian nationality was the fruit of a great national literature. Poets throughout the Middle Ages had kept alive the haunting dream of a revived national union of Italy around Rome. Florence, Milan and Venice had been the great Italian powers in Renaissance Europe. In those cities, and in Genoa, Bologna, Naples, were the masterpieces of Italian art and the famous academies and opera-houses. Milan had been the capital of Napoleon's 'Kingdom of Italy'. These, and not Turin, had been celebrated or denounced by Dante, Petrarch, Machiavelli, Foscolo as the vital centres of Italian history. For Piedmont it could at most be said that some Prince of Savoy, pitted against foreign competitors, had felt his efforts towards territorial expansion to be 'Italian' efforts and gained the poetic applause of a minor poet like Fulvio Testi. Such were the slender roots of Piedmontese primacy in Italian history. And even in the most recent times, prior to the adventure of 1848 the restored Piedmontese monarchy had to its own subjects appeared not less unmodern, not less oppressive, but only more efficiently and wilfully oppressive than the pro-Austrian governments of eastern, central and southern Italy.

Carlo Alberto's immediate predecessors had shown no desire to become the leaders of a national Italian movement. The sufferings of martyrs for liberty, and of illustrious exiles, marred the annals of Piedmont as of the other Italian states. The dynastic policy of Piedmont seemed as much an obstacle to Italian unity and liberty as that of any of the Italian states. Indeed when men looked round, in the second quarter of the nineteenth century, for an Italian dynasty to lead the way to Italian national unity, it was by no means only the House of Savoy that they took into consideration. The ascent of this dynasty to a position in which it appeared as the only possible Royal House for a United Kingdom of Italy was the achievement, as has already been described, of the enigmatic Carlo Alberto. But we shall see how little the Court of this king appealed to the instincts of certain young Italian patriots who were subjects of the Piedmontese kingdom.

It is useful first, however, to inquire whether Piedmont as a social and economic entity had any plausible claims to pre-eminence over the remainder of Italy. Was the forwardness of Piedmont simply the expression of an inflated dynastic ambition? Such was the view of Mazzini. That Piedmont should embark on the task of civilizing Italy seemed outrageous to those, like Mazzini, whose values were historical and poetical. The civilization of the early nineteenth century had to do, however, with the use of machinery in production and communications, and with the liberation of citizens from hindrances to its ever more extended use. In this material and mechanical civilization Piedmont had now come to excel.

Until shortly before the middle of the century Lombardy had been the farthest advanced of the Italian regions in industry and trade. The Austrian Government which in 1814 had superseded in Milan the semi-autonomous Napoleonic 'Kingdom of Italy' was not animated with the reactionary zeal of the dynasty of Piedmont. Lombardy had a quite considerable silk and linen manufacturing industry, and a developing cotton industry, slowly turning to steam-power. Some of the Milan cotton spinners by 1840 even made direct purchases of raw cotton in America. Piedmont exported raw silk in quantity: but Genoa and its province, which had previously had a respectable silk industry, almost ceased to practise the manufacturing arts in the first twenty-five years of its incorporation with Piedmont, under the elaborately paternalistic rule of Turin.

In the forties Piedmont began to outpace Lombardy. The Austrian Government impeded the transit of raw cotton across Lago Maggiore, and the Milanese manufacturers turned to Genoa, which soon became a great and well-organized importing centre for cotton and cereals. The first railway line in North Italy was constructed to connect Genoa with Turin. Cavour made railway construction a chief plank in his policy. Taking office for the first time immediately after the Italian political fiascos of 1849 he threw himself into the task of assimilating Piedmont to the great countries of the West, in whose support he saw the sole hope of a new and successful drive against Austria. Between 1851 and 1858, under Cavour, Piedmont's foreign trade was doubled, the coal imports—now required for the railway and the gas-lighting enterprises—more than quadrupled. The Ligurian coast developed a power-driven cotton industry to profit by the imports received in Genoa.

To promote external trading relations and the rise of large-scale industry as rapidly as possible Cavour was prepared to expose the existing industries of Piedmont to sudden and overwhelming competition. He precipitately concluded a treaty of free trade with England, and shortly afterwards one with Belgium.

To those who proposed the alternative of a gradual and considered abatement of the tariff, Cavour replied with the most
dogmatic proclamation of absolute free-trade principles. You
must choose, he said, between 'faith in the principles of liberty,
of free competition, of free development of man's moral and
intellectual nature' or alternatively the belief 'that Government
has the duty and faculty of putting its supposedly more enlightened
will in the place of the free will of individuals'. If you accept
this last doctrine you should carry it logically to a full doctrine
of Socialism; if you oppose Socialism (argued Cavour), which
demands a State interference in wages, you should oppose also
Protectionism or State interference in the use of capital. The
fact that the English treaty was followed in truth by a great
expansion of new industries and traffics enabled Cavour to live
down the damage which it had done to some of the established
manufactures. The Trade Treaty with England, and the alliance
and participation with England and France in the Crimean war,
also made the Kingdom of Piedmont respectable in the eyes of
the international bankers: the London banking house of Hambro
joined with those of Erlanger and Rothschild of Paris as inter-
mediaries for raising loans for the use of Piedmont for purposes of
peace and war.

By the time that the Piedmontese Government set up a claim
to leadership of the whole Italian peninsula there was no doubt
of its superior standing in the eyes of the governing classes of
the most prosperous and powerful of the European countries.
Piedmont was associated with western Europe by trade, by debt,
and by the possession of something unknown to any other of
the former autonomous states, or to Austrian Lombardy—that
is, of developing mechanized industries and of modern financial
institutions. And this, in the eyes of a Cavour, was worth a
great deal of ancient historical glamour.

II. THE GIOBERTIAN EPISODE

The men whom Italian historical tradition has canonized as
the fathers of United Italy were all born within the enlarged
frontiers of Piedmont as the Congress of Vienna drew them—
Mazzini and Gioberti, Garibaldi and Cavour. The two former
were the chief propagandists of the idea of a United Italy (though
both played also a highly active part in politics and conspiracy),
while the two latter were pre-eminently men of action.

Something has been said of Cavour's ambitions. Let us now

look at the ideas of Gioberti and Mazzini, and see where they led
them. Vincenzo Gioberti, an orphan reared in a Turin cloister,
marked out by his great gifts for high station, and early attached
to the Court, had hardly reached man's estate before he was involved in the schemes of conspirators against the royal absolutism
of the Savoys. He was arrested, and sought immunity from royal
wrath in a long exile (1833-48). Giuseppe Mazzini (born, be it
noted, in Genoa, in 1805) had already suffered two months of
fortress confinement by the age of twenty-five, and he was from
that time onwards almost permanently in exile. To have been
born a subject of Piedmont instead of another Italian state was
a matter of no advantage to young rebels against absolutism.
To both of these philosopher-conspirators in their first youth the
choice presented itself whether to serve the little monarchy or
to aspire after a greater Italy in which Piedmont would be
subordinated or merged. Both embraced the cause of Italy.
Mazzini had been initiated in boyhood into the rites of the
Carbonari, the most conspicuous of the various secret societies
whose adherents, throughout Italy, were pledged to work against
royal and priestly absolutism and, broadly speaking, for the
revolutionary Rights of Man. But Mazzini soon broke with an
organization which seemed to him to lack a defined purpose and
programme. He initiated his own brotherhood, the *Giovine Italia*,
Young Italy, to which Gioberti also for a while adhered. Gioberti
and Mazzini at this stage were inspired by one and the same
vision. They conceived that there could be one centre and one
only for a United Italy: Rome, which still, as the capital city
of Catholicism, claimed to be capital of the world. The cause
of the unity of Italy, in the minds of young men like Gioberti and
Mazzini, was on an entirely different plane from that of the
eighteenth-century politics in which dynastic ambitions had been
the moving impulse, and of which the Savoy kings were the heirs.
They felt themselves to be at a turning-point in human history,
and united Italy was to be the centrepiece of something like a
New Heaven and a New Earth. They debated in terms of
a vast religious regeneration of mankind to be brought about
instantly. The institution of the Church, not less than that of
the State, was to be renovated from top to bottom: and in this
vast drama the national resurrection of Italy was to be the brightest
scene.

'Success will be yours' (writes Gioberti to Mazzini and his
friends in 1834, commenting on the programme of the *Giovine*

Italia) 'if you can develop the germs hidden in Christianity so as to display (as it were) its full pattern, deducing the implications of its principles, and extending their application to the present age and its politics: and if, while doing all this, you can convince the peoples who believe or would fain believe in the faith, that Christ gave in his Church the symbol of political unity, equality and freedom. And for this you must constitute the Church on perfectly popular lines, dispelling every shadow of force or domination, choosing the heads of the Church by election of the most competent, holding to the principle of the authority of the people.' Warming to the dream of a democratized Universal Church Gioberti rails against 'the hypocrisy of the princes, who with monstrous blasphemy dare to call themselves Christians, Catholics, fathers of the people by divine dispensation, outraging the holiness of religion by their vicious homage to it.' Gioberti and Mazzini were united in their identification of the Italian cause with that of a world-wide spiritual awakening, in which Italy was to play a most special part: united also, therefore, in disgust for the petty ambitions of the Piedmontese kingdom from which they were fugitives. But their ways were to lie apart: they were to be suspicious rivals, not brothers in enterprise.

Like other young priests of his generation who set out on a gallant venture of marrying Catholic dogma to visionary romanticism, Gioberti, on a mature reflection, found it necessary to reaffirm the unassailable primacy of established dogma. A similar moderation overtook his views of the monarchical institution in the state in which he had been born. In his exile Gioberti found a post as teacher of philosophy in Brussels. Under the pressure of study and experience he soon forswore that vision of the regenerated Catholic Church which had made him an advocate of the dissolution of dogma in benevolence, and of the hierarchy in universal suffrage. In politics he now argued that one must build the new Italy on existing institutions. There persisted in Gioberti, however, a strong prophetic impulse. In return for his restored loyalty to Church discipline, he allowed himself the expectation of a great rôle to be played by the Papacy in the new age. 'I see' (Gioberti writes, in his famous essay *The Moral and Civil Primacy of the Italians*, 1843) 'religion placed at the summit of all things human. I see princes and peoples vying in reverence and love for the Roman Pontiff, recognizing and adoring him not only as successor of Peter, Vicar of Christ, head of the Universal Church, but as doge and standard-bearer of the Italian confederation, fatherly arbitrator and pacifyer of Europe, teacher and civilizer of the world, spiritual father of the human race, heir to Latin greatness, and amplifyer of it by natural and pacific modes.' And similarly, though on a lesser plane, he now expected great things of the Piedmontese monarchy. It was to play if not the chief, at least a most important part in the struggle for Italian freedom. Piedmont was 'the sentinel of Italy on the Alps, the reservoir of Italian military valour'.

With the publication of this essay Gioberti became suddenly famous in Piedmont and throughout Italy. It was a moment of intellectual and emotional excitement in Europe which filled even the conventional with a sense of impending change. Clerics and devout laity, loyal subjects of Piedmont, and their counterparts in some of the other states, found that by the dialectic of Gioberti the way was opened for them to sympathize with the progressive movement which they felt around them, yet to respect their vows and to cling to established traditions. King Carlo Alberto himself was moved to offer a pension to the exile: Gioberti accepted the pension, but passed it on to charity. The extraordinary success of this half-revolutionary, half-traditional propaganda filled the conservatives with alarm. The Jesuits, friends of reactionary Austria and of the established order, put up champions to plead against Gioberti, but their counter-propaganda only spread further afield the fame of Gioberti's appeal for the Italian confederation under the presidency of the Pope, with royal Piedmont as his secular arm. Agricultural societies and academies pressed honours upon him. Yet Gioberti took no steps to be recalled from exile, though influential citizens of Piedmont begged him to come and guide them. Not until early in 1848 did he set foot in Turin, which he had left as an obscure subversive, and now returned to as one of the most famous men in Italy.

There had also, meanwhile, been the most decisive change in the atmosphere of Turin. Carlo Alberto had now definitely taken his stand against Vienna, granting Piedmont a constitution on the French model: 'The legislative power,' it stated, 'is to be exercised jointly by the King and two Houses of Parliament.' Gioberti was at once elected Deputy for both Turin and Genoa, and was appointed to a post in the Government, of which he became at once the outstanding personality. Six months later Carlo Alberto took the supreme step of declaring war against Austria. It must here suffice to state that the choice lay between an armed defiance of Austria, or the submission of Turin to

Viennese policy, on the same footing as the duchies of Tuscany, Parma and Modena. Seldom can a philosopher have appeared to enjoy more favourable circumstances for putting theory into effect than Gioberti at this moment. Piedmont had now denounced and defied the whole Legitimist Settlement in Italy imposed by Austria in 1815. The Piedmontese king had become, if not the friend and disciple of the conspirators, at all events their ally against Austria. So far, Gioberti was abundantly justified in his doctrine that the Piedmontese dynasty was to be the instrument of the Italian national revolution.

But at that point the facts ceased to correspond to Gioberti's prophecies. On Gioberti's theory the recently elected and youthful Pope, Pius IX, who had not concealed his deep admiration for the philosopher-statesman, should have proclaimed that Piedmont's war against Austria was a Holy War for all Italy. Thereupon each of the Italian princes—daring at last to breathe freely—should have sent a powerful contingent to help Piedmont to foment and support the Italian national rebellion in the Austrian domains of Lombardy and Venetia. After a little uncomfortable hesitation the Pope and the princes opted on the contrary to support Austria. The Pope's indignant subjects frightened him away from Rome into voluntary exile. Piedmont was rapidly defeated and was forced to beg for an armistice. Carlo Alberto thus lost the fruit of plebiscites in which the inhabitants of the Austrian-Italian provinces and of the small neighbouring dukedom had voted their annexation to the crown of Piedmont. The Giobertian experiment had manifestly failed. As a last stroke, Carlo Alberto actually called upon Gioberti to lead the Government in order that his persuasive eloquence might unite the revolutionary forces in Italy. But the military position of Austria was now thoroughly restored. Piedmont was for the moment ruined, and Gioberti's failure marked also the doom of the heroic Roman Republic which Mazzini had instituted and of which Garibaldi had become the defender. For, as will shortly appear, the Piedmontese war against Austria was but one aspect of the Italian revolutionary struggle of the fateful year of 1848. A common disaster merged all alike when before the end of 1849 Austria had re-established the régimes of 1815 throughout the peninsula.

Both Gioberti and Mazzini returned to exile, and exile was also the lot of the defeated and abdicating Carlo Alberto. From the utter failure of his propaganda and his policy Gioberti proceeded to draw lessons for the future. He publicly repudiated the project of an Italian Confederation under the Pope. Gioberti declared that Pope Pius had severed himself once and for all from the people when he retreated from Rome in 1848 to place himself under protection of the King of Naples. Gioberti now advanced a new project. The temporal rule of the Pope must be abolished. The laity must be called in to administer the Papal States. The resurrection of Italy must be accomplished on the two hinges of Rome and Piedmont. Rome, though it must no more be administered by ecclesiastics, should still be the seat and centre of the Catholic hierarchy, the 'moral head' of Italy. Piedmont was incontestably the seat of the one Italian monarchy which had upheld Italian honour in arms. Led by Rome and Piedmont, the other Italian states could be drawn into federation. 'Let the royal crown and the triple crown get rid of ancient accretions and be freed of every stain: they will flourish anew, and be no longer the occasions or pretexts of schisms and scandals to the fatherland, but will help to consolidate and unite the various members in one body.'

Gioberti thus still aspired for a federation of the Italian states under the Church's blessing: but he now held that the Pope must enter it as a Constitutional Monarch, after submitting to a reform of his policy. Gioberti, ever an ardent dialectician, justified his project as having in it sufficient of revolution to satisfy the prophetic yearnings of Italian patriots: and sufficient of conservatism to keep contact with the world as it was in practice and in detail. But he was not too hopeful of success. He feared that the cruder revolutionary enthusiasts and the cruder conservatives would each do their bit to disturb this nice historical balance. He observed that there were weaknesses which arose out of the peculiar situation in which events had now left Piedmont. A Piedmontese by the mere fact of being anti-Austrian would be fighting in the ranks of progress, though he might be inspired by no more liberal motive than an ambition that the House of Savoy should acquire Lombardy at the expense of the House of Hapsburg. Were not these the motives of Cavour, the man who now seemed destined to sway the policy of Turin, where Carlo Alberto had committed the crown to his young son Victor Emmanuel? There was more than a touch of the old disciple of Mazzini in the attitude of Gioberti to the newcomer. Camillo di Cavour, Gioberti recognized, was brilliant, vigorous, active; but far from being a perfect Italian patriot he was

'English in his ideas, French in his language.' Gioberti exhorted Cavour to renounce the old policy of the House of Savoy and the petty ambition of enlarging Piedmont, which he suspected Cavour of preferring to that of saving Italy.

But if Gioberti now palely reflected the suspicions of Mazzini against the new Court at Turin this was as nothing to the suspicions which he harboured in regard to Mazzini himself, who had meanwhile gained fame throughout Italy as the hero of the 'Republic of Rome'. He frankly confessed that he was more afraid of Mazzini's overwhelming enthusiasm than of Cavour's cold cunning. This is the moment to turn to the figure of the other great ideologue and propagandist and to see what had become of the *Giovine Italia* since the days of Gioberti's youthful association with it.

III. MAZZINI AND CAVOUR

In distinction from Gioberti, Mazzini had not been educated to the ecclesiastical profession, and no links of sentiment bound him to the Kingdom of Piedmont of which he was legally a subject. A citizen of ancient Genoa, which the treaty makers of 1815 had assigned to Piedmont as a reward for the throne-and-altar orthodoxy of its dynasty, Mazzini at no time felt any intimate tie to the House of Savoy or to the semi-French Court and society of Turin. To a Genoese citizen Piedmont and its dynasty were not merely a portion of the tyrannical settlement of 1815, but were the direct usurpers of the sovereignty which the Republic of Genoa, though in decrepitude, had preserved until the day of Napoleon. As nobody could seriously desire to resuscitate the small and ancient Republic, the way was open for Mazzini to give all his passionate loyalty to the great Italian Republic of his dreams.

In him, the spirit of United Italy seemed to be naturally incarnate. In his thought and his eloquence, the whole tradition of Italian literature from Dante to Foscolo seemed to come for the first time into contact with a concrete political ambition. No task was real to him save that of fulfilling the prophecies of those revered voices. A thinker whose thoughts were rooted in the centuries!—yet their purport was nothing less than a complete overthrow of existing political institutions. A zest for fruitful change, for organic development, animated his whole consciousness. Not the beauty of the *Divine Comedy* itself could persuade him to compound with creeds or with heritages which in the flux of centuries had served their purpose and outlived it. There was, in his language, an implicit claim that direct revelations had been divinely manifested to him. Mazzini clung all the more obstinately to his personal revelation when Gioberti (and in due course almost every one of the conspirators of his generation) reshaped their early romantic theories to make room for the brute facts of the world as it was.

'Mine is no rebellious irritation' (Mazzini wrote to a friendly but alarmed Catholic in 1834). 'My whole nature inclines towards respect for every great unifying and organic concept: there is no youthful illusion, no aspiring dream which I have not at some time cherished in favour of that gigantic ruin (the Papacy). But it cannot be. Those ruins (Church and Empire) can bring forth nothing now but the poetry of expiation. It is not we but God who condemns the Papacy: God who calls the peoples to arise and establish the new unity in the two spheres of the spiritual and the temporal domination. We do but translate the thought of the Age. The Age rejects any power between itself and the source of life, feels itself able to stand in the sight of God and ask him, like Moses on Sinai, for the law of its destiny. The Age abandons the Pope and appeals to the General Council of the Church, that is of all believers, a Council which will be also what is to-day called a Constituent Assembly, for it will reunite what was hitherto always divided. . . . The Papacy must perish. . . . It has killed the faith with a materialism far more disastrous and abject than that of the eighteenth century. . . . Papacy and Austrian Empire must perish, the first for having, through three centuries at least, hindered the general mission entrusted by God to humanity: the second for having in that time hindered the special missions confided by God to the races.' Italy, Mazzini continues, has hitherto lacked nothing but a faith in great principles. This faith is dawning: it will spread and flourish because it is a religious faith, illuminating a banner which is at the same time national and humanitarian.

Unshaken by the disaster of the abortive republics of 1848, or by his own condemnation to almost perpetual exile, Mazzini dreamed on of Italy's mission in the world, of Rome's resurgence as Holy City of the new faith. For ten years later than the above declaration of faith he wrote, in one of his stirring but interminable manifestos:

'Bend the knee and worship: there beats the heart of Italy: there in eternal solemnity lies Rome. There juts out the capital of the Christian world—and a little removed from it the capitol of the Pagan world. Those recumbent worlds await a third world, vaster and more sublime than themselves, rising out of the mighty ruins. . . . This is the Trinity of History, of which the Word is in Rome. Tyrants and false prophets may delay the incarnation of the Word; none can prevent it. Many cities have perished from the earth, all can perish, but Rome, by the design of Providence discerned by the peoples, is eternal. Rome of the Caesars which unified much of Europe by Action, gave way to Rome of the Popes which by Thought unified Europe and America. Now Rome of the People will supplant the other two, to unify, by the faith of Thought and Action, Europe, America and the rest of the world. . . . This will happen when you Italians understand that the life of a nation is Religion.'

What could be the attitude of the author of such magnificent musings to the pretensions of Piedmont? Count Cavour, who appeared to Gioberti deficient in Italianity, and too much pledged to the petty ambitions of Piedmont, was to Mazzini nothing less than a full-fledged traitor and enemy of the Italian cause. Year after year Mazzini thundered at him:

'Italy, whatever happens, cannot assume the nature of Piedmont. The centre of the national organism cannot be transferred to the extremity. The heart of Italy is in Rome, not in Turin. A Piedmontese monarch will never conquer Naples. Naples will give herself to the nation, not to the Prince of another Italian province. . . . A royal house cannot overthrow the Papacy and annex the Papal dominions . . . or invade and recapture the lands held by Austria. . . . Your mission was to Italianize Piedmont and prepare it to melt into the common fatherland, of which it could have been the first province, and your King the first citizen. You have instead taught Piedmont to deny the common mother: to expect to survive as a State. . . . We represent Italy, you represent the old, greedy, timorous ambition of the House of Savoy' (1858).

Count Camillo Cavour, hard-working Piedmontese landowner, Minister of the Piedmontese Crown, and man of the world who knew the salons of Paris and the clubs of London could, and did, retort that Mazzini was a crazy visionary without knowledge or skill in affairs, for all his adventures and exiles. Utterly contemptuous of Mazzini's literature, imperfectly aware of the magnetism of his saintliness, Cavour attended to his job as Foreign Minister and Prime Minister of Piedmont: conducted the policy of that small defeated and debt-ridden state with a courageous determination still to achieve the aggrandizement of the Savoy dynasty, an aggrandizement of such scope as thereby to bring Italy, represented by Piedmont, into active partnership with the great powers of Europe. In this spirit he launched Piedmont at the side of England and France into the Crimean war, imposing upon his king's subjects a severe military and economic burden: in this spirit he negotiated a Free Trade Treaty with England regardless of the shock to established Piedmontese industries: and finally induced Napoleon III to attack Austria (1859), though his king had to pay with the cession to France of his ancient possessions of Nice and Savoy. He purposed in the first instance to drive Austria from northern Italy and to establish a North Italian kingdom to be ruled from Turin. As for the wider schemes of a total unification of Italy, Cavour envisaged—or professed to envisage—a federation under presidency of the Pope in accordance with the final version of Gioberti's doctrine. Firmly resolved to make Piedmont pre-eminent in Italy, hating Austria as the patroness of small, inefficient, antiquated states, Cavour regarded the progress of Piedmont and the cause of Italy as identical. Those who saw a contrast between them were perilous fanatics. Against Austria Cavour needed above all the help of France, that is of the Emperor Louis Napoleon: to gain this help he was ready on his part to barter the French-speaking regions of Piedmont. Nor was Cavour's alliance with the French Emperor merely mercenary: he admired him as energetic, efficient and modern. Mazzini, whose disciples were awaiting the signal to arise and sweep Papacy, kingdoms, but more especially empires off the face of the earth, cried 'Treason' to each deal with the Parisian despot: and little Cavour heeded him. A fierce warfare of mutual contempt and exasperation marked as long as they lived the relations of these two supreme actors whom Providence ironically destined to serve a single cause.

IV. CAVOUR, GARIBALDI AND VICTOR EMMANUEL

It was the function of a man whose adventurous heroism fascinated both parties to secure that Mazzini's disciples, though not Mazzini himself, should finally contract an alliance with Cavour. Giuseppe Garibaldi, too, was a fugitive subject of Piedmont, and had been condemned to death in 1834 for having participated in one of Mazzini's conspiracies. He repaired to South America, where he helped several of the new republics to establish their liberties against royal pretenders and outside interference. His exploits became famous among Italian patriots. In 1849 Garibaldi joined Mazzini in Rome and was general of the forces of the ephemeral Roman Republic of which Mazzini was the political inspirer and chief magistrate. When the Republic collapsed, Garibaldi led his small surviving force miraculously through the net of the Austrian and legitimist armies. Then he sailed away again to America, quietly returning to Piedmont five years later. His chivalry, his audacity, his personal beauty made a legendary figure of him everywhere in Italy. The Mazzinians admired him too much to cry treason even when he trafficked with a court: and on their side the courtiers, except the most bigoted, admired him too much to cavil at his association with Mazzini. To common Italians he was a legendary 'perfect knight'.

The first five years after the disasters of the Italian cause in 1848–49 passed in passivity and gloom, save for isolated and tragic exploits by individuals against overwhelming power. But Cavour was tirelessly nursing schemes for a new war to drive Austria from North Italy. He knew that such a war, unsupported by the party of Italian unity, could never bring the struggle against Austria to a final conclusion. He accordingly sought Garibaldi's support and aid, and in 1856 the two were in negotiation for a working agreement. Mazzini himself rejected the plan with horror. He even arrived in disguise in Genoa in order to frustrate Cavour's plans by engineering anti-monarchical uprisings in both Naples and Piedmont. But Garibaldi would now have nothing to do with Mazzini's plots, and many of Mazzini's other friends fell away from him and from the principles of the *Giovine Italia* in order to subscribe to those of a new 'Italian National Society' which implicitly accepted the necessity of Piedmontese leadership.

But Cavour had no intention of attempting to pit his Italian forces unaided against the Austrian might. In 1859 he persuaded the French Emperor to strike against Austria: the French Army advanced through Piedmont and in a few weeks Austrian resistance in Lombardy was broken down. In all the independent principalities of northern Italy (Tuscany, Parma, Modena, also the northern province of the Papal State) the Patriotic Associations asserted themselves, and the princes with their ministers fled, leaving the administration to provisional governments which declared in favour of the annexation of these states to Piedmont.

Cavour's plans for Italy were maturing excellently. This very fact filled Louis Napoleon with alarm. His own plan provided for an Italian Confederation under French influence. It now began to look as though there would be no room for that influence. Piedmont was acquiring not merely the Austrian provinces, but Central Italy as a whole.

Louis Napoleon resolved to act in his own interests while there was still time. Overriding Cavour he rapidly compounded with the Austrians, arranging that they should cede Lombardy, without Venetia, to himself, for transfer to Piedmont; the minor princes were to be restored to their thrones and the Pope was to preside over an Italian Confederation in which the Austrian Emperor should participate as the sovereign of Venetia. This, however interesting, was a thoroughly impracticable programme. The only part of it of which Louis Napoleon could really secure the fulfilment was the provision that Austria for the meanwhile should hold fast to Venetia. Short of turning his own troops against the North Italians, there was no hope whatever of reversing the decisions by which they had attached themselves to Piedmont. It soon transpired that things would move similarly even in the far south of the peninsula. It had not, perhaps, seriously occurred to Louis Napoleon that the ambitions of Piedmont might immediately envelop the largest of the Italian states, the Kingdom of Naples and Sicily. Indeed no such purpose had been in the immediate intentions of the Court of Turin. But the National Society—organization of the ex-Mazzinians now following the lead of Garibaldi—had extended its influence to the extremities of the peninsula. From the outbreak of the war of 1859 the patriotic groups in Naples, and especially in Sicily, had been stirring. The National Society was working in with Cavour, although its leaders sincerely repudiated Mazzini's taunt that the association was no more than an instrument for Piedmontese aggrandizement. Its members, in the south, comprised numbers of the gentry and professional classes of Sicily, who, whatever they thought of Piedmont, aimed at gaining independence from Naples. For that matter the Piedmontese crown was not without a pretext for showing interest in the southern isle. The Savoy dynasty had once for a brief while actually borne the crown of Sicily: and in 1848 the Sicilians, in the course of a sustained rebellion against Naples, had seriously negotiated for Carlo Alberto's second son to come to the island as a Constitutional King. Louis Napoleon had foreseen that in the long run Piedmont might try to annex Sicily as a first step to annexing Naples itself, which, together with Lombardy and Tuscany, would be the substance of that great Italian kingdom which he feared to see at France's door. On perceiving that this danger was now imminent he weighed the possibility of installing a Bonaparte on the throne of Naples, which two Napoleonic monarchs, Joseph Bonaparte and Murat, had occupied half a century before. But Cavour had no intention of seeing imperial France installed in the peninsula from which he was engaged upon expelling imperial Austria. He played upon British fears of French hegemony in the Mediterranean, and obtained British good-will for a plan by which Piedmont might anticipate and frustrate the French ambitions.

Cavour did not, however, propose at this stage to risk Piedmont's own forces in an expedition to the south: for this he was ready to utilize the men whom Garibaldi had detached from Mazzini, though he well knew that at heart they cherished the dream of Mazzini's Republic of the Future, and had accepted alliance with the Piedmontese dynasty merely as a tactical move.

Garibaldi, with the magic of his legend, was the only leader who might be able to gather into a united Italian movement the Mazzinian and the Savoyan and other discontented parties in Sicily: and Cavour decided to risk letting Garibaldi raise rebellion in the island, although this meant using Mazzini's methods, and appealing to Mazzini's men. Indeed the Sicilian upon whose knowledge and relations in the island Garibaldi had chiefly to depend was Francesco Crispi, Mazzini's chief correspondent in Sicily. A bargain was struck between Cavour and Garibaldi, by which the expedition to Sicily should proclaim its mission in the island in the name of Victor Emmanuel, but at the same time in that of the autonomy of Sicily. Garibaldi set sail from Genoa with his famous thousand volunteers, and with scrupulous loyalty he proclaimed the union of all Italy under Victor Emmanuel, in whose name he declared himself as Dictator and Crispi as Secretary of State.

Yet Cavour continued to watch the expedition suspiciously. Easily overrunning Sicily, Garibaldi with his amateur army passed to the mainland and soon marched upon Naples, amid the ruins of the great Neapolitan army and of an administration which scarcely moved to defend itself. The anxieties of Cavour at this prodigious over-success of Garibaldi's escapade were redoubled when the hero threatened to march straight on into the Papal dominions and to attempt to capture Rome also by simply provoking internal insurrection. Rome had a garrison of French troops and Cavour foresaw with the utmost alarm the possibility that France might turn her arms to make common cause with Austria in defence of the Papacy. He resolved to act quickly at whatever risk to his relations with Garibaldi. He dispatched a regular Piedmontese army to march across the Papal States, leaving Rome well to the west, and thence through the, Abruzzi to Naples. The King himself headed the army in its march across Italy. The position now was that the regular army of Piedmont was in control of two-thirds of northern and central Italy, while Garibaldi was the Dictator of the south. To render the tension between the Italian parties still more extreme, Mazzini himself arrived from exile in Naples and agitated for the summoning of a National Constituent Assembly. But Cavour had rightly guessed that the soldier Garibaldi would not risk a civil war for the sake of a political theory. Garibaldi in fact rode out from Naples to welcome the King of Piedmont and to do obeisance to him.

This meeting of the Monarch and of the former Republican Dictator is one of those picturesque episodes which come to stand symbolically for the history of an epoch. Popular prints of the scene are still found throughout Italy on the walls of country inns and old-fashioned houses: in virtue of it, the Piedmontese dynasty appeared to receive the obedience of the whole wider patriotic movement, only Mazzini and a few irreconcilable Republicans continuing to challenge his title. The King of Piedmont and Sardinia was now acclaimed by plebiscites in each of the annexed states or provinces as King of Italy by the grace of God and the will of the people, and was in fact master of the whole peninsula except the closer environs of Rome and of Venice. Mazzini was more or less forcibly embarked on to a ship and sent back to his exile in London.

It was now Garibaldi's turn to realize the meaning of some of Mazzini's remonstrances and warnings. The King had received him with a hearty and brotherly welcome. But the King was not master of his policy.

As soon as the Piedmontese army arrived on the scene of his triumphs Garibaldi was given to understand that his improvised army and administration were henceforth wholly superfluous. 'Be inexorable against Mazzini and against all Mazzinians, confessed or clandestine. Make an absolutely clean sweep of people like Crispi,' were Cavour's orders to a subordinate on the spot. By Cavour's orders the improvised Garibaldian army was to be disbanded immediately.

Garibaldi was impotent to resist these orders, which filled him with bitterness. He retired to his island property of Caprera— off Sardinia—violently embittered against Cavour and feeling almost as much an exile as Mazzini.

With the sudden, almost miraculous absorption of almost the whole of Italy into the domains of the crown of Piedmont, there fell to Cavour and his friends a vast field for accomplishing what had already been accomplished on a small scale in Piedmont. Economic reform and industrial development were the objective, and sentimental or historical politics must take a secondary place. There must be no paralysing political unrest. By the annexation of twenty millions of Italians to the crown of Savoy, the party of Cavour had outraged at one and the same time the sentiments of the Legitimist powers of Europe and those of the Italian Republican movement. Legitimists and Republicans stood waiting for their revenge. It was in such circumstances that Cavour proceeded to create forthwith an Italian State complete in its institutions, with no fundamental questions left open or deferred in such a manner as to offer scope for hostile interference. In post haste the victorious party imposed the internal laws and the external treaty relations of Piedmont upon United Italy. Garibaldi remonstrated that Naples and Sicily should remain separate under a local administration governing in the name of Victor Emmanuel, at least until Rome could be incorporated and given its place as capital. Cavour sternly opposed this measure, which would have left Mazzini an operating ground against the whole settlement as effected by Piedmont. In a fury of energy Cavour forced the pace of administrative unification, and when a year later he died, scarcely fifty years old, exhausted by his prodigious achievements, his followers were imbued with the inexorable determination of their master. A bare week before his death Cavour had sustained an impassioned attack upon him by Garibaldi. By this time the hero of 1859 was a more formidable critic of the new Royal Government than Mazzini himself.

V. THE UNIFICATION OF ITALY

Exhilarated and propitiated by the enticing propaganda of Cavour, all the ex-states of Italy had, by plebiscite, annexed themselves to the monarchy of Victor Emmanuel. Only a portion of the Papal States, garrisoned by the French Empire, and Venice, still held by Austria, remained outside the new Kingdom. In rural Tuscany the voters marched to the urn in military formation behind the tricolour flag. In Naples those who voted 'no' did so at the risk of their lives. The Piedmontese Statute of 1848 was declared in March 1861 to be the Constitution of Italy: and with a shock it was realized that the Piedmontese electoral law would exclude a great number of Italians, who in the plebiscite had voted for annexation, from voting in the election of Parliament. The new Kingdom had to shoulder a national debt of Piedmont larger than the combined debts of all the other constituent states. Lombardy and Tuscany were annexed to the Piedmontese customs area in 1860; the next year the Piedmontese free-trade tariff was at a sweep made applicable to the whole of Italy, with no more regard to the revenues of the State than to the disturbance of markets. The unified State started, for this and other reasons, with an expenditure double its revenue, though it was heir to the financial systems of states which had steadily paid their way, and to the intact resources of the country. The Turin Parliament, elected in 1861 by the half-million voters of Italy who alone were eligible under the Piedmontese electoral law, at once made the Piedmontese taxation system applicable to all Italy.

The southern half of Italy and Sicily were overwhelmed with measures to bring them into line with the north—taxes on personal income and succession taxes, things scarcely before heard of in the Kingdom of Naples, were suddenly imposed on an agricultural population which was simultaneously deprived of fiscal protection for its products. Tobacco-growing, a staple industry, was suddenly erected into a State monopoly. Within a year or two the tax payments on agricultural property were increased for the ex-Neapolitan and Sicilian provinces by 40 per cent. Even so the Piedmontese and the Lombards, who believed that southern Italy could be immensely wealthy if only the inhabitants would work, argued that the south was paying too little.

All this meant that the southern half of the new great kingdom was prey to an enormous discontent.

The Bourbon régime did not, for many years after 1860, give up its cause for wholly lost; the King and Queen of Naples retired to Rome, and as long as the Pope still continued to hold a remnant of his State they could use their Roman retreat as a base for expeditions of legitimist marauders into their lost domains. Small armies of a thousand men apiece lurked in the mountains near the Ionian Sea. Against these the new State had to wage a veritable internal war, shooting hundreds of them, destroying their villages, and imprisoning the priests and friars who befriended them. In parts of northern Italy, also, the new State had to affirm its authority against a double opposition of loyalists attached to the old régime, and of Italian patriots impatient of Piedmontese ways.

To meet the expenditure involved in bringing the country to order, the new State had recourse to the capital assets of those which it had inherited. Much of the State property of the annexed territories was at once made over by Piedmont to the local authorities as a politic act of largess. Next, the new State applied to the remainder of Italy the laws by which Piedmont, some years earlier, had already appropriated the surplus fortunes of religious communities. These ecclesiastical properties, together with the remaining State properties, were now thrown on the market: they were far more extensive in the ex-Kingdom of Naples than elsewhere. Speculators or local land-hungry peasants bought up these lands at cut prices and exploited their forests and other accumulated wealth for a quick immediate profit. The deforestation of the public and Church estates gravely affected the water distribution for neighbouring lands. According to F. S. Nitti the ex-southern kingdom provided much more than half a milliard lire (£25,000,000) for the needs of the Italian State out of these sales. A generation later, investigators of Italian agriculture still traced much misery in the south to that origin.

The south groaned that it had been utterly sacrificed to the north: yet the north failed to see that it had gained economically by the Union. Tariff barriers between the industrial north and the agricultural south had been thrown down, but the industrial north was too weak to hold the new Italian markets against foreign, especially French, providers. Then, like all the cotton industries of Europe, the North Italian industry was suddenly deprived of its raw material by the American Civil War: this just in the years of greatest internal confusion in Italy.

Even Piedmont itself gave vent to public discontent. Louis Napoleon still kept a garrison in Rome, and under cover of this French support the Papacy encouraged brigandage in South

Italy. It became a major purpose of Italian policy to gain the withdrawal of the French troops, and thus to get a more powerful Italian hold on the Vatican. With this intention King Victor Emmanuel and his ministers in 1865 removed the capital from Turin to Florence. This was to serve for a token that the King of Italy was not going to march precipitately into Rome. But in Turin riots and a sort of siege of the royal palace marked the removal of the Court and the seat of Government from its original home.

Meanwhile it became suddenly possible to make good one of the defects of the 1861 settlement which Garibaldi and Mazzini most bitterly criticized, and even to re-enlist Garibaldi's help. The outbreak in 1866 of the Prussian-Austrian war enabled Italy to join with Prussia and liberate Venetia from Austrian possession. But Prussia treated its ally much as the same ally had been treated seven years earlier by Louis Napoleon. Having gained its own objectives Prussia made peace over the head of Italy. Victor Emmanuel, once more incurring the bitter resentment of Garibaldi, had to receive Venetia, as he had previously received Lombardy, not by right of an Italian conquest, but as an incidental consequence of negotiations between more formidable powers. The Italian army and navy had an inglorious share in Prussia's triumph. Garibaldi, whose views were by now indistinguishable from those of Mazzini, revolted against this unification of Italy by dynastic deals, in which royal diplomacy seemed always to compound with the enemy and to remain beholden to him, before the Italian people had been able to show its strength or assert its rights. He raised an army of volunteers and attempted—it was the second of such attempts in defiance of the Government—to march into Rome and to stir up a popular revolution. This time luck and genius failed him. He found a well-appointed Papal Army with French auxiliaries drawn up against him and was defeated at Mentana. On recrossing the frontier he was arrested by the Royal Italian Government and committed to a fortress. A strengthened French garrison remained for the next three years in the neighbourhood of Rome.

These episodes gave unceasing sustenance to the agitators of the Garibaldian 'Party of Action'. Cavour's successors were girded at for their impotent tolerance of the French menace at Rome. But their domestic policy was no more popular. In the year after Mentana, in a supreme effort to raise revenue, the Government imposed a tax on the milling of grain. It was one of those taxes which the Piedmontese administration had found already in force in some of the annexed regions, and had amid the jubilations of the populace promptly abolished. The 'Party of Action', Mazzinians and Garibaldians, now declared that the monarchical Government had revealed its true reactionary colours by renewing the detested exaction. Mazzini, from abroad, continued to plot for an upheaval in Rome, the effect of which would be to shatter the prestige of the Savoy monarchy throughout Italy. Mazzini and his friends were, in fact, regaining power and influence: they accused the Government above all of base servility to the French Emperor. The Party of Action drew its support for these plots largely from the young officers who, after 1861, had been discharged from the army for reasons of economy and who now hung about Florence, useless to themselves and to the country, waiting for an adventure as glorious and important as that of Garibaldi's 'Thousand' ten years earlier. The men in the Government strained their utmost to prevent a clash with France which would once more align Paris and Vienna against the precarious new kingdom. They hoped in time to have Napoleon's approval for an occupation of outer Rome, leaving the narrower environment of the Vatican to the Pope.

The prospects were entirely changed by the outbreak in 1870 of the Franco-Prussian war. It happened with the incorporation of Rome in 1870 as it had happened with that of Venice a few years before. The overwhelming victories of Prussia allowed the Royal Italian Government to achieve at little cost what the Party of Action had been so obstreperously agitating to have attempted at all costs. As long as the Second French Empire kept its garrison in Rome, the incorporation of Rome into Italy could be achieved only in defiance of Louis Napoleon, and to this the Party of Action were continually trying to push the ministers of Victor Emmanuel. They believed that only an Italian régime of a flamingly revolutionary character could stand up to the French Emperor or take a share in bringing him down. Rising superior to his bitter disappointment, Mazzini had cherished the faith that national and revolutionary Italy would shake off the petty Piedmontese disguise when the moment came for the incorporation of Eternal Rome. But it was another Empire which now brought Louis Napoleon low. It availed nothing that on the first sign of the French collapse in the face of Prussia (1870) Mazzini reappeared in Sicily. The Italian authorities at once arrested him and sent him to fortress confinement in Gaeta.

The Roman crisis had lit up a brief glimmer of hope for the revolutionaries. The Party of Action raised small revolts in Lombardy, in Ancona and in the extreme south. Victor Emmanuel and some of his ministers, unable to shake off at once the recollections of their former intimacy with the powerful ally of 1859, were strongly inclined to take the field on behalf of Louis Napoleon. Lanza, the Italian Prime Minister, as late as August 1, 1870, denounced all suggestions that Italy should profit by the misfortunes of France to gain Rome. In general the more conservative politicians were for keeping close to France. A belated disciple of Gioberti, the Neapolitan Massari, warned the Chamber (August 22, 1870) that a Prussian victory over France would mean really a German triumph over the Roman Primacy exemplified in the Papacy. Intervention in favour of France was also advocated from a completely different quarter, through the mouth of the great Republican sociologist Giuseppe Ferrari. The overwhelming opinion of the governing class of the Italian kingdom was, however, that the French disaster should be exploited, so that the incorporation of Rome might redound to the glory of the monarchy and be removed for ever from among the incentives to a Republican revolution. The Government found itself impelled, by a vote in the Chamber of 214 against 152, to 'resolve the Roman question in accordance with national aspirations'. A fortnight after the battle of Sedan the Royal Italian troops marched into Rome, while Cardinal Antonelli, the Pope's Secretary of State, launched resounding encyclicals against the invading 'Subalpine' (Piedmontese) invaders, and refused to take any notice of that 'Law of Guarantees' which was passed in recognition of the continued 'sovereignty' and 'independence' of the dispossessed Holy See. Next, Rome was declared the capital of United Italy, spelling ruin for Florence, which was still busily equipping itself for that post.

The 'fair land which Apennine cuts in twain and seas and Alps surround' (Petrarch's still valid description of Italy) was now, save for the disputable frontier fringes of Trent and Trieste, united under a single Government established in Rome. The oncoming generations were conscripted for military service in the Army of the King of Italy, to expand the cadres of his dynastic Army of Piedmont. It had not come about (as Gioberti had dreamed) that the Pope, radiating a supernatural authority from the Holy City, should preside over a federation of autonomous Italian states. It had not come about (as Mazzini had dreamed) that the people of Rome should arise and wrest authority from the priests of dogma to hand it to the prophets and devoted servants of the new religion of 'Thought and Action'. Nor had Garibaldi sent the old Papal throne tottering at the mere sight of a few hundred Italic heroes. The Savoy Monarchy, with its parliamentarian institutions and its favours to commercial and industrial entrepreneurs, had migrated to Rome and was now in command of a great United Nation of 27 millions.

For just half a century the Liberal Monarchy was able, through fine weather and not a few tempests—which we shall now describe —to hold together a country which, when it aspired through the voices of poets and philosophers for national unity, had never dreamed that Providence would send its answer in the shape of a dynasty, an army and a bureaucracy from Piedmont. To the amazement of those who had looked for Providence to recreate Italy from its ancient centre, the Piedmontese State had been the instrument of the unification. Piedmont, they acknowledged, had effected it by brilliantly exploited external alliances, by the attraction of many eminent men who genuinely accepted the Piedmontese claim to stand for light and progress, but also (they would add) by hastily improvised understandings with those Italians in the various regions—not necessarily the most energetic and public-spirited—who made least difficulty about a change of masters, and most unquestioningly did what they were told, to keep their posts. Millions of Italians passively accepted the change without knowing how to protest when it proved, in their private lives, to be a change for the worse. Every organized protest henceforth appeared an act of treason against the Unity itself.

But it must never be forgotten that the unity of Italy was achieved by methods and in the name of principles which were execrated by the great Italian heroes Mazzini and Garibaldi. Not only does Italian history of the last half-century ring with their complaints, but they are implicit in the Italian politics of to-day, which could not be seriously studied without some understanding of them.

CHAPTER TWO

THE DOMINION OF DRYASDUST

I. SOUR FRUITS OF UNITY.—The summary methods by which the Piedmontese Liberals had forced the institutions of their kingdom upon unified Italy produced suffering and resentment. This ultimately found expression in the election of deputies who dismissed the heirs of the Cavourian tradition from office.

II. GOVERNMENT BY THE LEFT.—It was the turn of former followers of Mazzini and of Garibaldi. The more heroic and idealistic of these, however, proved singularly inefficient in office, and in deep disillusionment Italy accepted the rule of a prosaic administrator who, without ideals or a coherent policy, became the indispensable centre of the Governmental machine.

III. A PARLIAMENTARY DICTATOR.—Methods and measures of Agostino Depretis.

IV.—POLICY WITHOUT PRINCIPLE.—Drift into the Triple Alliance: Currency Troubles: and a taste of *Impero*.

I. SOUR FRUITS OF UNITY

Mazzini—to the moment of his death in 1872—remained irreconcilable to the Savoy Monarchy and cast scorn upon the version of United Italy which it had brought into being. But Mazzini was the lone apostle of a lost cause. His ablest follower, Francesco Crispi, broke finally with him some years before his death with the memorable declaration: 'The Republic would divide us, the Monarchy unites us.' Yet if Crispi was determined to preserve the union at the cost of accepting monarchical institutions he was also determined to complete it, with or without royal approval. When he forswore Republicanism Venice and Rome were still outside the new State, and until they too were gathered in, men of Crispi's persuasion would give the Royal Government no peace.

The loosely constituted 'Party of Action', of which Crispi was now the chief spokesman, incessantly urged Cavour's successors to risk the resources of the State on the conquest of Venice and Rome, and so to take the wind out of the sails of Mazzini and Garibaldi who were vowed to achieve it by private expeditions and insurrections. The arguments of the 'Party of Action' were rebutted by the Liberals of 'the Right', Cavour's old allies and colleagues, who if they were considered by legitimists and

47

clericalists to be violators of the rights of throne and altar were scorned by the Left as men of little faith in regard to the one purpose on which all—except legitimists and clericalists—were agreed: the completion of the Union of Italy. Party of Action, bent upon the quick liberation of Venice and Rome: Government Party, cautiously deferring those hopes until less hazardous times —such was the main division in the politics of the new Kingdom until Venice and Rome fell to it as a by-product of Prussia's advance in Europe.

But after Venice and Rome had been thus incorporated in Italy, the Party of Action, in order to maintain its identity, had perforce to turn its attention to the inner affairs of the completed State, and to challenge the Government on its general programme of administration. And the keynote of that programme of administration in the seventies was economy to the bone.

The completion of the unity of the Kingdom had cost twice the annual revenue of the new State. Cavour's successors were at one with constitutional statesmen throughout Europe in regarding the balancing of budgets as a supreme test of the respectability of a State. They therefore insisted upon treating the adjustment of revenue to expenditure as the supreme task before the nation. If this entailed piling exactions upon the heads of citizens who had been lured into supporting the new Kingdom by prophecies of plenty it was unfortunate. But there was, in the minds of these Liberal-Conservatives, nothing to be done about it. The new Kingdom, or rather the old Savoy Kingdom in its enlarged shape, was a fixed and unalterable structure. There was no help but to pay for the rapid unification of the country on the Piedmontese model by new and crushing taxation. This bred a discontent which within a few years reduced the public morale of the Kingdom to as low a depth as Mazzini (on much less prosaic grounds) had prophesied.

Men far removed from Mazzini's ideals uttered serious warnings. The Lombard Count Stefano Jacini declared that the financial stress should be met by a modification of policy. This authoritative personage, in his capacity as Minister for Public Works, opposed both the first shifting of the national capital from Turin to Florence and then the second shift to Rome, as in each case a costly, useless and economically harmful proceeding. He maintained that United Italy's first duty should be to refrain from sucking up the savings of the farmers and peasants for the sake of high policy as conceived in the towns. The more Jacini investigated the life of Italy under its new united Government, the more persuaded he was of the need for a profound modification of the institutions which had been imported from Piedmont.

Jacini's arguments made a great impression, but the men in power dared not relax Cavour's legacy of rigid unity and uniformity. Jacini made soundings for the formation of a Conservative party with a programme of decentralization. He described the Italian constitution as a 'monstrous connubium' of British Parliamentarism with French administrative centralization. He meant that Italy had been subjected by Piedmont to the institution of Prefects and sub-Prefects, direct representatives of the Minister of the Interior, charged with maintenance of public order throughout the kingdom. For this the model was France. But at the same time Italy was looking to England as the model for Parliament: to England, where Parliament kept the closest watch upon ministers' actions, and where the play of rival parties determined the fate of governments. But then in England governments scarcely interfered in local affairs. In Italy, on the contrary, it was only through Parliament that attention could be got for urgent local affairs. There was already taking shape, in the Kingdom of Italy, that type of Parliamentarism in which governments find their majorities for national policies by conceding what deputies come and beg for (in the antechamber of the Minister of the Interior or of Public Works) on behalf of their constituencies. Jacini, in fact, and others with him, already saw the Italian Parliament becoming a marketplace for bargains between the King's Government and the constituencies, and losing its prestige as a platform for airing and sifting policy. The characteristic failings of Italian Parliamentarism were a matter of common observation within the first decade of the completion of Italian unity. Already the rumblings of anti-Parliamentary agitation could be distantly heard.

For the time being, however, Piedmontism—the extension to all Italy of the routine of the small centralized Piedmontese Kingdom—rather than Parliamentarism, was the form under which the defects of the monarchical State were experienced and denounced.

Jacini was a leading personage of ex-Austrian Lombardy, and for the next half-century the demand for decentralization went forth ceaselessly from the Lombard capital, Milan, which though it was the wealthiest of all Italian towns, and had enjoyed the status of capital of the Napoleonic 'Kingdom of Italy', had been wholly passed over, at a time when Turin, Florence, Rome and even Naples were vying with one another for the status and emoluments of the capital of the new Kingdom. Despite the gravity of their arguments, men like Jacini, who seriously advocated the granting of local autonomies, and a general overhauling of the Constitution which had been thrust on Italy by Piedmont, were rare among the Conservatives. Most of their class felt that the relative preservation of order and of property rights through the struggle for Italian unity had been something of a fortunate miracle. This miracle they associated with the Savoy monarchy, and they would do nothing seriously to weaken the roots which it had thrust into the soil.

The discontent thus became incarnated in men of less distinguished status and of less certain disinterestedness. It fermented as a somewhat shapeless agitation against the direct successors of Cavour. And this agitation became localized in the regions of lowest culture and enlightenment.

The ministers who served Victor Emmanuel from 1860 to 1878 were men of high culture and stainless rectitude. The Legitimists and the Papalists might officially brand them as barbarian invaders, Mazzini might scorn them as trimmers, hovering helplessly between an old and a new world. But it was no light achievement to have carried United Italy through its first decade and a half, through a civil war against semi-political 'brigands', last remnant of the armies of the old régimes, through an external war against Austria, through schismatic uprisings of Garibaldians and Mazzinians. The rigid traditions of Piedmont had prevailed and survived through all this disturbance. But this very success had accentuated the cleavage and contrast between north and south which now came to be felt as one of the gravest weaknesses of Italy.

In their haste to unify Italy by the crudest conceivable method of extending the Piedmontese constitution and administration to the whole kingdom, Cavour and his successors had very severely damaged the more retrograde areas of the peninsula, dispersing their communal wealth by the hurried sale of Crown and ecclesiastical properties, and in the case of the ex-Kingdom of Naples, of the State railways, and in general by taxing the sparse fortunes of the south at the same rates as the frequent fortunes of the north (and it was said with a far severer scrutiny of the returns). The northerners had entered on the heritage of the southern kingdom with a vastly exaggerated notion of the fertility of the soil, and of the benefits to production which might be procured there by abolishing medieval servitudes. Forced to spend without stinting on the most elementary necessities of the State, and having exhausted the capital reserves which they had inherited, they had resorted finally to applying throughout the peninsula the most abhorred tax of the old régime in Sicily: the tax on flour-milling which they themselves had abolished with a flourish ten years earlier. The impost on salt (described sentimentally as 'the poor man's sugar') had been doubled. The reward of these devices, which had so gravely estranged the south, was that the Kingdom of Italy in 1876 could boast for the first time a balanced Budget, with expenditure not greatly different from that shown in the first Budget (1862) but with a revenue considerably more than doubled.

Discontent was rifest in the impoverished south, but throughout Italy the Garibaldians and Mazzinians kept sections of the population in a ferment. The Romagna (northernmost province of the ex-Papal States), where Mazzinian Republicanism never ceased to be the prevalent political persuasion, seethed with sedition. Alongside of the Mazzinian Republicans there arose other malcontents calling themselves Socialists and Anarchists. The Anarchist sect was greatly in evidence. The Russian revolutionary Bakunin, who in those years was wrangling with Marx and Engels for the leadership of the International Working Men's Association, had one of his most fertile fields of action in Italy. There were Anarchist sections of the 'International' in Romagna and Sicily. Petty insurrections, and even 'a march on Bologna', occurred in the name of Anarchist-Socialism in the seventies. One Alessandro Mussolini, father of the future 'Duce', was not without note among the hundreds of young enthusiasts whose hopes went out towards a vast and purifying upheaval.

Socialists in Italy of the eighteen-seventies belonged less to the world of organized politics than to that of unattached enthusiasts and dreamers. It brought them no nearer to any influence upon affairs that the great Garibaldi in 1870 designated Socialism as 'The Sun of the Future'. But if political Socialism was still a forlorn sect, many eminent and respected people in Italy were at one with the Socialists in rejecting *laissez-faire* economics and demanding an economic intervention of the State to give the afflicted poorer classes some tangible advantages as a reward for their acceptance of the much-trumpeted unification of Italy.

The eminent Neapolitan patriot Pasquale Villari denounced those who had deprived the south of Italy of the safeguards inherent in their local laws and who thought now that it was sufficient to have 'faith in freedom' and let time do its work. It was a widespread opinion that the throwing together of the old states into one large national market, the free admission of foreign commerce and foreign capitalist enterprise, had enriched a few people but had deprived the many of accustomed security.

Such considerations began at last to affect the new governing classes. The electorate of half a million in a general election in the year 1874 returned a bare majority of ministerial deputies. In 1876 a defection of Tuscan deputies, irritated by an affront to their regional interests, put the successors of Cavour in a minority. This Parliamentary vote of March 18, 1876, was felt to be historic. Ministries had been defeated and replaced more than once in the first sixteen years of Italy's union, but now for the first time a Government was challenged and defeated by an Opposition in which there seemed to be vested the power to speak for the classes and interests which Cavour and his followers, in their zealous haste for a monarchical unification of Italy, had overborne. Cavour's disciples and successors had at last lost control of Parliament: old henchmen of Mazzini and Garibaldi, their tireless and intractable adversaries, now formed a part— the most vocal part—of a new Parliamentary majority.

II. GOVERNMENT BY THE LEFT

According to the Piedmontese fundamental statute of 1848, which had in 1861 become the general law of Italy, power is exercised jointly by the King and two Chambers: the King alone has the executive power: he nominates and dismisses ministers. Nothing is said (and this was later to be constantly recalled and emphasized) of the Ministry being representative of a Parliamentary majority, though Parliament must assent to all legislation. However that might be, in 1876 King Victor Emmanuel, knowing that he was expected to behave like a British monarch, at once sought a Prime Minister from among the new Parliamentary majority.

The deputies of this majority were by this time generally known as the 'Left'. They were grouped round those several men who, after distinguishing themselves at Garibaldi's and Mazzini's side in battle, or in bold conspiracy against the old régime, had ultimately acknowledged Victor Emmanuel's all-

Italian Kingship, and had accepted election to the Chamber without renouncing their intention to give a different shape to the new Italy than the existing one of an enlarged Piedmont. Until the incorporation of Rome they had vaguely constituted the 'Party of Action'. Mazzini, who consistently rejected the Kingship of Victor Emmanuel, and Garibaldi, who grew in time to be scarcely less disaffected, were powerful influences among them, though most of them stopped short of a formal profession of Republicanism. They had gathered about them the discontented of all provinces and classes: and the Right, or Cavourian party, in its zeal for financial stability had never paused to consider how many they threw into that attitude. Into the ranks of the Left, moreover, there gravitated, especially in the south, men who had been thrown out of local position or influence in consequence of the national unity. Scarcely converted adherents of the old Bourbon régime flocked in to join those who had stood for the most extreme and revolutionary methods of national unification. The Left was powerful in number, rich in men, but lacking in a principle of coherence, in substitution for which they offered at the best moral enthusiasm, at the worst a windy rhetoric.

Each leader of the Left had his own following—Francesco Crispi, the hero of the revolt of Sicily: Benedetto Cairoli, who had been a Lombard conspirator against Austria and captain in Garibaldi's legion; Giuseppe Zanardelli, leader of the rebellion of Brescia against Austria in 1848, and again in 1859; Giovanni Nicotera of Calabria, who had been the executant of some of Mazzini's most desperate insurrectionary schemes in the south; Agostino Bertani, who alone among these had held unswervingly to Mazzini until the great conspirator's death (1872). It was for none of these full-blooded patriots, however, that the King sent, but for one of his old subjects, the Piedmontese Agostino Depretis. Depretis like the others had his Mazzinian past, but he had long since learned in the old Piedmontese Chamber how to square an attitude of Parliamentary opposition with an ultimate acquiescence in the acts of the Monarchy. In the final war of unity he had been with Garibaldi in Sicily, but he had acted there as an unofficial moderator between Garibaldi and Cavour: a very different rôle from that chosen by an intransigent like Crispi. The man whom the King sent for to inaugurate the rule of the Left was from his royal point of view the safest of the safe. Thus there entered into the seat of power one of the three or four men whose names, for a generation, came to con-note a dustiness and prosiness which hung fatally around the constitutional arrangements of the Kingdom.

Despite this damping circumstance Italy received the new Government with festal acclamations. The heirs of the 'Party of Action' were expected to abolish odious exactions on the poor, to admit to the Parliamentary suffrage the multitudes who had been allowed (and indeed marched in military formation) to vote in the plebiscites for the Savoy monarchy. They would, it was said, reverse all the injustices of the rule of the Right. They would redeem the stricken south, allow the regions to manage their own affairs. They would show firmness against the Papacy, which still kept up its shrill protest, and against those clergy who persisted in portraying the existence of United Italy as a temporary prevailing of the Gates of Hell.

Having taken over the Government, Depretis dissolved the Chamber, and men of the Left were now returned by over-whelming majorities to represent the expectant provinces of the south, and not these alone. But the mood of hopeful expectancy quickly vanished. The Parliament of men of the Left considered Depretis to be a timid man and a temporizer, and when he refused to be hurried into the promised reforms they endeavoured to transfer their support to men of bolder appearance, men more strikingly different from those who had held power in the previous twenty years.

The soldierly Cairoli was hoisted into office and with him, as the chief voice and brain of the Ministry, the noble, eloquent Zanardelli. Zanardelli is one of those politicians over whom it is worth while to linger a moment. He represents the abstract passion of liberty. At the Ministry of the Interior he showed a truly intrepid faith in freedom by putting a sudden stop to police surveillance over the groups of Republicans, Anarchists and other declared enemies of the constitution. Freedom for what is desirable, he declared, involves freedom for what is undesirable. One should repress disorders which happen, not try to prevent their happening. Zanardelli would neither restrain Republicans and Anarchists at home nor yet would he attempt to silence those Italian voices which were heard with displeasure abroad. Those Italians who wished to fulminate against Austria, and to claim the still 'unredeemed' territories of Trieste and Trent, were to be free to do so. No fear of complications was to be allowed to silence them. And Italy rang with wild speeches.

The Foreign Minister Corti resigned, declaring that such licence at home was incompatible with good relations abroad. The Ministers of War and of the Navy went with him.

The doubts which so soon tempered the enthusiasm of the Italian people for its rulers of the Left were now enhanced by a sense of their incapacity to give Italy the international standing of a Great Power. It was the moment of the Congress of Berlin, and at that council for determining the temporary preservation and the ultimate disposal of the Ottoman heritage, Italy had been too weak to stand alone, too doubtful to weigh by supporting any other power. Italy under the Government of the Left appeared to have nothing much to say or do in the wider affairs of Europe. It was a hard discovery for a generation taught by Gioberti and Mazzini to view the unification of Italy as the first act in a world drama of mounting intensity and significance.

Mazzini and Garibaldi had always abhorred the grasping diplomacy of empires, but this was because they had in their mind an ideal federation of the peoples which was to wrest power from monarchs and priests and to harmonize the direct rule of the peoples of each nation in the framework of a scheme for the betterment of mankind. Of such a federation of mankind the 'Third Rome' was to be the symbol. The makers of United Italy and their sons still felt, and were to feel for a generation or more, an abhorrence for the unregenerate diplomatic scramble. But the most enthusiastic patriot could not point to unified Italy as a prototype of European regeneration. The unity of Italy once accomplished, the Left found Europe inclined to forget that Italy existed at all. Certainly Europe was taking no lessons from the 'Third Rome'. The fact was that although Mazzini as the apostle of Italian ideals had played a quite indispensable part in overthrowing the old Italian régimes it was to Cavour's astuteness, and not to Mazzini's revivalism, that Europe had ultimately accorded recognition. Austria had acquiesced in the cession of Lombardy and Venetia to Victor Emmanuel under duress from France and from Prussia. France had only just tolerated, also under duress, the final stage of Italian unification, the capture of Rome. Germany and England had no reason to oppose, and had some reason to support, the formation of a large new state in Europe. But only romantic poets had conceived that the Union of Italy might be an event transcending the political plane. Only in Italy, and only in the circles of the Left, did anyone outside literary circles recall that the 'new

Italy' and the 'Third Rome' had been prophetically adorned with the significance of a symbol of human regeneration. There had been more than rhetoric in these prophecies. A few men, at least, had been ready to die for them. And there were men in the Italian Left who genuinely desired to conduct Italian foreign policy on a plane of the highest human morality. But in their inexpert hands the regenerateness of Italy looked too like a helpless meekness. The Italians of 1878 were not quite so saintly as to regard political virtue as its own reward.

Cairoli and Zanardelli were thrown out of office after a bare six months. Depretis ruled again for six months and made way again for Cairoli, this time without Zanardelli. A devastating object lesson now suddenly laid bare the diplomatic situation in which the Italian Left had conducted themselves so amiably. In 1881 the French Republic suddenly invaded and occupied the corner of North Africa lying opposite Sicily. Italian trading interests in Tunis were, if not large, much larger than those of France, and they were protected by treaties of the old states with the Bey. They had been expanding in a way which the French—who did not forget that Italy produces Cavours as well as Mazzinis —took to be a prelude to occupation.

The French conquest of Tunis, undertaken on the pretext of an Algerian frontier disturbance, caught Cairoli and Mancini so much by surprise that they resigned without meeting Parliament. Italy's international helplessness had been shown up all too startlingly. Romantic heroes suddenly seemed to be altogether the wrong sort of men to cope with the tasks of high policy.

III. A PARLIAMENTARY DICTATOR

So Depretis came back at the head of the Government for the fourth time. The great men of the Left were by now all in opposition to him—Cairoli, Nicotera, Crispi, Zanardelli and Beccarini, each with his group of adherents, known jointly as the 'Pentarchy'. The Left could not or dared not sustain any of these popular leaders in power. Only Depretis could count upon adequate support, and Depretis was of the Left in little more than name. What indeed could the Left now stand for? What was left of the old hostility to popes and emperors? Policy could not now be based upon these old prejudices, and the longer the constitutional settlement of 1861 stood, the less was the inclination to challenge it. The first King of Italy died in 1878, Pope Pius IX a few weeks later. Garibaldi died in 1881. The new

Pope repeated his predecessor's protests against the existence of the Kingdom of Italy, but with each year the renewal of the Temporal Power of the Popes seemed a more unrealistic ambition. The new Pope Leo XIII and the new King Humbert were the embarrassed heirs of their predecessors' quarrels. Anti-Papalism was no adequate policy for the Left to rally round. And Republican France, by occupying Tunis, had utterly alienated those Italian opponents of monarchy who looked to Paris for moral inspiration. For thirty years Cavourians and Mazzinians, Piedmontese and enthusiasts for the 'Third Rome', Royalists and Republicans, had been passionately divided on their attitude towards the Pope and towards France. The Pope now frightened only the most timorous: the French were no longer an Empire respected by the Right and their Republic was obnoxious even to the Italian Left. The Right had been dismissed for their heartless insistence upon the tax on milling. It was to be a temporary expedient, and thanks to it, after years of financial strain, they had at last (1876) balanced the Budget.

The world-picture of the Left, which in 1876 had conjured up the enthusiasm of the middle classes, had within five years fallen quite awry. The case was not much different with their outlook upon home policy. What had happened to so many promises of economic justice? Preoccupied in their turn with finance, the Left continued the exaction against which they had declaimed.

The fact was, the Left proved to have no clear principles of policy at all. This is the turning-point of the constitutional history of Italy. Making capital out of the national bewilderment, Depretis—the incarnation of spiritless competence—proceeded to ignore the distinction of the two parties. With half of the Left against him, he turned for support to the Right; and he knew very well how to win it, not by the allurements of personal bribery—for like the great majority of Italian Parliamentarian leaders he had clean hands—but by pledges of attention to their ambitions and aid for the local interests on which their prestige was dependent. The system inaugurated by Depretis became known, from the obliteration of political distinctions, as *Trasformismo*. It was bequeathed by him to his most eminent successors, and the constant theme of Italian politics up to the First Great War may be described as a struggle between *Trasformismo* and groups which endeavoured to gain power in the name of definite principles, or at least of highly coloured myths.

An early example of clear-sighted diagnosis of the system is found in the electoral speeches of a particularly earnest patriot in the extreme south. Depretis had extended the suffrage to two million voters and replaced single-member constituencies by large regional constituencies, a measure which in itself set a premium upon the talent for political bargain-driving. Giuseppe Fortunato, Deputy for Basilicata, informed the electors that he stood for State overseership and assistance, against *laissez faire*, and for emancipation of the country from Catholic prejudices (though not for some form of new religion or the adoption of Protestantism). In virtue of these principles he proclaimed himself a supporter of the Left. But there were few who felt such a call to intellectual clarity. In many centres the successful candidates were returned to the Chamber in virtue simply of arrangements between a nominal Right candidate, or group of candidates, and the nominally Left Government. A great many deputies returned as of the Right forthwith gave their support to Depretis. For the time being Depretis took care that the official spokesmen for his acts of policy should be always men of the Left: those Left leaders who opposed him could never pillory him as a confessed turncoat. There were in all eight Depretis ministries. Their composition was determined by this Parliamentary dictator's determination to have a Chamber progressively more subservient to himself. The political business of the subordinate ministers was to dangle the expectation of Government assistance in the constituencies (whether in the economic and social interests of the constituency, or in the personal interest of the deputy) in such a way as to secure the deputy's support in Parliament.

IV. POLICY WITHOUT PRINCIPLE

Policy ungoverned by any recognizable principle now prevailed also in the Italian Foreign Office.

As omnipotent controller of the administration of Italy from 1881 to 1887 Depretis committed the country to the Triple Alliance with the Emperors in Berlin and Vienna, and built a navy of big ships (four of the largest ironclads of the time) to confront the French navy. Depretis was answering the French occupation of Tunis. But this League with German Emperors was something that old Mazzinians, however disillusioned by the behaviour of Republican France, could not stomach. In Trieste, Istria and the Trentino the Austrian Empire still included a few hundred thousand Italians. It was with the despotic ruler of these 'unredeemed' territories, the old supporter of the Papacy and tyrant of northern Italy, that Depretis had tied the new Italy in alliance. Mazzinians denounced the Premier as an arch-traitor. A few ardent men broke away from the Left and constituted an Extreme Left, which included, besides a Republican group and a Radical group, one or two deputies who called themselves Socialists. A young Trieste student, named Oberdan, made himself the hero of the Extreme Left by firing a shot at the Austrian Emperor, not in a spirit of vengeance but in order to strain and frustrate the Italo-Austrian conciliation. Oberdan was executed in Austria and his blood imputed to the savagery of Italy's unnatural ally. In fine, after six years of power the Left was being execrated by an Extreme Left for just such misdemeanours as had in the sixties and seventies formed the basis of the agitation of the Left against the Right. The Extreme Left was scarcely less uproarious against Depretis' home policy. He had finally after long delay abolished the tax on flour-milling, replacing the revenue so lost by new heavy duties on coffee, sugar and imports in general. Otherwise he had left the country very much where it was before—poor and discontented.

Financial agitations and controversies loomed so large in this period of Italian history that some have sought in them the key to the whole drama. One episode, at least, is worth recording. Its significance may be found to be prophetic of later times.

Throughout the domination of the 'Left', and Depretis' Parliamentary dictatorship, the Finance Ministry was ruled by a brilliant orator, Agostino Magliani. He was the successor of a line of ministers who had made it a sacred duty to provide for expenditure out of revenue, even if the revenue had to be bolstered up by forced sales of public property. Magliani, however, was an expert in the art of viewing current expenditure as capital outlay which might be properly provided for by incurring debt. Magliani duly provided the wherewithal for the great national expenditure on the fleet against the French menace: for railway constructions which were financed by the State on a grand scale in regions of Italy where, for want of industry and commerce, no private enterprise could expect to pay its way: and further for abundant national subsidies to Florence, because it had suffered by a foiled expectation of being the capital of Italy, to Rome because it had actually become the capital of Italy, and to Naples because it had ceased to be a capital at all. While he provided for all this outlay Magliani was pledged to remit the chief special tax which had been imposed by his predecessors to pay for the preliminary costs of the Kingdom.

Magliani had promised something more. In 1866, the year of the war for Venetia, the Italian State banks (which still comprised the old national banks of Piedmont, Tuscany, Naples and Sicily) had ceased payments in gold and silver: the Italian currency was an unredeemable paper money, and was quoted with a depreciation sometimes reaching ten per cent on the French franc and other currencies. The economists of the time viewed the depreciation as a universal tax upon consumers, since prices in paper lire were correspondingly higher than in gold lire or francs. Magliani undertook to restore the convertibility of the currency and raised an Anglo-French loan of 800 million lire in gold, through the Banque d'Escompte in Paris and Baring's and Hambro's banks in London. The Italian banks resumed payments in specie. For a year or two the lira was again quoted at parity with the franc. But the Italian currency consisted largely in silver coins, of which quantities were held abroad. At that moment the great depreciation of silver, following on the change over of Germany to a gold currency, set in: the Italian banks had to be exonerated from the obligation to accept silver in exchange for gold, and the depreciation of the lira recommenced. To provide finance for the Budget and to reduce the import bill the Government resorted to a stiffening of import duties and this, since France was the largest provider of Italy, brought on a conflict with France. Italy denounced the existing Treaty of Commerce; France refused to negotiate another: each country imposed special taxes on the other's goods as the exchange between them was halved. From 1887 to 1888 Italy's entire foreign trade, imports and exports, was reduced by a quarter.

The north of Italy stood to benefit at least in some of the industrial centres, to which the currency depreciation had already given occasion for substantial new developments. The south of Italy was, on the contrary, largely bereft of the only market for one of its chief exports, the Italian wine, which was used in France in great quantities for mixing purposes. A year or two before this Count Stefano Jacini, the Milanese patriot, had drawn up the final report of an exhaustive State inquiry into agriculture throughout the country. The farmers and peasants, Jacini said, might be materially a little better off than they had been before the Unification of Italy: but in other countries agriculture had advanced much more quickly. Agricultural Italy was relatively worse off and (he added) morally worse off than it had been a quarter-century before. The State had taxed and borrowed away the savings of landowners for the setting up of its great urban organizations and for the conduct of high policy.

The disastrous end of the financial policy of Magliani led to a typical Italian agitation for the abandonment of the all too grandiose ambitions of the recent past. Attention became fixed, however, not upon fundamental features of the administration, but upon a very modest chapter in colonial enterprise which had been initiated in the enthusiastic period of the rule of the Left.

A colonial settlement had been established on the Red Sea, which the Foreign Minister Mancini declared in noble parlance 'holds the keys of the Mediterranean'. In the meantime, the settlement had brought Italy nothing but a military disaster. In 1887 the Italian forces suffered the massacre of a garrison of 500 men at Dogali at the hands of an Abyssinian Ras. The opponents and detractors of Depretis insisted upon bringing a general before a court martial. Shaken by the disaster, and by this time old and infirm, Depretis invited his old rival and critic Francesco Crispi into the Cabinet. Shortly afterwards the first Parliamentary Dictator of Italy died, and King Humbert called upon Crispi to form a Government. An honest patriot and a zealous administrator, Depretis had found himself recalled to office over and over again for the inestimable merit of having no general policy. Each of his rivals was identified with some policy which might split the country and bring United Italy to an abrupt end within a quarter-century of its foundation. He himself held the country together by putting politics—the art of gaining secure personal allegiances—before policy. And this —after an interval of different character which must now be described—proved to be the classic formula of the affairs of Italy until the year 1915.

CHAPTER THREE

GOVERNMENT BY MAN OF DESTINY

I. CRISPI'S WILL TO POWER.—Francesco Crispi, ex-Mazzinian, ambitious, dictatorial, energetic, succeeded Depretis. It was personal rule again, though the person was this time changeable, forceful and the object of fierce hatreds.

II. STRONG HAND ABROAD AND AT HOME.—Crispi quarrels with France: provokes economic upheaval: and copes with the consequences by the method of violence.

III. AFRICAN GLORY AND SHAME.—He attempts to build a Northeast African Empire: its ruins envelop him in disgrace.

IV. SOCIALISM AS MENACE AND HOPE.—Crispi leaves a heritage of confusion. The century closes on a note of alarm, though with some hopeful presages.

I. CRISPI'S WILL TO POWER

Francesco Crispi, the Sicilian, was in strong contrast to Depretis a man of policy more than of politics. At the moment when the Piedmontese army ousted Garibaldi from authority in Sicily and Naples, Crispi was banished by the Court from the higher reaches of public life. No severer treatment could have been meted out to a popular hero and a gifted leader who, after all, had accepted the monarchy at the cost of a harsh reproof from his old master Mazzini. Garibaldi on passing to the mainland in 1869 had left Crispi as the effectual dictator of Sicily, and had later called him to his side at Naples. Cavour promptly put a ban upon the employment of Crispi in any responsible position, and it was all that Crispi could do to find a constituency to venture to elect him to the first Italian Parliament. Crispi was far from being a safe man like Depretis. In the assembly he rose again and again to demand the completion of Italian Unity by the seizure of Rome. He never went back upon his acceptance of the monarchy, but when Rome was occupied, and the Government—to soothe Catholic consciences—promised still to recognize the 'sovereignty' of the Pope, Crispi protested that 'sovereignty' in Italy was only of the people: the King himself was not a sovereign, but the chosen mandatory of the people. How then could sovereignty be recognized in the Pope? ('Howls of joy from the anti-papal tigers' reported a clerical journalist.) In 1877 Depretis gave Crispi the Ministry of the Interior, and there

62

he was responsible for relations with the Vatican on the death of Pius IX. Some of the Cardinals planned to hold the Conclave abroad: but Crispi was not going to have the council of a hostile Roman Church deliberating outside his own jurisdiction: he threatened to occupy the Vatican with troops if the Conclave were not held there. Incautious in his private as in his public life, Crispi was never long immune from violent attacks on his person. He was forced to resign the Ministry of the Interior on a charge of bigamy which was preferred against him by a rival politician of his own complexion, Nicotera. It was an accusation which his opponents regularly trotted out along with accusations of financial duplicity whenever Crispi particularly provoked them. (The bigamy question—subject of a whole library of pamphlets—turned on whether a form of marriage which Crispi had gone through in youth at Malta was binding.)

In one respect, however, Crispi was the true heir of Depretis. When, at the age of sixty-seven, he succeeded him as Head of the Government, he had long ceased to take any serious account of political groupings. He provoked and sustained the simultaneous hostility both of the swelling and ever more vocal 'Extreme Left' and of the cautious, diffident elements of the Right. The Right saw in him a restless adventurer perpetually seeking changes and climaxes: the Extreme Left, who had once cheered him on fiercely as the spokesman of their own slogans (Down with popes, emperors, courtiers! Rome for the Italian people! Up the brotherhood of nations!), now spied on him in the seat of power with frantic hatred. It was not so much that he had thrown over their ideals. Crispi to the end of his long life did homage to Mazzini's great dream of a Europe of free and equal national states, each developing harmoniously, the spirit of the peoples heightened by faith in God's plan of history. But Crispi felt irresistibly called to the immediate clearing up of the public problems next in front of him. To gain power was his imperative instinct, and having marked down those whom it was necessary to have as allies or supporters, or to avoid having as enemies, he adjusted his day-to-day policy accordingly.

The impelling urge to power had already caused him to forswear Republican principles. He was equally ready to abandon Mazzinian intransigence against the Holy See. A few weeks before Depretis' death, when Crispi was already taking charge of the Government, he prepared to come to terms also with the Papacy. He received a Benedictine prelate, Monsignor Tosti, whom he believed to be a qualified negotiator on behalf of Leo XIII. The Pope, however, publicly emphatically disclaimed Tosti. Crispi thereupon reverted to his pugnacious anti-Clericalism and for two years worked to reduce the influence of the clergy upon national education. Late in 1887 he suspended the Mayor of Rome for offering congratulations on the Pope's ordination jubilee-day. In the municipality, as in Parliament and in the Palace, there must be (wrote Crispi's journalistic mouthpiece) a single heart and a single will. In 1889 he gave full official approval for a tercentenary celebration of the burning of Giordano Bruno, a grandiose anti-Clerical ceremony which was staged almost within hearing of the Vatican precincts. These menacing attitudes were opportunistic. Crispi was quite ready to have the Church as an ally. Only that Italian statesman (he said) who succeeded in reconciling Italy with the Papacy would have a great name in history, and he was reported to have asked a prelate: 'Why cannot I have a direct talk with the Pope? We could patch up so much between us.' A year or two later, two Cardinals appeared to officiate at Crispi's daughter's wedding. It was the anti-Clericals' turn to revile this treason to their cause.

II. STRONG HAND ABROAD AND AT HOME

Depretis had drawn his followers from Left and Right alike. His readiness to accept support from any side had become known as 'Trasformismo'. It was a system which presupposed the permanence of Depretis. But with far more passion than Depretis Crispi felt himself to be indispensable to the country, and like Depretis he was for a certain time regarded as indispensable even by those who hated him. Depretis, venerable, full-bearded, a master of gentle ridicule, had eluded opposition by his flexibility: Crispi exposed himself and every cause to so much opposition that followers felt forced to support him for fear of the State collapsing if he were to fall. On forming his first Government Crispi kept on the Home Office and also took over the Foreign Office. He was not going to have home policy and foreign policy confounding each other. In foreign policy he drew closer and closer to the German and Austrian empires, and in his inextinguishable anger against France for the occupation of Tunis he drifted into a 'tariff war' between Italy and France, which did Italy much damage and France very little. Crispi inherited Mazzini's indifference to economic problems and ignorance of them. From 1887 to 1888 the commerce between the countries was about halved on either side: but for Italy this meant a shrinkage of the entire foreign trade of the country by a quarter. France was quickly and easily able to make up for the Italian market, both on the buying and on the selling side, Italy could do nothing to replace the French market.

Taking France to be Italy's irreconcilable enemy, Crispi resolved that he would allow no undisciplined shows of patriotism to disturb the Triple Alliance with Germany and Austria. He treated 'irredentists' not as heroes but as public nuisances. He supplemented the Austrian repression of Italian societies in Trieste by himself dissolving the irredentist clubs on Italian soil. He was capable of naïve errors where his passions were engaged. He believed on the evidence of tittle-tattle that France intended suddenly to pounce on Sicily or some other exposed portion of Italian coast, and on one occasion sent signals of alarm to London and Berlin. His old fellow-Mazzinians regarded him as a turn-coat, and soon enough as a tyrant, a madman and a criminal. In 1890 the leader of the Radical, Republican and Socialist groups entered into a pact for united action against him. The 'Extreme Left' was thus given permanent form: a Mazzinian orator, poet, agitator and indefatigable duellist, Felice Cavalotti, presided over it. And since suspicion of France was Crispi's permanent passion Cavalotti went to France and in the name of his group swore friendship with the French Radicals and Socialists.

The world of Crispi's imagination bristled with conspiracies inside and outside Italy. Now it was the French, another time it was international freemasonry (in the bosom of whose gatherings undoubtedly the Italian democrats responded to French inspiration), or yet again the Republican Separatists or the Atheist Anarchists (among whom Crispi classed all Socialists and organizers of trade unions) who excited his suspicions. But he inveighed also against the surviving politicians of the old Cavourian Right, ferociously exhuming the controversies of twenty years earlier. At last they too joined the league to withdraw Parliamentary support from him. He was forced out of office. But none of a number of transient successors could hold together a Parliamentary majority—not even a Piedmontese of the notable name of Giovanni Giolitti; and this though Giolitti in 1892 followed up his appointment with a general election in which Government organization and favouritism were used with

a thoroughness far exceeding the practices of Depretis. Crispi
had still his great name, and in a great name the leading classes
still had more confidence than in any programme. Even the
disastrous results of some of his own measures made his presence
at the head of affairs indispensable. The tariff war with France
had thrown the silk industry, which employed about 200,000
people, into disorder and cut off the chief market for the wines
of the south. The middle classes were thoroughly alarmed. For
the first time proletarian organizations were beginning to count
in politics and were experimenting with the social weapon of the
strike. Plots for declaring an independent republic were suspected
in Milan and Turin, while in Sicily the peasants flocked to enrol
themselves in a movement known as the Fasci Siciliani (Sicilian
groups) to force the landlords to listen to grievances.

Landlords and employers called loudly for the strong hand,
and Crispi was nothing if not ready to answer the call. The
Extreme Left made a practice at this time of always voting
against the Government, and its votes combined with those of
the Conservative wing sufficed to eject Giolitti and to open the
way for Crispi's return.

Crispi now proceeded to reduce the country to obedience.
He sent 50,000 troops to his native Sicily, instituted special
tribunals, suspended newspapers on the strength of special powers
allowed by the Constitution in national emergencies. Grave
disorders meanwhile had been discovered in the chief Roman
bank and in the chief banks of Tuscany and Naples. It was
revealed that Crispi and other politicians had received credits
for somewhat inscrutable purposes. Crispi tried to direct the
main suspicion against Giolitti—and it illustrates the tension of
the moment that this ex-Premier evaded arrest by a quick retreat
to Germany. The Extreme Left tried to force an open inquiry
into the transactions of Crispi and of his family. Cavalotti
proclaimed that the unresolved 'moral question' against Crispi
was the source of all the mischief and degeneration of Italian
politics and enumerated Crispi's malpractices in four hundred
pages of print.

III. AFRICAN GLORY AND SHAME

But Crispi's energy was not fully, perhaps not even primarily,
absorbed in the furies of reciprocal accusation, or in the subtleties
of squaring the practice of repression with the theory of the
Liberal Constitution (for he neither desired nor attempted any

change of the constitutional forms). He had vowed himself to a policy of grandeur, of assertion of Italy's right and duty and ability to compete successfully in all fields against France. Depretis and his counsellors had with bashful timidity promoted a small settlement on the Red Sea, but it had not entered their minds to enter seriously into the race for the partition of Mediterranean Africa. Prior to the French march on Tunis, they had refused to let themselves be encouraged by Prussia to go in there first, and they had rejected an overture made by England in 1882 for Anglo-Italian co-operation in Egypt. The French seizure of Tunis had provoked deep but impotent mortification. Even when Depretis assented to the small settlement on the Red Sea coast at Massowah troops and supplies were sent only intermittently. After the disaster of Dogali in 1887 Depretis was faced with a choice between forswearing all colonialism or backing up the policy with adequate means. It was while he was weighing the alternative that unpopularity, age and exhaustion overtook Depretis.

On taking office, Crispi loudly proclaimed it to be one of his special tasks to vindicate Italian honour in the Red Sea, though adding that he had not in the first place favoured expeditions in that quarter.

At first Crispi was not only successful, but successful without effort or cost. A rivalry had developed between various Abyssinian chiefs for the 'Emperorship' of that tribal federation, and Crispi by extending support to the winning candidate, Menelik, was repaid with that personage's signature to a treaty (Treaty of Uccialli, 1889) in which he appeared to recognize Italy as Protector of Abyssinia. Crispi had the pleasure of being recognized, in at least one series of European negotiations, as the authorized spokesman of Abyssinia to the outer world.

Soon this easy success was revealed at its true value. Having obtained a small loan from Italy, Menelik, who had French, Russian and other advisers at his Court, repudiated the Italian protectorate, declaring that the Ethiopian text assented to by his advisers gave him merely the option of asking Italian help when he needed it. Menelik stirred up the coastal tribes to resist Italian encroachments. The Italian Commander in the Red Sea, Oreste Baratieri, dealt successfully with these tribes, and touring round Italy played the popular hero. He was a fascinating writer and speaker and a considerable demagogue. His command comprised about 20,000 men in the Red Sea coastal garrisons. It was no force with which to challenge the unknown strength of the teeming inland tribes of Ethiopia, but Crispi's Finance Minister vetoed any greater outlay.

Crispi, however, was determined to avenge Dogali with military triumphs on the Red Sea. He spurred on, or rather maddened, Baratieri with insulting telegrams about his slow progress. Finally—as it happened, at the very moment when Menelik himself was advancing towards the coast with a huge army— Crispi secretly decided to supersede Baratieri. It seems that a leakage of information about his successor's nomination determined the unhappy Commander to risk his whole forces in a gamble in which he might re-establish his credit. Baratieri and his chief subordinate were certainly at variance. The brigades of the Italian force of 15,000, instructed to assemble on the heights over the town of Adua, near which Menelik was encamped, lost touch with each other owing to faulty maps, misunderstanding of local names, or deliberate trickery by the guides. Menelik's hordes fell upon the isolated brigades, which fought bravely but were almost wholly massacred or taken prisoner. Baratieri himself escaped back to Asmara, whence in a folly of despair he began to throw blame for the disaster upon his associates.

The defeat of Adua—than which few military disasters have ever been more directly traceable to faulty statesmanship— instantaneously broke Crispi's hold over Parliament and the country. For years manufacturing Italy had accused him of ruining trade and taxing away profits in order to vent his rancour on France and to conduct a war of magnificence in Africa. Cavalotti and his friends reiterated that Crispi was morally malign, politically ruinous and psychologically a megalomaniac. It was a Conservative politician who threw this last epithet into circulation, and when Crispi came to the Chamber to communicate the news of the disaster of Adua, Conservatives joined with the Extreme Left in howling him down. So strong was popular fury that Crispi's carriage had to pass by a circuitous route to avoid outrage. The rank and file of the deputies from the south, Crispi's men by personal compact as long as Crispi through the Ministry of the Interior commanded the officialdom of the remote provinces, deserted him hurriedly. He was old; he had incited the country to look away from its domestic miseries to splendour in Africa, and now the foothold in Africa was all but lost. Crispi's more level-headed opponents called for Italy to take the lesson to heart and to terminate, once and for all,

the unhappy venture in colonial power politics.   Frantic agitators
went further and shouted: 'Long live Menelik!'

The only Government which could be formed to succeed
Crispi was a miscellaneous committee of men of all opinions.
Once again, as in the intervals, fifteen years earlier, when
Depretis had been transiently dispossessed, so now each successive
Government that was formed by Crispi's opponents came
quickly to grief through the withdrawal of one of the group
chieftains.   Crispi waited to be summoned, but King Humbert
judged that his career as a man of destiny was closed.   Not so
the passions which his personality had aroused.   Felice Cavalotti,
Crispi's sworn enemy, author of a four-hundred-page list of his
crimes, was killed in a duel just two years after Crispi's fall: vast
processions of students and working people followed him to his
grave, and demonstrated throughout Italy against the broken
old Sicilian who was held somehow responsible for his death.

IV. SOCIALISM AS MENACE AND HOPE

The parties and movements which Crispi had repressed, the
men who had refused to enter into compacts with him, thrust
themselves boldly forward—Republicans, Radicals and Socialists.
It was now that 'Socialists' came to be viewed as belonging to
the political world.   The mid-nineteenth-century Socialists of
Italy had been obscure conspirators for a prophetically conceived rebirth of humanity through upheaval.   This was still the
character of the Socialist agitator or apostle in remote provinces.
In Romagna, the local agitator and organizer Alessandro
Mussolini, father of the future Duce, emitted in 1891 the following
definition of Socialism: 'Science illuminating the world: reason
mastering faith: free thought overthrowing prejudice: free
agreement between men to live a truly civilized life: true justice
enthroned on the earth: a sublime harmony of concept, thought
and action.'   There had been Socialists also drawn from the
higher social classes, spirits aloof from the world, estranged from
official religion, preaching only a Franciscan contempt for wealth
and power.   Such evangelists renounced honourable positions
and careers to preach human brotherhood, and it is a testimony
at least to the spiritual tension in which they lived that several
of the most ardent of them succumbed to incurable mental
diseases.   But an entirely different sort of Socialism was now
dawning.   Among the Milanese workmen, impatient alike with
the revolutionary doctrinaires of remote country regions and with

the unworldly evangelists, a small Trade Union Party had struggled into existence: it rigidly excluded from its ranks all but wage-earners. Italian Socialism was already developing a wing of middle-class intellectuals and a wing of trade unionists who could not easily tolerate each other.

Crispi had a horror of the name of Socialist. It conjured up to his mind the image of fanatics modelled on the nihilist-terrorists of Russia. It was a common enough valuation in 1890. Even the Radicals of the Cavalotti school regarded Socialism as something infamous until Crispi's persecutions disposed them more kindly to the victims. In the north of Italy, as Crispi made himself increasingly abhorred, Socialism was increasingly tolerated in Radical circles, and it appeared to young bourgeois in the radiance of a faith of the future.

This rhetorical Socialism, and the grimmer spirit of revolt that was kindling in the workshops of industry, joined to give a new character to the rapidly growing cities of the north. Milan, Genoa and Turin, towns where factory-workers were numbered by tens of thousands, began to appear to foreign observers as centres of tumult and unrest, directed permanently towards dimly imagined upheavals. Brilliant university students became known throughout Italy for defiant harangues delivered in the special court before which they were haled as Socialists or accomplices of Socialists.

The uproar was intense at the moment of Crispi's fall. His successors endeavoured to mitigate it by somewhat milder treatment, but they soon resorted again to special courts and martial law. General Pelloux, who assumed the Premiership in 1898 with the reputation of a liberal, popular and indulgent military commander, soon outdid Crispi himself in harsh and arbitrary action.

Amid this tumult the development of the Italian Parliamentary régime in the past quarter of a century was anxiously scrutinized. Parliamentary democracy, the supreme convenience of civilization which Piedmont had brought to Italy, no longer bore the faintest resemblance to that systematic alternation of strong and mutually corrective parties in office which had been so much admired in England as a model for universal imitation. Landowners and manufacturers called for the suffrage to be restricted. There was a demand for something like a royal dictatorship. Sonnino, a politician who had started on his career as the spokesman for the poor peasants of Sicily, and had been an advocate of universal suffrage, re-read the Piedmontese Constitution and found that according to its letter the King's ministers should be held responsible to the King and not to Parliament. He urged that the King should take to himself a power which had been considered obsolete even in pre-1860 Piedmont, rather than let the 'Extreme Left' of Socialists, Republicans and Radicals get through Parliament a free field for their own experiments.

The nineteenth century closed, for Italy, in an atmosphere of official lassitude broken by tremors of revolt which were magnified rather than offset by hints of an impending era of economic expansion. A grave material and moral crisis seemed to threaten the foundations of the political structure. It was a crisis of frustrated imaginations: a typically Italian crisis, for it is in the Italian nature to approach the future with a clear pictorial anticipation of things to be. Mazzini, Garibaldi, Gioberti and Cavour had each struggled to create a united Italy in the image of a preconceived design. Thus Mazzini cherished, and bequeathed to his admirers, the clear-cut image of an Italy springing spontaneously from a republican revival of all the great old decayed cities. These were to group themselves round a regenerated Rome, whence there would radiate new metaphysic and moral truths for all mankind. Gioberti's version had it that Italy would be formed by the federation of Piedmont, Tuscany, Naples, Lombardy under a Papal presidency, the hierarchical tradition of Christendom giving its consecration in this chosen land to freedom and reform. In a singularly different spirit, but with the same pictorial clarity, Cavour sighed after a modern liberal and industrial Kingdom of Italy to be formed by the assimilation of all its regions and of all their institutions to those of westernized and progressive Piedmont. It was Cavour's extraordinary achievement to utilize the moral energy generated by Mazzini and Gioberti for the lightning realization of his own programme. It was an Italy of Piedmontese prefects and generals that Mazzini, Gioberti and other apostles of Italian unity had unwittingly brought into being. The spectacle filled such men with resentment, and the heritage which they bequeathed to their disciples was one of scorn for the abortion. Yet, as it was repeatedly shown, sooner than wreck what had been achieved, all the patriotic Italian factions would in the last resort rally round the Savoy monarchy and the institutions which it had brought with it to Rome. Depretis and Crispi, old henchmen of Mazzini, identified themselves utterly with the maintenance of the monarchical régime, the former dedicating to it his incomparable skill in co-involving the interests of local groups with those of the bureaucracy in Rome, the latter his energy, imagination and ruthlessness at home and abroad. Throwing over their party allegiances, picking supporters and co-operators wherever they found them, Depretis and Crispi consolidated throughout a quarter-century a body of upper- and middle-class Governmentalists who stood for keeping the new kingdom as a going concern, and preserving it against the risks of disintegration which any affirmation of broad principles would bring with it. Government of thirty millions by three thousand for the benefit of three hundred thousand it was called. With the turn of the century there came a new and stronger endeavour to transform it into something nobler and better—doomed to quick frustration, we shall see.

CHAPTER FOUR

POWER WITHOUT GLORY: GIOLITTI

I. AN END TO REPRESSION.—The end of Crispi was not the end of repression. Pelloux tried to rule by violence. But Socialists and Radicals raised a standard of revolt, and Pelloux was driven from office. There followed the democratic Zanardelli, with a bold programme of reforms. But these included the legitimization of divorce, and excited animosity in the Church. On Zanardelli's broken health Giolitti climbed to supreme power.

II. GIOLITTI: MAN AND METHODS.—Giolitti plays off the parties: he nominates his own 'opponents': he is all things to all men— at a price.

III. MASTER OF ITALY.—Tranquillity breeds prosperity. Giolitti's Italy grows in population and wealth. There is a shady side. The tranquillity is a fruit of obscure bargains and discreet doses of persecution. Dead men at the polling booth.

IV. FROM CAVOUR TO GIOLITTI.—We briefly reconsider how Italy had changed in half a century.

I. AN END TO REPRESSION

Here, then, is Italy at the beginning of the twentieth century visibly on the way to material enrichment. But the prime beneficiaries were a class of politicians intimately connected with land speculation and with finance, men without notable character or popular appeal. It was almost a universal impression that the fatherland, whose formation had called into play the highest gifts of the Italian people, now offered scope only to mediocrities. The saints and heroes and geniuses of a great Italian generation had given their lives to create a United Italy: the best men of a less brilliant generation had then taken over their heritage: but in the last quarter of the nineteenth century the men of clear outlook and single purpose had given up the struggle. An unworthy clan had dug itself in to the places of authority and could successfully defy challenge from any quarter.

The atmosphere was prohibitive of any grand affirmation of principle, whether for or against the constituted order. For example if the State was in formal opposition to the Church, and its growing educational system was alienated from the dogmas and practices of religion, yet the fervent Catholic was restrained from pressing the cause of religion in public life. For the Vatican did not wish to provoke new tension and it advised fervent Catholics to abstain from political activity. There was no scope in politics, either, for the humanitarian religiosity of a Mazzini. His ideals were still celebrated in verse and in oratory, but they seemed irrelevant to the social and economic problems of the new times. But neither did the energetic and earthy Liberalism of a Cavour retain its power to project a pattern on to the current of affairs. It bore the blame of having left the south of Italy to decay in face of the outside competition suddenly thrust upon it. A grey disillusionment lay upon the mind of a generation. It was no company of missionaries, no school of thought, who represented Italy before the world. Astute and forceful managers of men alone gave their character to that 'Third Italy' which had been ushered in with sacred enthusiasm.

Such was the lament to be heard on all sides: but one group, on the fringe of the constitutional life of the country, made bold to declare itself the heir and resuscitator of great human ideals. It was the 'Extreme Left', known for short simply as *L'Estrema*, which claimed to bridge the gap between ideal conceptions and practical politics. In the Parliamentary 'Extreme Left' a remnant of obstinate perpetuators of Mazzini's Republicanism joined with enthusiasts for universal suffrage and world pacifism ('Radicals'), and into association with these there gravitated also the few men who were returned from time to time by certain Parliamentary constituencies under the description 'Socialist'.

Persecution by Crispi and Pelloux gave to this miscellaneous assemblage of the Extreme Left a cohesion and a consistency in the eyes of the country at large. In the atmosphere of the times it stood for something broader than a political doctrine. Sympathy with *L'Estrema* usually connoted, among the professional men and school teachers, an enthusiastic approval of the gospel of the perfectibility of Man through science.

The Extreme Left took on the spokesmanship in Italian politics of the Positivist idea. They sought power in order that Italy might be made safe for the beneficent activities, discoveries and fruits of experimental science. Their outlook was broadly international, and had more affinity with the English school of Herbert Spencer than with the French positivism derived from Comte. They were no mere mirrors of foreign influence. The Italian positivist criminologists, headed by Cesare Lombroso, were making a stir in all Europe. This school placed upon 'environment' almost the whole responsibility for the criminal or anti-social actions of individuals. They believed that the re-education and transplantation of maladjusted individuals might almost wholly replace punishment of the criminal. Such were the ideas which Enrico Ferri, Lombroso's chief disciple, had in mind when one day in somewhat portentous style he declared himself to be a convert to 'scientific' socialism. The relation between these anthropological doctrines and the economics of Marxism was vague: but both were somehow fitted into the edifice of a 'Religion of Science'. The Extreme Left thus laid claim to be the trustees of a humanitarian creed. The most admired confessor of this religion was Roberto Ardigò, a learned and eloquent Catholic priest who had resigned his benefice on account of religious doubts. Ardigò pleaded powerfully for an open and frank repudiation by the educated youth of any sort of dogmatic religion. And the Socialist leaders of the generation which was young at the turn of the century, men like Filippo Turati and Leonida Bissolati, modelled themselves upon Ardigò, raising the banner of a new and austerely 'scientific' outlook upon life, coupled somewhat awkwardly with a profession of faith in a coming miracle of social revolution.

Under Crispi and Pelloux the university students, who followed these currents, suffered some degree of police persecution. This heightened their fame. In the north of Italy groups of students made it their Sunday duty to repair to remote villages and to preach the Kingdom of Science and Socialism to countrymen in the piazza in front of the church. Scarcely a man of intellectual note in that generation eluded the fascination of this gospel of Socialism. It was embraced by the flamboyant Gabriele d'Annunzio, who after getting himself elected as a deputy of the Right suddenly announced 'I go towards Life' and took his place in Parliament among the Socialists: and in contrasting sobriety it was embraced by the exquisitely learned and meditative Benedetto Croce in his library in Naples. Guglielmo Ferrero, another brilliant representative of the same generation, was often found in the forefront of scuffles with the police, and landed himself more than once in gaol for his zeal as a popular propagandist.

The Extreme Left though few in Parliamentary numbers (sixty to seventy members in 1900 supported by a quarter of the electorate) was the Party of Youth, and in the measure that it successfully defied Governmental persecution it attracted those who described themselves as the Moderate, or Constitutional, Left, from their place in the colourless Governmental majority. Without a Depretis or a Crispi this majority was losing that working coherency which had so long served it in lieu of a definite policy. In Parliament the Extreme Left paralysed Pelloux by perpetual obstruction: Pelloux tried to retort by the summary rushing of measures through the Chamber without giving time for discussion. But the Constitutional Left supported the Extreme, and Pelloux was constrained to resign. Jubilation over this event was suddenly checked, and new incitement to repression was, however, afforded by the assassination of King Humbert by an anarchist in Lombardy in the first year of the new century. But the ensuing critical situation enabled the gathering strength of Left sentiment to reveal itself. An attempt to resuscitate Pelloux roused fierce opposition on a national scale heralding, it seemed, a democratic dawn.

The new young King Victor Emmanuel III showed himself remarkably sensitive to the hopes of his own generation. He entrusted the formation of the new Government not to a master of repression, but to the most representative man of the Left. It was the venerable Giuseppe Zanardelli who now again attained office, a survivor from among the combatants of 1848, no orthodox Mazzinian but a fervent rationalist democrat, an unshakable believer in man's power and ultimate inclination to live wisely in freedom if only he were left with his responsibility and not corrected and dragooned on the first sign of error. Zanardelli, as has already been recounted, had, many years before, held for a brief spell the Ministry of the Interior, where he greatly alarmed his colleagues by the withdrawal of police measures against Republicans and by tolerating even the extremest expressions of opinion. In the intervening years, from his seat in the Chamber amid the Moderate Left he had denounced the repressions of Crispi and Pelloux with all the force of an earnest philosophy of freedom. This philosophy now fitted closely with the mood of the young generation and Zanardelli was not going to shrink from the boldest applications of it. On taking office he at once planned a new marriage law to admit of divorce, a measure which was demanded by sociologists, psychologists, and in general by those who claimed reform in the name of science, but which at once excited hot protests from the Church and other guardians of the tradition of the indissoluble family.

It has been said [1] authoritatively that, in the entire course of a half-century of Italian Parliamentary Government after 1870, two effective Parliamentary parties confronted each other for the first and only time at the turn of the century, when Zanardelli took the place of Pelloux. Around Pelloux were gathered the landlords and industrialists, who held that there was only one possible method of governing Italy: striking with the strong hand against every movement for radical reformation of institutions, and against every association for asserting the peasants' and workmen's claims to economic betterment. A foreign policy of close attachment to the Central Empires, and of the greatest possible distance from France, fitted in naturally with the home policy represented by Pelloux.

Such was the first of the two great divisions which for a short spell bore the aspect of national parties competing for power. The other one was grouped around Zanardelli. It comprised all those whom Crispi and Pelloux had persecuted: Republicans and Socialists whether of the political or of the trade-unionist persuasion; and along with them traders who believed that freer trade with France was Italy's best economic opening, professional men and students whose scientific rationalism harmonized with that of 'Dreyfusard' and masonic France. Zanardelli, righteous, fervid, laborious, seemed the man to gather behind him a party or at least a group of parties like that of the French Left. With Giolitti as his Minister of the Interior he allowed labour movements to spread their agitation in a freedom previously undreamed of in Italy: the Ministry refused to intervene even when on one

[1] By Luigi Sturzo.

occasion two hundred strikes were in progress on a single day. Zanardelli was accused by his opponents of giving rein to the forces of anarchy. He retorted that those opponents had persistently thrown the forces of the State on the side of oppressive landlords and employers until the reasonable demands of the people had become charged with seditious bitterness.

But the incorruptible Zanardelli was old and infirm. He was soon no match for his Minister of the Interior, Giovanni Giolitti, himself a former Prime Minister, and a strong-headed devotee of the realities of power. And with the abrupt failure of the grand old radical's personal powers, early in 1903, his singularly dissimilar lieutenant comes on the scene as its dominator. With this, as will be seen, the brief interlude of true party politics quickly loses its outlines.

The profile of one man progressively dominates the scene, typifying a material prosperity more than ever divorced from the sense of a high and healthful discharge of a national mission.

II. GIOLITTI: MAN AND METHODS

Giovanni Giolitti has already figured in this narrative.

Giolitti (as he tells in his *Memoirs*) renounced intellectual speculation early in life after a surfeit of metaphysics. There followed a brilliant civil service career and a rapid rise through Parliament to ministerial rank. As bureaucrat, deputy, minister, Giolitti prevailed in ever-wider fields by his matchless assiduity in mastering problems, his serene and detached sense of public opinion which saved him from ever wasting energy upon the unattainable, and his skill in bargaining, composing differences, and in framing tacit yet reliable compacts with nominal opponents. Zanardelli pursued great purposes regardless of the opposition which they would rouse. His proposed divorce law was a bold affirmation of the principles of the religion of science. His lieutenant totally lacked this impulse. Giolitti would say: 'Personally I am for divorce laws of the greatest latitude: politically I must take account of the agitations this will arouse in the country.'

Giolitti's detached efficiency fitted him perfectly for the task of holding together the Italian State which had been so quickly and ruthlessly compounded. A Piedmontese magistrate's son, brought up in a remote mountain village, he had come of age in time to enter the service of the Italian State immediately after the unification. Almost at once he became the confidential

assistant of high officials and ministers. To him it fell to superintend in detail the incorporation of certain southern regions
into the fiscal system imposed upon them by Turin. He was
chosen to superintend affairs in Naples because the Government
desired to be represented by a civil servant who had never met
a single Neapolitan. He pitted his brains in a game of skill
against southerners, and not southerners only, who were determined to elude the new fiscal discipline. Tax evasion was on
an heroic scale: not only individuals but whole cities were
officially reported by the local authorities to be 'untraceable'.
An everlasting battle of wits against opponents with whom
ultimately one must reach a good-humoured understanding, and
not try to impose upon them the crude rigour of the law—such
was the exercise in which Giolitti learned to view his task on
behalf of the State, and his attitude never changed through long
years of power when he was triumphant, or during his brief
attempt, after humiliation and eclipse, to resuscitate it in the
post-war crisis. He dominates our next chapters.

In his first Premiership in 1892, though it lasted only a few
months, he showed himself equal to Depretis as a maker of
electoral pacts and as a controller of local affairs from his headquarters at the Ministry of the Interior in Rome. In the first
general elections 'made' by him, troops of deputies were returned
in consequence of such pacts: a comic paper gave a picture of
the Chamber in which every deputy was a tall, spare, hook-nosed
replica of Giolitti. But Crispi, at that time, was still the ultimate
dictator; those serried ranks of Giolittians were after a while
constrained to recall Crispi as the Man of Destiny to cope with
riots and revolts by the strong hand. Between Giolitti and
Crispi there had arisen, at that time, a fierce contest of mutual
accusations: each bore some ministerial responsibility and each
was to some degree personally involved in a chain of banking
scandals in 1893. Afterwards Giolitti had assumed the style
of a democrat (signifying a position in the 'Left' which
approached, without actually reaching, the 'Extreme Left').
He had taken up the cause of all those whom Crispi oppressed:
and on being assigned the Ministry of the Interior in Zanardelli's
Government he gained the loud applause of the Left, moderate
and extreme, for calling off police measures and permitting the
activities of the extreme parties in a way that they had not known
for years. Turati, the most eminent Socialist leader, proclaimed
Giolitti to be the greatest Italian statesman since Caesar. Giolitti

did not trouble much to explore and expound the merits of democracy: he was satisfied with feeling convinced of its inevitability. The millions of struggling peasants and the growing myriads of industrial workers appeared to him as the potential controllers of the Italy of to-morrow, whether he or anyone else should welcome them or not. To negotiate their entry into politics as collaborators with the existing powers, and as reformers of institutions, not as exasperated revolutionaries, was what he saw to be his duty. Never did Giolitti open his mouth as spokesman of a movement in whose passions he shared: never did he proclaim himself the irreconcilable opponent of others' demands. Cautiously he established a domination over Parliament, such that in a dozen years it was scarcely challenged, for the brief premierships of Fortis, Sonnino and Luzzatti were but stop-gaps during Giolitti's voluntary retirements. Raised to power on the tide of the parties of the Left, Giolitti became more and more the moderator of all groups and parties. From the Palazzo Braschi (Ministry of the Interior) he so wholly dominated the local affairs of remote and backward regions that a hundred or so deputies, elected by these regions, and known as the 'Askari' (coloured troops), were simply Giolitti's pledged henchmen—the Parliamentary whip of this legion of back-benchers was a most dignified-looking old gentleman, but, according to gossip, he could not read or write.

With the Socialists Giolitti refused to enter into any theoretical controversy. He told them that Karl Marx's works were now 'in the attic'. To prove, in fact, that the class struggle was out of date Giolitti gave abundant material assistance, both directly through the organs of the State and indirectly through the banks, to the Socialists' own practical experiments in co-operation. Energetic men in the Socialist movement who became officials in the co-operatives found themselves in charge of a large and expanding business which was promoted in every way by the State. It was hard in such circumstances to proclaim the imminence of revolution.

Throughout the course of his Parliamentary dictatorship (which can be dated 1903–15, omitting his earlier Premiership and his great power as Minister of the Interior under Zanardelli) Giolitti picked and chose his adherents, shaping his policy to the end of keeping an adequate troop of Parliamentarians at his command. On becoming Premier he wanted to introduce Socialists into the Ministry; when he failed to bring this off he found compensation not by strengthening his ties with the Zanardelli group, but by making offers to the Right. But the Right, and in general all Conservatives, were greatly disturbed when in September 1903 Giolitti let the troops and police force stand by without interfering in a general strike: he was obviously still playing for support of the proletarians. However, to ensure that the strike should not extend to the railway service, Giolitti took out powers to call the railwaymen to the colours. The strike was called off without having achieved its objects and Giolitti dissolved the Chamber. He had needed, in the outgoing legislature, the support either of the Extreme Left (Radicals, Republicans and Socialists) or of men of the Right. It suited him now to curb the exuberance of the Extreme Left. To this end he had dissolved the Chamber during the aftermath of the ill-fated general strike. But finding that the Socialists were less discredited by the futile conclusion of the strike than he expected, Giolitti at the last moment reached an understanding, in view of the impending elections, with some of the high clergy. Devout Catholics were in consequence instructed by their hierarchy to depart from the attitude of abstinence from politics, which had been officially recommended by succeeding Pontiffs since 1870, and to vote for the Giolittian candidates to keep out the Reds.

At this stage Giolitti performed what was to become a well-known recurrent feature in his technique. He withdrew from the overt tenure of power to strengthen his position in the background. An exceedingly complex and intricate controversy about the railway system provided the occasion.

At the formation of the Italian State those parts of the railways which were the property of the ex-sovereign states had been sold off to meet their current expenses: but a few years later the Italian State had been obliged to take them over again, and then it had once more passed them into private hands under a concession which was due to lapse in 1905. Many of the Conservatives now demanded that the railways should be taken over by the State in order to render railway strikes illegal: the Socialists opposed nationalization because they preferred to retain freedom to strike. Sooner than tackle this problem in person Giolitti imposed upon the Chamber a lieutenant of his own, Alessandro Fortis, as Prime Minister. Fortis was to re-acquire the railways and to deflect the annoyance of the Socialists from Giolitti's person. Giolitti's command of the Parliamentary milieu was not fully perfected, for the Chamber, irritated by the incompetence of Fortis, threw him out, and in a confused moment accorded its confidence to a man entirely unsusceptible to Giolitti's influence, the austere, unbending, half Anglo-Jewish Baron Sidney Sonnino. The experiment was short-lived. Sonnino proved quite unable to negotiate the personal and local deals which would have been necessary to wrest the Chamber's obedience from the man in the background. Giolitti was loudly summoned to return and take charge. Again he presided over a 'long Ministry' (1906-9), which left behind it what a friendly critic calls a 'beneficial but inorganic' record.

His detachment from any party or current of opinion was shown anew. He invited into his Ministry Bertolini, formerly Under-Secretary in the Pelloux Government, the man who had put his name ten years earlier to the notorious repressive decrees against the Extreme Left. Even the show of consistency had ceased to count in the recruitment of Giolittian ministers: Governmentalism was the only political qualification needed for taking a share in the Government.

After reducing the groups of the Right to impotence and dependence upon him, Giolitti decided to compass a closer relationship with the Socialists than had been possible since the general strike. He found his occasion in the popular agitation for universal suffrage, supported, of course, by the Socialists. He first provoked or took advantage of an insignificant vote by the groups of the Right against a tax-reform proposal espoused by himself. The uncompromising Conservative Sonnino was put into the position of vainly attempting, once again for only a few weeks, to govern against Giolitti: on him followed the eminent Jewish economist Luzzatti, transparently representing the absent Piedmontese master. This, as it was called, 'Giolittian Ministry without Giolitti' having aired some far from radical proposals for extending the electorate, Giolitti without warning rose from his seat to demand not merely a greatly widened suffrage (the voters then being some three millions) but implementation of the full principle of universal manhood suffrage (an effective electorate of eight millions). The makeshift Luzzatti Ministry at once understood Giolitti's admonition that their term was up, and took their departure, on March 29, 1911.

III. MASTER OF ITALY

Twenty years earlier Sonnino had advocated universal suffrage and men of the Left had resisted it: for at that time the new

voters would have been almost wholly submissive peasants ready
to vote as the landlord or even the priest advised them.   But in
1911 the quickly expanding industries of North Italy were employing hundreds of thousands of wage-earners.   The cotton industry
by now was the largest, with 200,000 employees (less than half
of these, it is true, were adult males) ; the iron and steel industry
which employed 15,000 men in 1902 paid wages to almost 35,000
ten years later;   there were 100,000 railway employees;   about
12,000 men in the new automobile industry, and much larger
contingents in the manufacturing branches of the silk and woollen
goods industries.   In a few districts of Tuscany and Umbria,
and more sparsely in the Neapolitan region, factories had sprung
up to attract men from the land into towns which were now
self-conscious industrial centres with trade-union and socialist
newspapers.   The sulphur miners of Sicily—an important fraction
of the industrial class—remained, it was true, as illiterate and
helpless as any of the peasantry.   On the other hand the peasants
of some regions of North Central Italy were as alert and as ready
to combine as any of the industrial workers.

Giolitti now opened the suffrage to five millions of new voters,
among whom hundreds of thousands were sure to vote for the
Socialists.   Conservatives quaked to see the ultimate power thus
surrendered to the masses and to the revolutionaries who claimed
to speak for them.   Giolitti, on the contrary, felt altogether equal
to bringing the masses, as he had brought so many of the old and
proud classes, into the great political combine of which he was
the moderator.   He had bound the landowners of the south to
himself by deals between Palazzo Braschi (Ministry of the Interior)
and the local administrations and political committees.   He was
binding the Socialists by deals between the Treasury and the
Socialist Co-operatives.

Giolitti thus formed his fourth Government in 1911, with a
pledge to legislate for manhood suffrage and—another decided
concession to the Socialists—to institute a State monopoly of life
insurance, with a further undertaking to prepare the way for
national unemployment insurance.   In Parliament no one
seriously opposed his authority.   He had leagued with him the
prevailing landowners of the south : he was able, when he needed
them, to make bargains with leading men in the Church : he
had by direct legislation and by pressure upon bankers and
industrialists enabled some four thousand co-operative societies
to take a large part in the production and distribution of the

country. The general economic situation was favourable. Since the end of political repression, and the renewal (around 1900) of close commercial relations with France, Italy had prospered materially as never before since the days of the national unification. Industry indeed was expanding too quickly for steadiness of employment, but all acknowledged that the quick development of water-power, electricity and other industrial applications of science were bringing wealth to the country. Italians, between 1898 and 1908, bought back far the greater part of the large quantity of Italian State securities originally issued abroad, and they had acquired foreign state securities sufficient to balance the remainder. Several hundreds of foreign enterprises were working in Italy (chiefly French, Belgian and British) and were on the whole prospering. If three-quarters of a million emigrants were leaving the country yearly, yet at that time most Italians viewed this process as a mode of Italian participation in the resources of richer countries. Many of the emigrants came back rich and trained to a new vigour, and able to buy and develop land from half-derelict great estates: meanwhile with their remittances from abroad they often maintained their parents and relatives, while they left fewer poor labourers to compete in Italy for the humbler jobs. The stay-at-home industrial workers and agricultural labourers were the better able to achieve, in the first decade of the twentieth century, a general wage increase.

Few European statesmen in modern times, enjoying such undoubted political control as Giolitti had exercised in the first decade of the nineteenth century, could claim to have presided over so unquestionable a measure of progress towards the satisfaction of their countrymen's human needs. But there was no widespread spirit of satisfaction: the all-powerful Parliamentarian enjoyed little popularity or prestige. An Opposition, all the more inscrutable for its disorganized condition, was discovering new modes of thought and feeling. It was not a clear-cut Opposition such as had confronted Crispi in the time of his omnipotence. Crispi had aroused frantic hatred, and his enemies were the Republicans and Socialists whom he had persecuted, and in general the whole Left which looked towards liberty, equality and fraternity: to these a group of personally resentful Conservatives had joined themselves and thus once and for all annihilated Crispi's primacy the week after Adua. Giolitti persecuted nobody for his opinions, sought agreement with all. He was the supreme regulator of a concern to which all were invited to bring their contributions and from which all might extract some advantages. The smooth external perfection of the situation was a profound irritant to men of forthright and independent nature, irrespectively almost of their political and social origins and bent.

Every holder of a seat in Parliament, a ministerial office, a co-operative managership, kept somebody else out: and for his exclusion that man held Giolitti personally responsible. Men of gifts and integrity indignantly saw a shady banker or a voluptuary absentee landlord enjoying the permanence of a seat in Parliament because that inferior or corrupt citizen would sell his obedience for a tangible price. Giolitti stood aloof from every earnestly held belief or passionately pressed programme. The free-thinking Positivist saw how he shunned any conflict of principle with the Vatican—Giolitti would never use his power to further Zanardelli's project to legalize divorce, nor would he assist the poor communes of the south to bring into each parish a lay schoolmaster to resist the dictatorship of the village priest. Giolitti would no more have consented to lose touch with the Church as an occasional electoral ally than he would have associated himself with a movement for religious revival, whether from orthodox or from reforming quarters. The young and ardent Socialists on their side saw the well-paid bureaucracy of the co-operatives lowering the standard of revolution, and proclaiming the inevitability of gradualness. The same absence of clear-cut principle prevailed in foreign policy. Giolitti renewed the Triple Alliance, because, as one student of his politics says, in the name of fidelity to this inherited programme he could dispense with any further definition of Italy's purposes in international politics.

Foreign policy was a field in which Giolitti certainly did not intend to experiment: he wished only that it should not complicate his tasks at home. There was no obvious motive for apprehension. Italy seemed firmly set upon peace with all the great powers, and if Giolitti set value upon Germany as a formal ally this was partly explicable by his interest in having German help for developing a great Italian bank, the Banca Commerciale Italiana, comparable with the great banking concerns of Germany and France. Giolitti's foreign policy included, however, as a factor offsetting the Triple Alliance, which had always symbolized Conservative Italy's support for the principles of authority and established religion, a not less faultless understanding with France such as had, since 1870, always been demanded by the Extreme

Left to affirm Italy's sympathy with secularist democracy. Both parties in Italy now had the forms of the foreign attachments which they desired: neither could claim that the forms in fact signified what they meant by them. Giolitti in fact aimed in his foreign policy as in his home policy at the efficient daily discharge of the problems of the day. He displayed an equal measure of scepticism towards all professedly organic programmes of foreign policy.

The problems of the day he tackled with incomparable energy and promptness. The country and the State were perceptibly richer year by year, the people (as travellers judged) more contented and orderly. But to tackle the problems of the day Giolitti must have and hold power, and to hold power, un-challengeable, immovable, against the fiery and enthusiastic of all persuasions, the disappointed of all parties, Giolitti had his technique of 'making' elections. An abundant literature of the time preserves the records of Giolittian electioneering. Two British observers, King and Okey, writing in 1909 described the elections of that year as 'a mere parody on representative govern-ment as far as a large proportion of the 169 southern constitu-encies are concerned'. They have put on record some of the methods employed. First bribery: this might sometimes be rendered a safe investment by giving half a bank note together with a piece of blotting paper to the voter entering the booth. On the evidence of the blotting paper, on which the Government candidate's name had to be visible, he received the second part. Then more elaborate tricks: 'The absent, the illiterate, the dead vote by hundreds.' Sometimes the election officer would stuff into the ballot boxes enough forged votes to turn the scales. Inside Italy, a brilliant assault on the Giolittian system came from Gaetano Salvemini, later the most voluminous writer among the exiled enemies of Mussolini. He directed against Giolitti a spirited and formidable act of accusation in a pamphlet, *Il governo della mala vita* (Government by Criminals), based on his own observation of an election at Gioia del Colle (in the heel of Italy): a story of arrests, of suburbs placed in a state of siege, train services interrupted, to ensure the election of one of Giolitti's 'Askaris'. Needing only a sufficient group of personal followers in the Chamber to hold the balance between other groups, and content if these were elected by small majorities, Giolitti left the more progressive regions of Italy to vote in freedom: even in the constituencies which he needed to secure, his prefects and agents interfered only at the particular points where, for a bare majority in the constituency as a whole, the opposing candidate's voters must be barred, or fictitious votes introduced. Even the violence and fraud which Giolitti's opponents denounced in his system were applied in minimum doses at the least sensitive or at all events the least conspicuous points.

If by such methods Giolitti ensured himself a permanent personal following, for the rest he relied upon the bargains which he 'struck with the Church or with the Extreme Left according to the opportunities of the moment. That in Italy, and in all the world, the masses must be given full citizenship he did not trouble to doubt: never did he imitate Crispi in attempting to stabilize his dictatorship by repressing popular movements. The admission of five million new electors to the polls required a tremendous effort for holding them to a sufficient degree under control. His own lieutenants, more than anyone else, disliked the reform, but Giolitti was not greatly interested in their opinions. It was their obedient support that he wanted, and knew how to obtain.

IV. FROM CAVOUR TO GIOLITTI

Giolitti's Parliamentary dictatorship may be considered to have culminated in his autocratic imposition upon Parliament of manhood suffrage. He remained, for five years more, the unchallenged dominator of Italian politics. But adversaries were already gathering their forces in a variety of quarters. The end, not merely of the Giolitti system, but of the Parliamentarism of which that system was the logical outcome, was near at hand. Before examining the manner of its collapse, let us again examine its nature.

Italy had been united in the mid-nineteenth century by the statesmen of the Savoy dynasty: the ancient military organization, the hastily modernized civil administration, and the very new industrialism and free trade of Piedmont had been rudely thrust upon the entire Italian peninsula.

Some Neapolitan gentry, travelled and cultivated aristocrats, or enlightened reformers from among the Bourbon officialdom, especially in Sicily, accepted the new system with little or no remorse: so did some representatives of the upper classes of Tuscany and of the ex-Austrian and ex-Papal domains. The indigenous Roman Church, which under the shocks of French Revolution and Empire had thrown up men of respectable energy and intellect, had had no share in bringing the Italian Kingdom into being. On the contrary the Church had been left to take up an attitude of injured hostility towards the new authorities. The prophets of an Italian religious and philosophical reformation, who had by their criticism and conspiracy sapped the moral foundations of the old régimes—these and their followers had been exploited by the realistic politicians of Piedmont, only to be, in the hour of triumph, thrust aside and viewed with suspicion. They had never fully made their peace with the monarchy which plucked the fruits of their own audacity and idealism.

In every province of Italy there were men who hankered after the old régimes, but far more who, while accepting the fact of National Union, criticized the uniformization decreed by Piedmont and demanded a restitution of local autonomies. The passage of time intensified their grievances. For the first sixteen years, while the existence of the new State was still ill-secured against its enemies, differences among Italian patriots were held in check by the common determination of all the schools of patriotism to complete and preserve the unity and independence of the peninsula against foreigners. But once this task was completed, and external menaces began to fade from view, the Constitutionalists of the 'Right', who bore the direct responsibility for the drastic regimentation of the peninsula, were forced out of power amid loud reaffirmations of popular sentiment. But the 'Left' of Republicans, Regionalists and half-converted ex-Legitimists quickly disintegrated into groups and factions. The change from 'Right' to 'Left' instead of reviving the Mazzinian vision of a third Italy, or even the aspirations of the federalists, led through confusion to the personal domination of Agostino Depretis, the master of personal pacts and combinations, who alone succeeded in ruling Italy with support gathered indifferently in all quarters, while all conflict of principle was laid aside. On him followed a dominator of very different temper, Francesco Crispi, unmistakably a leader of men and a dreamer of great enterprises, but the slave of personal antipathies, and of an antiquated outlook upon the world around him. Almost without his being aware of it, the economic development of the new country had thrown up factories, and a proletariat, and small traders claiming their place in society. Crispi could see no scope for great achievements in the solution of economic problems: he sought greatness for Italy (and as an old Mazzinian he had always conceived that a United Italy would be great) in colonial conquest, while at home he dealt with 'social agitators' by repression. When his colonial ambition miscarried he was hounded out of place and power. Then once again discordant groups contested for office amid alarming unrest in the country: smaller men than Crispi tried to cope with it by repression. Their clumsy harshness almost brought into being a new and more coherent party of the Left, with a popular mandate for a social-democratic programme. For a moment Zanardelli gave expression to the common aspirations of the trade unionists, their middle-class Socialist spokesmen and the Radicals who had joined with them. But this brought him to a grave conflict with that great power which the revolution of 1860 had neither suppressed nor yet absorbed into the body of Italian life—the Church. Zanardelli's divorce law would have initiated a struggle between Church and State on a wholly new and treacherous ground. The political conflicts between the House of Savoy and the Papacy had been disputes over sovereignty and property. The social principles of Catholicism had not been at stake in these quarrels. The Piedmontese constitution, which had become the constitution of Italy, provided that the Catholic Apostolic and Roman Church was the sole religion of the State.

Zanardelli's proposal threatened to provoke a conflict which would have profoundly stirred the Italian people. Age and ill-health prevented him from carrying it out and once again it was in the power of a single man, Giolitti, that the State found the one possible mode of preserving order and tranquillity. Giolitti's mode was to invite all parties and classes to share in the responsibility of the State, while himself exercising the full ultimate power in their name. He was a pure politician, unencumbered by faiths, hatreds, prejudices, vices, or extraneous ambitions. But the pure politician was not a great and commanding figure. Indeed he could hold the country at peace only at the cost of symbolizing all that noble (or morally pretentious) men should detest.

CHAPTER FIVE

NATIONAL SOUL-SEARCHING

OFFICIAL Italy was wedded to Giolittianism. This gave rise to exasperation in the most diverse quarters: Socialistic, Nationalistic, Catholic, Heretic, Philosophic and Artistic. All this variegated opposition flowed somehow together into a single mood of rebellion.

I. SOCIALIST REBELS, and among them Mussolini.

II. NATIONALIST MALCONTENTS AND RELIGIOUS INTRANSIGENTS.

III. A PHILOSOPHIC GOSPEL.—In Benedetto Croce and Giovanni Gentile Italian philosophy finds a voice which affects ways of thought, and unwittingly anticipates future political cleavages.

IV. ART AND BOMBAST.—The Futurists as fanatics: the true poet d'Annunzio as debaucher.

I. SOCIALIST REBELS

The success of the Giolittian Parliamentary dictatorship in winning allies and auxiliaries in all the classes, all the regions, the parties and the organizations, excited the simultaneous and convergent dislike of everyone, of whatever class, region, or professed persuasion, who remained outside that system of bargains and understandings. To be of ardent and sanguine temperament was to be anti-Giolittian, for Giolitti stood neutral, aloof from all faiths, enthusiasms and agitations. He dismissed faith and enthusiasm as a psychological compensation which those too immature for practical politics conjured up out of the exuberance of their own fancies. He believed that he knew how to render agitations innocuous, by producing something tangible from his pocket at crucial moments, to satisfy some fragment of the demands of each party and school. The Socialists should have pensions and national insurance, the Radicals and Republicans universal suffrage and friendship with secularist France, the Catholics should have measures against Freemasonry and a continuance of the Triple Alliance. In addition to these, a new party was now emerging on the crest of a wave of industrial prosperity and natural prolificity. For it must be recalled that Italy in half a century had added ten million souls to her population—five times as many as France. The group taking its inspiration from these facts called itself the Nationalist party. It clamoured for external aggressiveness and territorial expansion.

As an electoral or parliamentary power it was in itself negligible. But support was gathering around it. The mood which it represented seemed to call for some recognition by Giolitti, by way of reinsurance, and in due course, in 1912, he agreed to embark upon a small war of conquest in Africa. Before examining the circumstances of this war let us look further into Giolitti's technique.

It was a patient alternation of concessions made to all sides which succeeded in holding the bulk of all parties, groups and persuasions in a working arrangement with Giolitti. But there remained in each of them a remnant of intransigents and purists. Each party had its wing of tempestuous rebels against Giolitti. He observed them with superior tolerance, expecting that they would tire of their heroic attitudes in good time or that their own more accommodating fellow-partisans would gradually educate them into the ways of realism.

The Socialist party was the most clear cut of the various political persuasions, and within it the division between Giolittians and anti-Giolittians was—by the date at which this narrative has now arrived—increasingly perceptible.

The Socialists, in the ten years since the repressions of Crispi and Pelloux, had built up an elaborate and powerful organization, with a Parliamentary group, a General Confederation of Labour, a conspicuous daily and weekly Press, and an associated co-operative movement with its stores and factories established in thousands of towns. There was a countervailing loss of internal harmony. When under Zanardelli they regained freedom to organize and to propagandize, the Socialists felt free also again— as in the times of their earliest origins, before repression had thrown them into a united defensive front—to dissent loudly and publicly from each other. Gradualists once again confronted insurrectionists in a perpetual conflict of theories and ambitions. Ancient animosities flared up. The United Socialist party of Italy, when it took firm shape in the nineties, had excluded from its ranks the sect of the Anarchists; the latter then absorbed some remnants of the old Mazzinian groups, and cultivated the doctrine of a sudden regeneration of mankind to be brought about by a social upheaval. The United Socialist party also repudiated in its initial career the doctrine of certain pioneer trade-unionist leaders who desired to limit the objectives of the Socialist move- ment to the development of the unions and thus to confine it to the class of organized wage-earners. The excluded anarchists and syndicalists had remained an ineffective dissident group on its fringe as long as the main Socialist party was suffering persecution and meeting it boldly. Many of them thought better of their individual views and drifted back to the party ranks. But when, at the turn of the century, the persecution ceased, the heretics regained influence, and rated the orthodox party leaders for their readiness to relax in the new atmosphere of tolerance. To hold the peace between the 'Syndicalists' and the 'Reformists' (or law-abiders) there arose a group calling itself 'Integralist', pledged to hold the party together. It was a hard task. The Syndicalists were continually promoting strikes, sometimes on a great scale and with much violence, which the party disclaimed. After a while the Reformists overcame the Integralists: the Syndicalists were ousted or fell away from the party, though returning to penetrate it, from time to time, through the allied labour organizations. By 1910 the leading Syndicalists were officially outside the Socialist party. But within the party there were extremists whose language was scarcely distinguishable from that of the Syndicalists. Prominent among them were Costantino Lazzari, veteran founder of the earliest exclusively working-class political group in Milan, and at his side a leader of the young generation, Benito Mussolini. What these near-Syndicalists felt about the Reformist domination of the party was expressed about this time in an article by Mussolini in a small weekly Socialist paper. The quotation illustrates in high relief the spectacle of the affiliation of the main body of the Socialist party to the Giolittian system, as seen by these Socialists who were ferociously anti-Giolittian.

'The picture of the Third Italy,' Mussolini wrote, '. . . is complete. Giolitti stands in the midst of the scene, behind him and flanking him comes the vast retinue of his *bloc*, in which are seen the Freemasons' triangle and the priest's shovel hat, Nathan [the Jewish Mayor of Rome] and Romolo Murri [a leader of the Catholic 'Modernist' movement]. A great game with electoral and banking customers—that is Giolitti's parliamentarism: neither reaction nor revolution. This tight-rope walker, this hopelessly mediocre Piedmontese [Giolitti] has conquered. The spirit of rebellion in Italy is extinguished. The official Socialists hug Madam Freemasonry in a sterile embrace under the approving eye of the Great Architect of the Universe. Past are the days of concentration camps, almost past are those of the prison-house. . . . *Ave Giolitti, morituri te salutant.* . . . Perhaps a healthful tempest is nigh to sweep away Giolitti, Giolittianism, and all this sickly social philosophy which is the ruin of genuine socialism.' Such was the language of the rebellious Socialist. But it was not language peculiar to a Socialist. Similar laments and hopes resounded from the extremer wing of other groups which shared with Socialists like Mussolini a sense of suffocation amid the compromise of Giolittian parliamentarism.

II. NATIONALIST MALCONTENTS AND RELIGIOUS INTRANSIGENTS

The Nationalists were a group who stood to the remnant of anti-Giolittian Conservatives in much the same relation as the Syndicalists to the Socialist party. And although the Nationalist movement, founded at the beginning of the century, and constituted as a political party ten years later, claimed to exercise the function of stiffening the governing classes against the infections of Socialism and Internationalism, yet by 1900 Corradini, the founder of the movement, had openly recognized the Syndicalists as kindred spirits. There was a model outside Italy for this meeting of the extremes. The approval of the Italian Nationalists for the 'spirit' of the Syndicalists (their 'heroic and anti-bourgeois' spirit, as Corradini wrote) followed upon a fraternization in France between the royalist Action Française (the chief though not the sole model from which the Italian Nationalists had borrowed their formulae) and the French Syndicalist movement. Both in France and in Italy at about this time some of the Syndicalists at variance with the main Socialist party began to drift into the Nationalist organizations. The founders of the Italian nationalist movement were literary men. The ideal which they pursued was that of a severe and masterful authority worthy to be the object of upper-class sentiments schooled in the classics. In Giolitti's Italy, with its spreading clans of 'pampered' Socialists and of Freemasons, they saw the extreme negation of such a concept. Proselytes flocked to their cause. Exalting the military values, honouring the memory of Crispi, and continually harking back to the shame of the unavenged defeat of Italian arms in Abyssinia in 1896, the Nationalists soon found allies in the army and among armament manufacturers. With the support of the heavy industry they were enabled to equip themselves with party newspapers, and by 1913 to launch their own party candidates, and to gain seats for some of them in Parliament.

The Syndicalists, then, formed a wing of Socialism hostile to the Giolittian system, and the Nationalists a wing of Conservatism for the most part similarly hostile. Giolitti had enemies also in yet another camp. By certain young Catholics their leaders' complacent bargainings with Giolitti were not less unsparingly denounced. Pius IX, the Pope who had been despoiled by Piedmont, and his successor, Leo XIII, the brilliant inheritor of a problematic situation, had passed away. The next Pope, Pius X, though he reiterated their remonstrances against the Pontiff's situation as 'Prisoner of the Vatican', was felt to have uttered a merely formal protestation against the 'usurpation' of the House of Savoy. Stage by stage the Vatican abated the ban which Pius IX had proclaimed against the participation of devout Catholics in the affairs of the State which had seized upon the patrimony of Peter. Giolitti was more than ready to blunt the edge of inherited animosities. At intervals he administered large or small concessions to the Vatican—at one time an improvement in the economic conditions of the parish clergy, at another military honours to a Cardinal, State participation in a Eucharistic Congress, the promise of restrictions on the influence of the Free-masons, or aids to Catholic education. In return, Giolitti was able to call Catholic voters to his support in 1904, and on the still more important occasion of the first elections with manhood suffrage in 1913. This play with the Catholic politicians was as vital a part of Giolitti's Parliamentary dictatorship as his play with the Socialist party officials.

The rebellious temper which stirred the Syndicalists and the Nationalists also stirred a wing of militant Catholics. Eclipse seemed to have overtaken, in 1849, Gioberti's ideal of a Holy Italy which should draw its political inspiration from a modernized yet still Catholic Rome. But half a century later these ideals found new life in a 'Modernist' movement within the Catholic Church. From about 1900 the Vatican became anxiously concerned over the more or less open confession, by priests and by Catholic laymen of standing, of a philosophy in which Catholic dogma was given a purely poetic or symbolic value. Pope Pius X hunted down the heterodox clergy with ruthless energy: they were condemned by Vatican writers in language which the present-day student finds strangely familiar. No political propaganda office of the present day has found more lurid terms for the execration of Reds, Whites, or Jews than these Vatican spokesmen a quarter-century ago for their campaign against the Modernists. The Modernist clergy, in rebellion against high clericalism, threw out feelers for support in the Socialist party, without getting much response. 'I know young ecclesiastics,' wrote one of the most prominent of the Modernists in 1908, 'who passionately follow the Italian working-class movement, and are even enthusiastic for that special brand of Socialism which is now so much in vogue, and stands for its extreme wing—Syndicalism.' As a movement for dogmatic reform Modernism was soon crushed. But meanwhile men like Don Sturzo, a brilliant young priest and mayor of Caltagirone in Sicily, were at work marshalling supporters for an Italian Catholic party capable of standing by itself within the Italian State. Political Catholicism would then no longer represent mere voting power to be bartered by the Vatican as payment for favours received from a Parliamentary dictator. By 1910 the reverend mayor of Caltagirone was a well-known personage anxiously watched by the dominators of the State. By an intense devotion not only to the local government of his own town, but also to the affairs of a National Association of local authorities, Sturzo was continually challenging the local dominion of the big landlords and hereditary leading citizens who managed elections, in remote parts of Italy, by agreement with the Government. Meanwhile some southern landlords themselves participated in the struggle against southern electoral feudalism and against the bankers and manufacturers of the north, whom they accused of selling their political support to Giolitti in return for high tariffs. 'The radical party has let itself be caught and devoured in the meshes of Parliamentary trans-formism, Giolitti's masterpiece,' proclaimed a great southern landlord and leader of a National Free Trade movement, Marchese de Viti de Marco. 'The Italian people are still waiting for the solution of old problems according to the old formula of individual liberty and social justice: but they look for it from a new man.'

III. A PHILOSOPHIC GOSPEL

The rebellious Socialists who became Syndicalists, the young Conservatives who became Nationalists, and even the young Catholics who became Modernists, were in rival political camps, but all of them shared some literary enthusiasms. All thrived upon the philosophic works of the Anglo-American pragmatists, William James and F. C. S. Schiller, and Blondel's *Action*. And all of them felt the fascination of the flourishing philosophic school which had gathered round Benedetto Croce and Giovanni Gentile in Naples since the beginning of the century. The influence of this school radiated far beyond the libraries and classrooms: its authors were by 1910 national figures.

Benedetto Croce, by birth a Neapolitan landowner, by family connexions a Cavourian Liberal of the Right, began his career as a representative of the aristocratic, literary erudition in which Italy is perennially so rich. By a revulsion from what he felt to be a narrow and frigid pursuit, he turned to seek an informing principle by the light of which historical research could be vitally related to the movements and aspirations of the day. This principle he struggled for some years to discover in the works of Karl Marx. Many of his young Italian contemporaries, at the turn of the century, drew comfort from the prestige of Marx as the author of a 'scientific' demonstration that the world's next age belonged to Socialism. Few of them, like Croce and Gentile, made a deep study of Marxian 'science'. Socialism was for the better among them a courageous crusade on behalf of the poor, for the cheaper spirits it was beginning to rank as a quick way to honours and salaries. Croce, bringing an incisive philosophic intelligence to bear upon *Das Kapital*, soon threw over an original profession of discipleship to Marx, and found himself, in the pages of International Socialist reviews, in alliance with Georges Sorel, the theorist of French Syndicalism, who was also engaged in overhauling and jettisoning the rigid Marxian doctrine. Croce (who by 1905 had risen to the first rank in Italy as a recognized master both of literary criticism and of social ethics) himself procured the publication of Sorel's works in Italy, and thus bore his share in popularizing a graceful type of Socialist extremism which substituted the heroic 'myth' of the general strike for the cumbrous ambition of a strategically planned class war.

By the time that he was introducing Sorel to Italian readers, Croce himself had risen to such intellectual eminence as to be allowed, by general consent, to stand above political controversy. The Italian of 1910 found in Croce's thought (then already expounded in a whole series of volumes) a confident conciliation of the spiritual with the social purposes of man. In the energetic pursuit not only of duty but also of a noble ambition, man—as Croce saw him—was always realizing the design of the Spirit, of Providence, of God as truly known to those who can liberate faith from the trappings of theology. Croce's bold and elegant coupling of religion and science came to thousands of young men as a liberation from an incubus: religion, then, for which one's heart cried out, need not mean the swallowing of creeds and syllabuses; and science need not mean the pursuit of ever-elusive truths, truths at the cost of a shaking of all standards of conduct and of all accepted loyalties. A factor of austere and restrained optimism entered into the public life of Italy with the diffusion of Croce's doctrines: but the austerity and restraint were not always preserved.

The activities of these philosophers had its fiercely personal side. In the review *La Critica*, Croce and Gentile summoned to the bar, man by man, the principal academic and literary personages of the day. The powerful clan of Positivist philosophers and sociologists were weighed up and found wanting: these included figures, like the venerable Ardigò, whom the Socialists had for a generation regarded as men of light and leading. From a different angle Croce assailed the two most influential poets, d'Annunzio and Pascoli. Meanwhile, however, Croce and Gentile fell into disagreement, at first in regard to somewhat rarefied philosophic issues, which surprisingly proved to be the index of a profound contrast in the whole range of their ideas. Croce distinguished Intuition from Thought, Thought from Action: Gentile—in his more elaborate and abstruse system of logic—absorbed all mental activity into the single manifestation of 'Pure Act'. As each of the eminent thinkers followed his own way, this rarefied intellectual dispute was seen to symbolize a differing judgement upon men and movements in the practical sphere: Gentile's glorification of 'Act' became a gospel for the promotion of cultural and political experiments which Croce condemned. Gentile was on the way to becoming 'the theologian of futurism' as a critic later dubbed him: though it was some time before either Gentile or the Futurists could have understood the affinity between them, which was to lead both into the Fascist camp. Nor could it have been foreseen in 1910 that Croce would in 1920 accept office as a minister in Giolitti's last and least successful Administration.

For the moment, the idealism of the Croce-Gentile school was to be reckoned as an inspiration among those which encouraged thoughts of a cleaner and more vigorous Italy which might be attained by an overthrow of the Giolittian clans and their obscure inter-attachments. It was left to a Florentine literary school, centred round the review *La Voce*, to draw such political conclusions from what was implicit in the higher intellectuality of the Neapolitan idealist.

IV. ART AND BOMBAST

The Italian Futuristic movement began to make a noise in the world about 1910. It resolutely threw its poetry and its politics into a single bag. Futurism was an exasperated exaggeration, a naughty and nightmarish caricature of the movement of rebellion surging among the student youth of Italy against the pastors and masters whom they found installed in the universities and editorial chairs in the years of Giolitti's uncontested authority. The Futurists bellowed abuse at the successful figureheads of every party and persuasion. Their head man, F. T. Marinetti, was an Italian born in Egypt and educated by French priests. In extravaganzas written in French blank verse—a fact which illustrates the close connexion with Montmartre which was then favoured by the bright young ultra-patriots of Florence—Marinetti indulged dreams of swooping over the Vatican in a monoplane, kidnapping the Pope, and dropping him in the Adriatic. Other futurist dreams which he celebrated in these 'poems' concerned the dragging of ministers and deputies out of their comfortable assembly hall at the Palazzo Montecitorio to explain themselves to the 'real representatives of the people', in the person of murderers, thieves and prostitutes: and the gathering of the students of Milan for a midnight stone-throwing raid on all the great houses. For the moment these ambitions were purely theoretical. 'I am light, free and powerful, an Italian suddenly rid of his Christian ballast, of his heavy Catholic chains,' exclaimed the hero of one of Marinetti's dramas. These wild pages were perhaps more prophetic than their author at the time sincerely believed.

The Futurist mood, on some sides, was shared by a far more seductive spokesman, a poet of gushing exuberance who gave expression to the personal and collective appetites of his generation. Gabriele d'Annunzio had by his fortieth year toyed with every major movement in Italy, the Nationalist, the Socialist, the Christian and the vaguely humanitarian. The Futurists, though they railed against him for his conventional forms of Art, responded to his temperament. This splendidly gifted poet of endless shifting amours and not less numerous debts has been described as the loneliest man of his generation, seeking in notoriety a compensation for the intimacy and respect which he could not gain. As early as 1904 Croce delivered a solemn warning on the significance of d'Annunzio's ascendancy. There grew out of d'Annunzio's loneliness an imperious appetite to draw the nation, as he himself had been drawn, into the glamour of adventure for adventure's sake. Like Marinetti, d'Annunzio was Parisianized and wrote in French as well as Italian. Yet his birth and breeding had been on the remote sea-coast of the Abruzzi, in the ex-Papal States. Rome of the Popes and of the Renaissance was the atmosphere in which he indulged his dreams.

No man could have been more remote than d'Annunzio from the ideals of austere efficiency which the best of the Piedmontese had sought to inspire into Italy. His wide acceptance as the national poet of Italy signified an extraordinary gap between even the ostensible ideals of the constituted State (let alone the humbler realities of it) and the ideals which the new generation welcomed in its literature. Like that of Croce, his name bore connotations which loom large in the political history of Italy.

If Giolitti in 1910 was at the height of his political domination of Italy, in virtue of his system of dark deals with the great land-lords, the Parliamentary Socialists, and the diplomats of the Vatican, the ardent and intellectual youth of Italy, to whatever philosophy of life they attached themselves, were unanimous in an attitude of impatient dismissal of the man and his work. Both Giolitti and those who hoped one day to undermine his Parliamentary dictatorship were aware of this, and for the time Giolitti was able, by widening the scope of his multiple alliances, to frustrate any design of marshalling these new forces into some sort of unity for an assault upon him.

CHAPTER SIX

WAR AND REVOLUTION: A REHEARSAL

I. THE TOUCHSTONE OF WAR.—In pursuance of his practice of pleasing everybody, Giolitti gave way to industrialist and cleri-calist pressure and launched a small war of African conquest. The Socialist party was split by the question whether to accept the war as part of the general bargain with Giolitti, or to break with Giolitti. No clear decision was reached but the advocates of a radical anti-Giolittian policy gained great prestige in the party. A chief agitator was Benito Mussolini, who now first emerged on the national stage.

II. INSURRECTIONARY PRELUDES.—While the Mussolinian agitation causes some stir, and notable disorders occur, Giolitti takes a rest, and his locum tenens tries out the policy of the strong hand. This has a measure of success, but the mood remains one of confused expectation of indefinable changes.

I. THE TOUCHSTONE OF WAR

Long before 1911, Italian diplomacy had staked out a reversionary right to Tripoli, the last territory in Africa which still remained under an attenuated form of Turkish sovereignty. And since the Turkish Empire was generally supposed to be collapsing by a process of internal decay, this claim that Italy should enter upon the heritage in Tripoli was in the circles of European diplomacy generally considered to be reasonable. In anticipation that Italian sovereignty would some time be proclaimed over these desert sands, Italian interests established flour-mills and other equipment in the coast towns of the vast and mostly desert region, and confidently awaited Turkey's breakdown. But the Young Turkish movement, which in 1908 won the sympathy of enlightened Europe by inscribing on its banners the promise of a regeneration of Turkey from within, at the same time began strengthening the decadent suzerainty of Constantinople over Tripoli. Germany, moreover, was at this time cultivating Turkey as an important auxiliary for her policy of predominance in the Near East. Such developments threatened to frustrate the anticipated reversion of Tripoli to Italian sovereignty. The Banco di Roma, a great bank dominated by friends of the Vatican, was particularly committed in the financing of pioneer Italian enterprise in Tripoli, and Giolitti's supporters among the clericalists pressed him to see to the safeguarding of these interests. It was in these circumstances that Giolitti decided to occupy Tripoli even at the cost of war. He had no taste for war, but he was not the man to deny its place among the ineradicable habits of humanity. The purposes of this war were reasonable, and it was desired in the most varied quarters for the most different reasons.

The Catholic Conservatives had certain highly material interests at stake, which harmonized well with the historic purpose of thrusting back Islam from the Mediterranean. They thus favoured an attack on Turkey. The Nationalists on their part

wanted to see Italy's African disaster of Adua avenged, and
Italy sharing at last, after the frustration of her Tunisian and
Ethiopian adventures, in the prestige of the conquering white
races in Africa. This Nationalist aspiration harmonized with
the interests of a nascent heavy industry eager to turn its plant
on to the production of shells. But there was support for the
Tripoli war from much less likely quarters, and for subtly
contingent motives. Many of the Radicals and Republicans
welcomed the war as a mode of breaking away from Austro-
German tutelage, and sharing in the world responsibilities of
democratic England and France. The peasantry of South Italy,
stirred up by an unblushing campaign of Government propaganda, thought that a new field for emigration was being found—
America was to be brought to their doorway and the horrors of
the Atlantic trip and the English language would be rendered
obsolete in the annals of emigration. D'Annunzio and the
Futurists, on their part, loudly celebrated this minor war as
the preface to a coming war against Austria for Trieste and the
Trentino, though some bickering with France brought forth at
the same time, from the circle of the Nationalists, reminders that
Corsica, Nice and Tunis might also be listed as 'unredeemed'
Italian territories.

For Giolitti the project of a conquest of Libya, whatever there
was to be said for and against it on the merits of the case, had
the supreme advantage of distracting and neutralizing much of
the impatience that was stirring in the country. In the event,
however, the declaration of war against Turkey had the serious
and not wholly foreseen consequence of risking his working
understanding with the Socialists. The Socialist party's placid
expansion through the foundation of co-operatives, with the
financial assistance of the Government, was rudely interrupted
by the Libyan war. In one prosperous decade Socialism had
become unrecognizably respectable. The leaders of this alleged
'revolutionary' party were now in the habit of explaining that
'revolution' was but a convenient formula for the sum of infinite
detailed changes which could in due course be achieved through
Parliament and through trade-union action. The forty Socialist
members of Parliament were in practice a constitutional group
with a grievance, more traditional than practical, against the
Government. The keenest individuals among them felt painfully
the embarrassing contrast between the Marxist theory (which they
could not eradicate from party programmes and speeches) and

the daily practice of constitutional democracy. The political managers of the party put value in the slogan 'revolution', and insisted upon its retention in the party's journalism and oratory. This did not deceive men of genuinely revolutionary taste and outlook. The Syndicalists and the young aspirants to power within the party denounced at each Socialist congress the divergence between the theory and the practice of the party. They called loudly for a return to revolutionary methods. The Libyan war was now presented to the Socialist leaders as a test of their intentions. It was to be seen whether they would sacrifice Socialist principle to the extent of acquiescing in an imperialistic war.

In point of fact not only some Socialists but some among the stormy Syndicalists supported the Libyan war. A few Socialists pronounced in favour of it because their peasant constituents believed it would make them landed proprietors: a few Syndicalists did likewise on the grounds that war of any sort was the best possible preparation for revolution. Arturo Labriola, the chief theorist among the Syndicalists, had played for some time with the theory that social revolution was to be obtained through the disaster of an unsuccessful war: and some of the Syndicalists did not hesitate to favour a war, regardless of its outcome, as the best school for revolution. It is hard to be for war without falling into line with the war mood. The Nationalists had already won over several leading Syndicalist intellectuals: in the Libyan war other Syndicalists veered strongly round to a Nationalist standpoint. On the other hand, certain leading Syndicalists advocated a policy of active sabotage. If the Syndicalists as an independent power in the country were negligible they reflected moods which were found also in the Socialist party.

The enormous majority of the Italian Socialists condemned the Tripoli war. But the party was sharply divided about the degree and duration of the resistance which it ought to show against the war. Many of the established leaders of the party wished to limit the protest to an expression of regret that the war had been begun. This was denounced as the height of time-serving treachery by those who shared the mood of the Syndicalists. Benito Mussolini stood out as the chief of the school of militant pacifists. During the war he came into national prominence as the promoter of disturbances to obstruct the campaign in Tripoli. When it was concluded it was Mussolini who led the onslaught against the Socialist 'traitors' who had supported or tolerated the war.

The profound disturbance caused by the Libyan war in the directing circles of the Socialist party afforded the opportunity for a sudden leap from local eminence to national notoriety. Mussolini was at this time still not thirty years old. He had been born and brought up in the Romagna, the outlying northern province of the former Papal States. The politics of this region bear a particular stamp. From 1815 to 1859 the Popes had shared its government with an Austrian garrison, and the Mazzinian Republicans had found this doubly despot-ridden region a most fruitful field for their agitation. Extreme discontent bred an agitation for the most sweeping changes. In the Romagna, with more persistence than anywhere else in Italy, Mazzinian devotees continued after 1859 to denounce the monarchical Government of the Piedmontese as an interloping tyranny which blocked the way against a truly Italian revolution. As Mazzini and his generation departed from the scene, the scattered villages transferred their revolutionary allegiance to the first preachers of Socialism, a Socialism of sheer rebellion which had little contact with the movements of organized workers in Lombardy and Piedmont. By contrast, the more comfortably situated farmers largely continued to style themselves Republicans. Thus in the Romagna both the better-off households and the poor village people, except those under the influence of the clergy (who also in their way were for a long while 'subversive' in regard to the Italian Kingdom), were the declared partisans of an upheaval against the established constitution. Crispi, in the nineties, regarded it as an extraordinary achievement to have piloted King Humbert safely across this turbulent region in the course of a royal tour.

In the Chamber in Rome the Republicans sat beside the Socialists on the benches of the 'Extreme Left', but at home in Romagna the Socialist and Republican factions confronted each other with violent words and sometimes violent deeds. Benito Mussolini's father, Alessandro the blacksmith of Predappio, was a tough and, on occasion, a rowdy and violent ringleader of the poor labourers of his region. His more particular bugbear was the priesthood, though his schoolmistress wife was a devout churchgoer. Yet he was in continual wordy conflict also with the local Republicans. Several times he was in gaol for disturbances to public order: in the main he was a blunt people's champion against local abuses, who held that kings and priests were everywhere and always the enemies of mankind. Such were the doctrines that his son Benito received by heritage. But since by his mother's efforts he received the education of a secondary school, and became qualified as an elementary State school teacher, Benito was able to step easily out of village politics into the higher ranks of Socialist leaders. Alessandro Mussolini was a humble reporter of village affairs and affrays for small local weekly journals. Benito, after a juvenile sojourn in Switzerland to try his luck at odd jobs and to evade (as his principles required) compulsory military training, was soon in demand as an editor of small Socialist periodicals and as a revolutionary and anti-religious lecturer and pamphleteer in northern Italy. For a brief time he did similar work in the Italian-speaking Austrian province of Trentino, until he was expelled on the suspicion of complicity in a dynamiting plot.

Intense and tumultuous as an orator, somewhat withdrawn and morose in manner, uninterested in comfort or in respectable appearances, indulging the widest intellectual curiosity, Mussolini broke into the ring of high Socialist leaders during their embarrassment over the Libyan war.

He was editor at this time of *La Lotta di Classe* (The Class Struggle), the Socialist weekly in the Romagnole city of Forlì. He at once spoke out for a policy of revolutionary obstruction of the war. Meanwhile the General Confederation of Labour—in which the associations of a quarter of a million organized workers were now united—joined with the Socialist party to proclaim a protest strike. It was a mild enough affair, in most of Italy, but the Socialists of Forlì—the capital of Mussolini's native province—with other sympathizers, cut telegraph wires, and laid a telegraph pole across a railway line to stop a troop train. Mussolini personally, according to the police, took part in tearing up tramlines. Arrested, Mussolini based his defence on the allegation that his own part had been purely literary—consisting in the composition of 'theoretical' justifications of the general strike and the revolution, as he said—and he argued that those who desired a 'rich and free Italy'—as true Socialists did—were more truly patriots than the Nationalists who wanted a big Italy. Italy, he said, was full of 'internal Tripolis' which needed colonizing: that was what Italians should be making their first concern, instead of careering over Africa.

The official Socialist daily paper, the *Avanti* of Milan, declaimed against the war. But the opposition which it expressed was circumspect. It did not strike the note of a total rebellion of the

Socialist party against the power of Giolitti. Margherita Sarfatti, Mussolini's later confidante, claims to have heard her fellow-Jew, Claudio Treves, the distinguished lawyer, and at the time chief editor of the paper, declare on the first day of the Libyan war: 'We must now be more Giolittian than ever: we must keep Giolitti dependent on our support . . . and make him moderate and restrict the Libyan enterprise. If we desert him, he will fall into the clutches of other Parliamentary groups and be forced into an extreme reactionary and colonialist policy.' Treves, this witness asserts, was overborne by Anna Kulishoff, one of the Russian Socialist refugee women who at that time, in the heyday of the fashion for the great Russian novelists, held court among the Italian Socialist leaders. Thus Treves and Filippo Turati, the most brilliant and authoritative of the Socialist Parliamentarians and journalists, publicly declared in favour of a breach with the master of Parliament. But their close associates Leonida Bissolati and Ivanoe Bonomi, younger men in the first rank of the Socialist intelligentsia, dissented. They would not, said Bissolati, in Parliament, amid cheers from the pro-war benches, acquiesce in the Socialist party and the working classes isolating themselves henceforth in hostility against the rest of the nation. They argued that Italy, by invading Tripoli, was simply taking up a position among the West European powers, all of which had in turn sought an expansion in Africa. They gave weight to the argument that unless Italy took Tripoli another power, probably Germany, would take it. They recognized that the peasantry of the south hoped to find lands across the Mediterranean, and they even entertained the view that Italy might have a 'civilizing mission' in Africa. But above all they insisted that Giolitti's Italy was quite another country than Crispi's Italy: They implored the Socialists to think twice or three times before courting a headlong conflict with the Ministry. Through Parliament and the Government—they said—the Socialists could do much, and were doing much, for the working classes. They recalled further that the Socialists, by local agreements with other parties, were in control, or part control, of many provincial and municipal administrations. If the Socialists now planned a revolutionary head-on attack on the Central Government they should logically give up also their local privileges and positions. Bissolati and Bonomi claimed to stand for the continuation of the work which Turati and Treves had been conducting for years, work which the revolutionaries were now stampeding these leaders into throwing over, for the sake of the demagogic appeal of a revolt against the hardships of war. In any case, if the revolutionaries imposed their policy on the party then the revolutionaries should take on responsibility for executing it. Turati and Treves were no longer the men to guide it. Such were the expressed views of the 'Reformist' wing.

The Socialist party held stormy sessions to thrash out these dissensions, which came to a head at Reggio Emilia, in July 1912. At these congresses Mussolini, but lately set at liberty after five months in gaol, came forward as the spokesman of the Socialist Federation of Forlì. This local group had recently abandoned the party, and proclaimed itself an autonomous revolutionary unit, but had then rejoined it to act as a gingering element from within. The principal national figure among the extremists at Reggio was, however, Costantino Lazzari, a name which recurs in each chapter of the history of Italian Socialism on its way towards Communism and Fascism.

In a long, turbulent and somewhat tortuous political life, this pioneer trade unionist never tired of one doctrine: the true proletarians should exercise ceaseless vigilance over the lawyers, doctors and literary men who were almost its only Parliamentary spokesmen. At Reggio he now thrust forward young Mussolini to be the spokesman of a proletarian demand for the expulsion of Bissolati, Bonomi and their friends from the Socialist party. It was Mussolini's first appearance on a national platform. In a tumultous speech Mussolini arraigned the reformists not only for their general policy, but for a recent particular act of solidarity with the Parliamentary régime: Bissolati, Bonomi and others had proceeded to the Royal Palace among the deputies of the Giolittian majority to congratulate King Victor Emmanuel on escaping from an attempt made on his life early that year. Mussolini, who had frequently in his papers applauded bomb-throwing and dynamiting exploits, gained the endorsement of the congress for a bitter denunciation of this visit to the Quirinal. The Reformists withdrew from the congress and the party to form their own independent and definitely ministerial group.

Turati, Treves and the minor office-holders of the party were left behind in uneasy collaboration with Lazzari, Mussolini and the other extremists. The success of the latter had gravely impaired their powers and position in the party. The General Confederation of Labour and the co-operatives continued to give their confidence to Turati and Treves and even, especially in the south of Italy, to collaborate with the expelled faction of the Reformists. But Treves was forced out of the editorship of the *Avanti*, and, after various attempts to find a better-known man, Mussolini was named editor of the official national organ of the party. It was an immediate ascent from provincial fame to a position of recognized importance.

II. INSURRECTIONARY PRELUDES

After this success, Benito Mussolini began to group around himself a nucleus of Socialists in revolt against the moderation of the admirers of Giolitti. The Mussolinians made it their aim to purge the party of moderates and of 'intellectuals'. Margherita Sarfatti has left on record how Mussolini would at that time pronounce this last word, slowly and scornfully, intending a bitter insult to those described. The new editor of the *Avanti* imposed a change of style on the national organ of the Socialist party, and the new style was the distinguishing mark of a new type of leadership. Affrays between the wretched peasantry of backward southern provinces and the police gave occasion for articles of inflammatory protest. The *Avanti*'s columns were closed to the elaborately argumentative articles of Treves and his friends. Mussolini published at the same time a personal review for the closer circle of his friends, entitled *Utopia*. In close discipleship to the Syndicalists (who as a separate political organization were, as has been said, negligible) Mussolini interpreted the class struggle not in economic terms as a tussle between profits and wages, but idealistically as an exercise in heroism in which a minority of leaders might form their characters and revivify society. 'Syndicalism,' he wrote or approvingly quoted in 1909, 'restores to its place in history the creative value of man, man who determines and is determined, who can leave the imprint of his force upon things and institutions which he changes as he pursues the purpose he himself has chosen.' And he quoted from an essay in praise of Syndicalism: 'Better a new consciousness than a fuller purse, better a gain of will-power than a life insurance policy.'

The older Socialist leaders manifested distrust and alarm in the face of this romantic sort of Socialist gospel which Mussolini was bringing into the pages of the *Avanti*. Treves, the ex-editor, maintained that Mussolini in throwing over the philosophy of historical materialism had jettisoned the fundamental standpoint of Socialism, having abandoned the theory of ideas as the product of environment in favour of a 'fatuous revolutionary idealism' which expected miracles from the ideas and will-power of a few representative men. This Mussolinian doctrine, according to Treves, expressed itself in an uncultured clamour, in which all distinctions between republicanism, socialism, syndicalism, anarchism were lost. A reversion, Treves called it, to the old infantile Socialism which Marx had swept out of court when he promulgated his 'Scientific Socialism'. Mussolini, said Treves, was appealing to the ignorant mob. Mussolini retorted that those who professed to disdain the mob were really backing out of the risks of revolution, and that this was what Treves and the elder Socialist intellectuals really meant to do.

While Mussolini had thus wrested the official party organ from the veterans of intellectual and Parliamentary Socialism, and was engaged upon assimilating it to the Anarchist sheets of his native region, the Socialist party was still pushing its way into local government, trade and production. Forceful local leaders, encouraged by the revolutionists at Party Headquarters, spurned the mild triumphs of electoral and economic progress and set their hopes upon a new type of agricultural trade unionism, which in some districts not merely made itself the sole contractor for bringing labourers in touch with employers who had jobs to offer, but established a monopoly as the sole supplier of goods to wage-earners. In some places in Emilia and Romagna the municipality paid its employees not in money but in credits at the local co-operative store. Socialist chiefs made themselves virtual dictators in small agricultural towns of that area.

The local civil authorities, and even the army authorities, interpreting Giolitti's purpose, went warily about the business of interfering, even when Socialist organizations or local bosses in remote provinces exercised an unconstitutional sway, or even when with violence they wrested power from the official guardians of the peace. Something new and highly disturbing was being witnessed in the internal affairs of the kingdom. The local dictator was a common enough figure in the south of Italy, where he stood leagued with the Ministry of the Interior in a more or less unholy bond for electoral purposes. But now little dictators were establishing themselves in north and central Italian districts, not in virtue of pacts with the Government but by dint of the growing power of Socialist organizations tolerated by the Government even in their breaches of the law.

In 1913 general elections were due to be held, the first in

which the new electorate, swollen by the manhood suffrage law, was called to the polls. Giolitti, following his usual practice of 'trimming', reached an explicit agreement with the high clericals —to ensure against an excessive triumph of Socialists and their sympathizers. The pact was concluded in deep privacy, a certain Count Gentiloni secretly negotiating for the clericals. At the end of the elections this aristocrat openly boasted that he had made two hundred seats safe for the Government candidates. On Giolitti's side the agreement with the clericals was entirely opportunistic. Where clerical votes were insufficient, or not required, Giolitti made his agreements with the most outright anti-clericals. None the less, he had stretched the compliance of his 'Left' supporters uncomfortably. The Socialists, who now came back with fifty seats in the Chamber, were at least in their open profession anti-Giolittian, while the Radicals, seventy strong, and the dozen or so of Republicans, were severe critics of the conduct of the Libyan war which, after dragging on indecisively, had been concluded with lame and indecisive terms of peace. All of these 'Extreme Left' groups cried out against the part played in politics by the Banca Romana, the clerical bank which had been so deeply concerned for the armed furtherance of its interests in Tripoli, but which none the less had suspended payments.

Had the Extreme Left joined with the scattered groups of his Conservative opponents, Giolitti would have been hard put to it to command his majority in the Chamber—though none doubted that in the last resort he could contrive a combination to oust any supplanter. He determined, therefore, as he had done before in 1906 and 1909, to bring into office an alternative and easily replaceable Premier, to carry on the Administration while he himself watched out for a new programme behind which he could rally a thoroughly reliable majority. It was his known practice to wait for a newly elected Parliament to become manageable before he harnessed it to the service of one of his own long ministries. Antonio Salandra, whom Giolitti recommended to the King as his successor, fully recognized that Giolitti was arbiter of the Chamber, and in the last resort of the Ministry itself. Salandra consulted Giolitti on his ministerial appointments, and by Giolitti's permission he retained in his Cabinet the Marchese di San Giuliano, the Giolittian Foreign Minister.

While the Salandra Government was finding its feet, the

Revolutionary Socialists, with Mussolini as their chief spokesman and inspirer, were making steady progress in their defiance of the authority of the State in certain regions. Already in 1913, in the turbulent Romagna and neighbouring provinces, 'Committees of Action' had organized the besieging of barracks to keep garrison troops off the streets while the proletariat (as a chronicler described it) 'sacked a few farmyards, knocked in a few church doors, kidnapped a few generals.' The Ministry of the Interior discouraged the prefects and garrison commanders from getting involved in any clashes with these irresponsible demonstrators. 'A sort of semi-anarchist agitation' Giolitti called it, and he left it to take its course. But here Salandra did not follow him. Scarcely had he taken over Palazzo Braschi, the all-powerful Ministry of the Interior, from Giolitti, when the Socialists of the same region—Mussolini's region—carried out still more extensive revolts. The city office of the great town of Bologna was occupied by demonstrators, who hoisted the red flag without the prefect or the chief of police in any way interfering: a railway strike was proclaimed in direct defiance of the law, and the Ministry of Justice proposed taking no action against its instigators until Salandra himself insisted upon a show of firmness. At Ravenna the chief of police was killed: the prefect kept the troops at his disposal indoors, and let bands of peasants, captained by Socialist officials, have the run of the town. At Foligno the railway station was destroyed. Salandra was much readier than Giolitti to repress these tumults by force, and Giolitti perhaps was pleased that a makeshift Ministry should have responsibility for unpopular disciplinary measures. In July, to avert a general railway strike, Salandra called a class of conscripts to the colours. The Socialists manifested intense indignation.

The Socialist party was in reality deeply divided. Its partisans in the turbulent towns of Bologna, Ravenna, Ferrara and of the smaller centres of the Emilian region (which includes Romagna) were peasants who had organized themselves successfully against the predominance and arbitrary economic pressure of the land-lords and big farmers. Successful organization had made of these Socialist peasants and day-labourers a power in their corner of the land. It was they who responded so readily to the propaganda of upheaval for upheaval's sake preached by their tribune, the editor of the *Avanti*, in the columns of this national organ of the Socialist party. The policy of sporadic violence was entirely contrary to the ideas of Turati and Treves, the great Parliamentarians of Socialism, who waited meanwhile for the insurrectionary school of Socialist leaders to exhaust their credit in these petty revolts. Turati and Treves had not, indeed, publicly reconciled themselves with Giolitti after the Libyan war: but while the Salandra Government took in hand the suppression of the outbreaks in Romagna and Emilia, the law-abiding Socialists—followed by the great mass of trade unionists—could only look forward to resuming their peaceful penetration of the State when the insurrectionists had had their fling. The outlook of Turati and Treves was fundamentally identified with that of Giolitti waiting to resume the power.

The restoration of order in the Romagna caused Salandra no great trouble. The powers of the State were able, in a few brief weeks, to put an end to the petty outbreaks of the agrarian extremists. Only a superficial judgement could, however, mistake this suppression of symptoms for a cure of the Italian *malaise*. Salandra privately declared that he was the successor to ten years of misgovernment: but neither he nor any Parliamentarian thrown up by the 1913 Legislature could hope to initiate a political renewal. The reasons lay deep in the history of a half-century of United Italy.

The *malaise* was rooted in profound scepticism about the destiny of the country. The creation of the United Kingdom of Italy, by the sudden extension of Piedmont's statute, laws and institutions over the tenfold area of the peninsula, had been generally acclaimed a miracle. Since its accomplishment, politically conscious Italians had shown an unshakable determination to preserve the new national independence and unity. But this led them no further than to a resigned acceptance of a constitution which was felt to exhibit deep and perhaps mortal defects. The institutions of Italy were those which little Piedmont, the Alpine borderland, had evolved for itself in its own particular circumstances. Even Piedmont had adopted its modern political structure by imitation of England and France, not without a second motive of gaining British and French help in the struggle against Austria. A half-century of Italian history had brought no conviction that the Piedmontese foundations were adequate to sustain the stress of the political life of a nation in sight of a population of fifty millions. Only such consummate bargainers and negotiators as Depretis and Giolitti had been able to hold the country together in relative peace and order:

and if Italy, under Giolitti, had made notable economic progress, the price paid for the Giolittian peace was one which the younger generation, the most self-confident and hopeful that had been born in United Italy, protested that it would no longer continue paying.

Yet what possible mode of change was open? The electorate was now, indeed, eight millions strong; in the national elected assembly all regions and all classes of citizens could hope to make known and to gain support for their programmes of reform. Already Giolitti's opponents had in their power an instrument which Giolitti had never taken very seriously: the Press. If the Italian Parliament was to be transformed from what Depretis and Giolitti had made it—a centre for the conclusion of effective clandestine bargains masked by splendid but ineffective displays of oratory—great political parties must learn to outmanœuvre Giolitti's official and unofficial staff of election managers. The choice for Giolitti's opponents lay between democratic renewal and insurrection. It was certainly a grave matter that professed insurrectionists had in their hands the popular Press of what seemed the one great party of the masses. The alternative in 1914 appeared to be the following. Either some strong Parliamentary party, such as Italy had not known in the half-century of unity, must succeed in breaking through Giolitti's electoral defences—his understandings with local bosses and high powers behind the scenes, the influence of his astutely disposed corps of prefects and sub-prefects, at the orders of the Ministry of the Interior, scattered through the kingdom—and must get adequate support from the new eight-million-strong electorate. Or insurrection must be attempted on a greater scale. Giolitti, to whom the very notion of a national political destiny was alien, probably felt equal to either menace, and was firmly persuaded that he still held the sole secret for governing a country which had been so surprisingly patched together, out of feudal fragments, into the semblance of a great power.

The world-shattering events of August 1914 impinged upon more than one local national crisis which had seemed to be coming to a head by its own logic. A month before the war England stood on the verge of civil strife over Ireland, while in France the figure of Caillaux focused upon itself the defiant fury of the upper classes. In Italy the ferment in such various quarters of the national life as the Church and the trade unions, the arts and the philosophic schools, portended a grim trial of strength against the established power. The impact of war appeared at first sight to relegate these local national crises to irrelevance. In reality it did no more than complicate the manner of their consummation.

CHAPTER SEVEN

WAR AND REVOLUTION: THE GREAT TEST

I. ACCLAMATION OF NEUTRALITY.—Italy's diplomatic engagements with the Triple Alliance, offset by understandings with England and France, made neutrality the necessary policy in 1914, and for this there was at first general approval. Socialists, Clericals and the Parliamentary majority were all at one in support of the policy.

II. THE INTERVENTIONIST CAMPAIGN.—The prospect of a long war rendered neutrality delicate and dubious. Republicans, Radicals, Freemasons opened the agitation for war at the side of the Entente. The Socialists constitute the bulwark of neutrality.

III. THE PART OF MUSSOLINI. — Mussolini breaks with the Socialists to join the Interventionist campaign. What sort of war? Nationalist or democratic?

I. ACCLAMATION OF NEUTRALITY

Italian foreign policy, like Italian home politics, appeared to have assumed under Giolitti a static fixity. In home politics a system of bargains linked the big forces of all the parties to an immobile centre; and so too, in foreign policy, there was no prevailing purpose, but a series of engagements on all sides which cancelled out each other's motive efficacy. To expect— in 1914—that Italy might preserve neutrality in a great European conflict was not unreasonable in the light of the history of the Italian national movement in its relations respectively with Vienna and with Paris. The wars of independence had been fought primarily against Vienna, but to balance this Rome had been absorbed into Italy in defiance of pro-Papal governments of France. After 1870 the eagerness of France to put a check on the seaward expansion of Italy in the Mediterranean had at times been felt to be yet more vexatious than Austrian pressure on dry land. France was held responsible for the frustration of Italy's expansion in Abyssinia, and even in the recent Libyan war France had exhibited suspicions which at one moment expressed themselves in open wrangling with Italy. Austria in herself was, by a strong tradition, viewed as the hereditary enemy; but by the early twentieth century Austria's status was that of the brilliant second of Germany. Prussia and the German Empire were in no sense hereditary enemies of Italy. On the contrary Italy had from the days of the unification sought and found support (conceded to her—in the event—with an unpleasing air of condescension) in Berlin. If not greatly liked, the Germans were greatly respected, and not only by one party or faction of Italians. The Italian army looked to the Prussian as its model, the Italian Socialists admired and envied the prestige of Prussian Socialism, and the Italian university professorate that of the academic institutions of Prussia.

But if Italian hostility to Austria was mitigated by the identification of Vienna with Berlin, still more did the fact of the Anglo-French Entente assist in smoothing the course of Italo-French relations. With scarcely a dissentient voice Italian statesmen had ever looked upon collaboration with England as the best guarantee for Italy's integrity in the Mediterranean. The native antipathy of the Italians against Austria and France was thus held in check by these countries' respective alliances. Vienna and Paris had also their respective attachments inside Italy, a pro-Austrian Vatican on the one side, and a pro-French Freemasonry on the other. The commercial world wanted peace.

It was in perfect accord with this complex play of forces that Italy's attitude, on the outbreak of the European war in August 1914, was one of unqualified neutrality. Diplomatically Italy was the ally of Germany and Austria, yet these allies did not seriously contend that the pledge of assistance which the Triple Alliance required in case of a defensive war was called into play by the Austro-German proceedings of August 1914. By a footnote to the Alliance Italy had at its very outset stipulated against being drawn into war upon England. But Italy also had secret commitments amounting to a promise never to join in an attack upon France—which had not prevented the Chief of the Italian General Staff, General Pollio, from pressing upon the German General Staff, as late as March 1914, offers of an Italian expeditionary force on the Rhine if the Alliance should come into play.

(The Italian Staff had even offered, in such an event, to assist Germany by a surprise march across neutral Switzerland, which the German Staff had on political grounds refused to consider.)

The link with England was, above all, a strong brake on the notion of Italo-German collaboration. At the moment when a war involving the Germanic partners of the Triple Alliance became obviously inevitable, Salandra notified her Allies that Italy could not allow that the circumstances foreseen in the Treaty had arisen. The war declared by Austria was not 'defensive'. An unwonted unanimity manifested itself from end to end of the Italian peninsula. The declaration of neutrality was applauded by all the serious powers in the land—by the Socialists, revolutionary and reformist alike, by the Vatican and the Clericals, by Giolitti himself and by the leading anti-Giolittians. The alternative to remaining neutral would be joining in the war, but on which side could Italy join the war? The leading newspaper of the Nationalists for a few days argued the case for going into war on the German side, but their motive was emotional—sheer admiration for the frank 'power-policy' and military might of the Central Powers, and instinctive antagonism to the out-and-out pacifists of the recent Libyan war —such as Mussolini—who now luxuriated in the national policy of peace.

Much more numerous and popular than the idolaters of Prussia were the highly miscellaneous groups which regarded Austria as the predestined enemy, if Italy was to come into the war at all. At the very least they demanded that Austria should pay a stiff price for Italian non-belligerence. A million Italians in Trieste, Istria and the Trentino were under Austria: for them a German and Austrian triumph—unless Italy could first make her weight felt—would mean perpetuation of a rule which was traditionally odious, and at that moment showed signs of a deliberate hardening against all Italian manifestations in local government and culture. Not only did Austria cling to these remnants of the old Italian-speaking domains; a deliberate policy of sacrificing the Italian middle class to the Slav peasant peoples was in favour at Vienna. Virtually all Italy was united in the determination to use the European war to secure a triumph for Italian nationalism in Trieste and the Trentino. There was no question of making war on behalf of Germany and Austria so as to establish a claim of gratitude upon the partners of the Triple Alliance. Therefore Italy could achieve her purposes in regard to Trieste and Trentino only in one of two ways: as a price to be paid by Austria for Italy's neutrality, or as the spoils of an active Italian contribution to the defeat of Austria in war.

To strike a bargain for neutrality was in the eyes of the prudent leading citizens of hundreds of Italian cities beyond all comparison a wiser course than to rush headlong into the conflict. Much living tradition favoured the method of an intelligent exploitation of the rivalries of the stronger great powers. A generation which was still alive in the Italy of 1914 had seen United Italy come into existence by dexterous playing off of the great powers against each other. The unity of the country had afterwards been preserved not by force but by the skill of consummate masters in bargaining. Thanks to the adroitness with which stable government and balanced relations with the wider world had been achieved, Italy was at last rising to a modest prosperity, with prospects of a rapid overtaking of the better-equipped countries in a promised age of electricity and automobilism—new technical branches of the world industrial system in which Italy was actually in the vanguard. It was true that Italy had but recently concluded a local war, but the adventure of the Italian State in Libya, like the adventures of the revolutionary wing of the Italian Socialists in Romagna, were discounted as fleeting indiscretions. Such was the attitude, such were the hopes, of Italians of undeniable patriotism. That Italy should peacefully attain an equal standing with the other great powers in a Europe where none was strong enough to domineer and play the bully—that was the only sense in which such prudent Italians would accept the message of the new Nationalism. The Italian Socialists in general did not dissent from a 'national aspiration' of that sort. They desired gradually to have more influence themselves in an Italy which should gradually have more influence in the world. Even the Mussolinian Socialists, fresh from agitations to stop Italy from finishing a war in Africa of her own making, could not for the moment dissent from the widespread and, among the Socialists, the unquestioned determination to keep her out of a war of other people's making.

On the issue of war and peace the important category of Italians who regarded themselves as positive and emphatic 'Catholics' were at one with the Socialists. The high clergy of Italy had attained a practical conciliation with the Italian kingdom. Not one of them, perhaps, dreamed of hearkening for

an Austrian voice which might have offered, in case of war, to
release the prisoner of the Vatican from his Piedmontese gaolers.
The Vatican, however, from its unnational standpoint, still
viewed the Austrian monarchy as a pillar of the Church.   In
Trieste and Trentino the Italian high clergy were at least by
comparison with the local Italian professional and business
classes loyal to Vienna and indifferent to the appeal of Italy.
The Vatican, which had been benevolent enough towards Italy's
Libyan war, was thus ranged along with the Socialists, and with
the Giolittian Parliamentarians as a whole, to demand that Italy
should remain neutral, and should agree to accept from Austria
as the price of that neutrality—rendered precious by its
uncertainty—a transaction to Italy's advantage about the
'unredeemed' territories of Trieste and Trentino and about
Albania, which the Balkan wars of 1911–13 had now thrown up
as a further annexable remnant of Turkish heritage.

II. THE INTERVENTIONIST CAMPAIGN

Such were the advocates of neutrality—a block which included
Giolittianism as a whole, but also such extraneous elements as
the philosophic circle of Croce and the revolutionaries of the
school of Mussolini.   But the recovery of the Allies on the Marne,
and the ensuing prospect of a prolonged war, rendered the
prospect, for nations intent upon detachment and impartiality,
highly delicate.   The appeal of the Allies for the solidarity of
all civilization sounded loud and clear.   First in Italy to respond
to it were the Republican party, clinging to memories of Mazzini
and Garibaldi; the closely associated Radicals; and the Reformist
Socialist party, those recent countenancers of the Libyan war,
and partisans of a compact with the monarchy whom Mussolini
had succeeding in ejecting from the official Socialist party two
years before.   These groups led the way in openly advocating
war at the side of France and England against Austria.   The
Masonic lodges were exceedingly active propagandists on this
behalf.   Their traditions and their interests ranged them whole-
heartedly on the side of war.   Freemasonry in Italy in the early
nineteenth century had been a rallying-ground for those who
cherished the traditions of those reforms which Napoleon had
brought to Italy and which the legitimist restorations of 1815 had
annulled.   The conspirators against Austrian and Papal rule
were largely Freemasons, and through the lodges they were in
correspondence with the Freemasons of France.   The religion of

the immortal triangle (Liberty, Equality, Fraternity) was what
the Freemasons offered in replacement of Catholic dogma:
and the Freemasons of France powerfully attracted those of Italy
towards support of the aims of French policy. From Garibaldi
to Crispi and Zanardelli many of the leading Italian politicians
were Masons: and the presence of Crispi's name among these
indicates clearly that membership of the brotherhood held a
statesman under no occult constraint to follow a single line of
policy. Yet the Freemasons, as an organized fellowship, inspired
greater and smaller organs of the Italian Press, and they were
believed to be influential in the making or breaking of careers
in the armed forces. Giolitti had rendered membership of the
lodges illicit for naval officers. The Freemasons exercised in the
background an influence which none could assess: membership
was in Italy more genuinely secret than in the Freemasonry of
other countries. The Socialists too sensed the influence of
Freemasonry in their ranks, and Mussolini, following his triumph
over the Reformists, had in 1912 moved a national Congress of
the Socialist Party to prohibit Socialists from being at the same
time Freemasons—a tactical stroke to weaken those leaders of
the party who profited by their associations outside it. The
breach was rendered more effective when in 1914 the Freemasons
ranged themselves decisively on the side of a war in aid of France.
  The war was in its earliest phase when a number of young
men led by a member of the Garibaldi family (name illustrious
in the Masonic annals) departed to offer their services as volunteers for France. It was, in the eyes of their sympathizers, a
noble protest against the drab utilitarianism of the majority.
The country as a whole seemed to stand fast by absolute
neutrality. Giolitti approved Salandra's actions step by step.
But by September 1914 the interventionists had begun to move
the country. In such circumstances it was of great importance
that Giolitti and his friends had no extensive grip on the Press.
The most modern and powerful daily papers in the country,
those considered to be 'Masonic' and also some others, were
favourable to Italian intervention in the war. The Socialists
were vigilant. On September 22nd the Socialist party issued a
manifesto of warning against the 'warmongers', which Turati,
the chief parliamentarian and legalitarian, and Mussolini, the
most conspicuous insurrectionist, were said to have composed
jointly. The party appeared more united than ever in its history. In this manifesto the Socialists were urged to withstand

the incitements to war which were now pouring forth from the mouths and printing presses of the Reformist Socialists, the Masonic Radicals, the Republicans and the Nationalists.

For the Nationalists too, by a rapid switch-round, had aligned themselves on the interventionist side, though on grounds peculiar to their own group. To start with, at least, they had no preference whatever for the countries with whom they now clamoured to become allies. They proposed making war with a cold calculation of advantage to be gained indifferently at the expense of Italy's allies and of Italy's enemies. As they did not doubt that at the end of the war the nations would again confront each other in eternal competition, they summoned their country-men to look beyond the winning of this present war, at the side of the Entente, to times when they would be glad enough to have Germany at least, if not Austria, as an ally again.

A very young agitator for war, who shared the basic views of the Nationalists, Dino Grandi, publicly lamented the historical contingency which required that Italy should fight against Germany. The 'natural' alignment would be, he said, that of the prolific and unsated Germans, Italians and Russians against England and France. He broadly hinted that a war of that description would follow ultimately upon the anti-German war which was necessitated by Italy's historic claims against Austria.

In August 1914 the Nationalists had favoured fighting on the side of Italy's Germanic allies. When that was impossible they had stood momentarily for neutrality. But soon they became convinced that when five of the European great powers were testing their strength in war, a sixth alleged great power which remained outside the struggle would be pushed aside and exploited by all at the making of the peace. These devotees of the 'Goddess Italy', for whom the strengthening of the Italian tribe against all challengers stood out as the one stable purpose, held themselves free to seek victory wherever it was offered. It had been reasonable, until the battle of the Marne, to hold that Germany was invincible: but when Germany failed to reach Paris the contending groups of powers seemed evenly balanced, so that intervention on the side of the Entente should give the victory to that side. The Nationalists were, indeed, a little concerned lest the Entente might gain a rapid victory without needing to call in Italy and pay the price for that help. They pressed therefore for immediate intervention as momentary allies of France and England, but talk of a war against imperialism and militarism as such moved them to scorn. Their view was that Italian imperialism and militarism should take advantage, for its own nourishment, of the German miscalculation of the balance of power.

There was thus, within the ranks of those who advocated Italy's entry into the war, the profoundest disagreement about the meaning of the proposed intervention. The other interventionists, Radicals, Republicans and Reformist Socialists, and in general the adepts of Freemasonry, far from viewing the protagonists of the European war with calculating indifference, denounced Germany—with its satellite Austria—as the breaker of peace, the plotter of a world hegemony which it was as much to Italy's interest as that of the other great powers to frustrate. They argued that the eclipse of Germany's military might would enable Italy and all other European nations thenceforth to devote their resources to material well-being and the progress of civilization. Should the crusade of the Entente fail, a German victory would leave Italy in the effective position of a satellite nation, even if, as a matter of form, Italy's neutrality were to be recompensed by some transference of territory by Austria. But the democratic interventionists developed an argument of a still more intimately Italian character. It was argued by them that the Giolittians—from whom they did not yet dissociate the Premier by Giolitti's sufferance, Salandra—might profit by Italy's isolation from the democracies at war, to smother the political renewal for which manhood suffrage had opened at last a promising prospect. To force the Giolittian clique to align Italy with the countries of truly democratic régime would be (they argued) to break Giolittianism itself. On the other hand, if the Giolittian clique were left to strike a bargain with the Central Powers there might follow an authoritarian reformation of the Government of Italy, the institution of a Chancellorial régime in which (said the Radicals) the great Italian Socialist party would acquiesce as submissively as the German Socialists had done when war had been declared by the Imperial Government.

III. THE PART OF MUSSOLINI

The Socialist party remained, during the first three months of these discussions, solidly united on the neutralist side. All of a sudden—within a few weeks of the Socialist manifesto against the 'war-makers'—Benito Mussolini swung round to the war-makers' point of view. There was no scope for his talents or for his turbulence among the opponents of this war.   He had been thoroughly at home when, in defiance of the State, he could denounce the Libyan war as a senseless massacre.   He had declaimed in favour of neutrality while this cause bore the aspect of an active policy of breach with the Triple Alliance.   But he now found himself as one among a miscellany of editors pushed into an alignment with the Vatican, the Conservatives, Giolitti and the Giolittian Parliament, and, what perhaps he found hardest to endure, with the constitutional Socialists, Turati and Treves, upon whom—since the grave spectacle of the war had put an end to the era of petty insurrectionism—the prestige of leadership of a united Socialist party had again descended.   By holding fast to the programme which he had drawn up in accord with Turati, Mussolini would in effect have accepted a subordinate collaboration in a policy of buttressing up the locum tenens of Giolitti.   In the very first days of the neutrality Mussolini's *Avanti* had declared it to be a 'strange irony of events' that the Salandra Government had defined a policy which was supported by the Proletariat.   And soon the apostle of the Proletariat could stand it no longer.   In all the sincerity of a heartfelt vocation to break up the counsels of prudence, and to rise on the crest of incessant agitation, Mussolini tried to argue his fellow-members of the Socialist Executive into reinterpreting their manifesto.   His intelligent confidante and panegyrist, Margherita Sarfatti, has left a vivid description of Mussolini as she saw him that autumn, visibly distraught and not concealing his unhappy irresolution.   He was perplexed to square his own recent slogan 'War and Socialism are profound and irreconcilable opposites' with the unquenchable urge to captain another revolt of the Socialist party against leaders who had made this very maxim the foundation of their policy.   He solved it by the timely discovery that there are wars and wars: there are wars for conquest with which Socialism is indeed irreconcilable; but there are also wars to end war, and to overturn the makers of the other sort of war.   These wars to end war Socialism should not oppose but should make its own.

The 'conversion' of Mussolini caused exasperation and rage. Only two years had passed since Mussolini had successfully incited the party to expel the Reformist Socialists, and now the same Mussolini sought to drag it in the direction of the policy which the Reformists had adopted to mark their breach with it— collaboration with Radicals and Republicans to push the Government into the war of the Democracies. The convert was assailed with bitter irony. He failed to induce any interest or sympathy among his fellow-leaders of the party. There was nothing for Mussolini save to resign from the party committee and from the editorship of the *Avanti*.

Not, however, in a resigned spirit. If his party rivals believed that they had driven the Romagnole into silence and impotence they were very soon disillusioned. To the astonishment and mortification of his ex-colleagues, within a month Mussolini produced a rival Socialist daily paper in Milan, which was pledged, from the first number, to the cause of war. 'To you, youth of Italy in workshops and universities, young in years and in spirit . . . to you I address my greeting, a word which I would never have uttered in normal times. But now I utter it loudly and clearly, without ambiguity, in sure confidence—the dreadful fascinating word War!' The Socialist section of Milan now expelled Mussolini from their midst. He was accused of accepting French money to start the *Popolo d'Italia*. He was also accused, now that he had left the *Avanti*, of irregular operations with the party paper's funds. The accusers brought forward no reason to explain why Mussolini, if it was money he wanted, should have abandoned the editorship of a great daily to found and conduct a small one. Mussolini had in the past given the clearest proof that on the financial side he sought for no more than a living wage from his political work. The accusations of irregularity at the *Avanti* were, it seems, simply malicious gossip. But the party chiefs were furious with him, and with their connivance he was expelled for 'moral and political unworthiness'. When he appeared before an assembly to justify himself the accusers made no detailed charges, but howled him down. To this Mussolini replied with the most definite threats of revenge against those leaders who had failed to come to his defence: there would be 'no pardon and no pity' for those who held their tongue—cowards and hypocrites! He followed with an article in the *Popolo*: 'It is not against the proletariat that I shall fight. The proletariat know . . . that I have spent myself in an indomitable urge for action without caring for danger or measuring my fatigue. But you, Sirs, you who are the leaders of the party . . . you shall pass through the toils. . . . I am there to spoil your game. . . . The case of Mussolini is not finished as you think. It is beginning now: it is growing larger all the time: I raise the standard of schism.'

With these oaths and threats of revenge Mussolini attached himself to the interventionists, vowing that he was still a Socialist, shrieking that if the proletarians could get bayonets in their hands they might use them for their own purposes. The organized trade unionists and the party as a whole remained quite unmoved. Caldara, the Mayor of Milan, was one of the few notable Socialists who joined with Mussolini.

The rebel at once sought for allies outside the party ranks. There were easy avenues for sympathy among other schismatic Socialists, including, if not those whom Mussolini had personally helped to drive out of the party, men whom until recently he had belaboured with invective. The group of Syndicalists were captained by a few restless spirits who had in the course of a few years repeatedly passed into and out of the ranks of the official Socialist party. At the moment of Mussolini's wandering into the wilderness they too were out of it. Filippo Corridoni was a striking figure among them, a man of thought and action—organizer of strikes in defiance of the staid Socialist Confederation of Labour; theorist of the strike as not merely a means of raising wages but at the same time, and more fundamentally, a school of heroism for the worker. Such teaching was very close to Mussolini's own doctrines. Corridoni had an organization and some thousands of working-class followers. He struck an alliance with Mussolini and their movement, which was said soon after to have 50,000 adherents, took the title Fasci di Azione Rivoluzionaria, or Fasci di Combattimento. Nobody thought this an unusual or significant title. The word *fascio*, or group, was as common a word as 'group' in English to describe a political movement usually for some limited purpose. Under Crispi the Sicilian peasantry formed 'Fasci Siciliani' to express their grievances. More recently a 'Fascio' had been formed in Naples by leading citizens, who were then known as 'Fascisti', to put an end to abuses in the local administration. The workers' party in Milan had an organ in the eighties with the title *Il Fascio*. The Corridoni-Mussolini 'Fasci' now proceeded to take a busy and noisy part in the agitation for Italy's entry into the war.

The agitation waxed month by month. Political Italy fell into two hostile camps, but the aggressive spirit was manifested, naturally, by the camp which demanded Italy's entry into the war. Its propaganda took on a fierce tone. Neutralists were branded as renegades to the nation and similar anathemas fell upon those who sought to place themselves outside the clash.

Thus a group formed by eminent men of learning called 'Pro Italia Nostra', professing in theory to desire a policy for Italy's own advantage, and to withstand the pressure of either of the two national factions, was forced into effective alignment with the neutralist faction, and its members laid themselves open, towards the end of the period of neutrality, to physical violence. Common hostility to the neutralists blurred the extraordinary differences of outlook in the motley ranks of the interventionists. Though continuing to disagree as much as ever on the purposes and methods of the intended war they formed a single vast movement of agitation, and could not but be considerably infected by each other's phrases.   Thus the Nationalists were soon crying out against Germany for the destruction of the cathedral of Rheims, though a few weeks before they would have cheerfully marched beside the Germans through the ruined courtyards of Louvain.   Advocates of the war against imperialism discovered, on the other hand, hitherto unsuspected inclinations towards imperialism of their own.   But while the issue of war or neutrality remained undecided, the advocates of democratic war and those of nationalist war sunk their differences and continued in agitation and uproar.

CHAPTER EIGHT

EXIT GIOLITTI

I. BOSS, PREMIER AND KING.—Giolitti, omnipotent in peace-time Italy, loses his hold when it falls to the locum tenens, Salandra, to negotiate supreme issues of foreign policy.   The part of Sonnino and of the King.   Italy deals with both sides: and two voices speak for Italy.

II. D'ANNUNZIO AND 'RADIANT MAY'.—Giolitti attempts to reassert his power.   D'Annunzio's agitation.   King Victor Emmanuel repudiates the Leader of Parliament, and Giolitti's 'dictatorship' breaks before the triumph of the war party.

I. BOSS, PREMIER AND KING

While war raged in Europe, and popular agitations traversed the wider public life of Italy, the political system characterized by Giolitti's dominance was moving almost imperceptibly to a

crisis. Antonio Salandra had entered upon his office as little
more than a locum tenens for Giolitti, though by contrast with
others who had fulfilled that function he differed from the
Piedmontese in mood and in method.   It was quite in accordance
with Giolitti's statecraft to stand aside while a weak rival tried
his hand at strong methods.   And in the sphere of foreign policy
it was Giolitti's nominee, Marquis San Giuliano, who guided the
Salandra Cabinet through the convulsions of August 1914.

There was a distinct weakening of Giolitti's influence when
San Giuliano, Giolitti's colleague and nominee, died in October.
As successor at the Foreign Office, Salandra chose the Baron
Sonnino. Sonnino perhaps differed little from his predecessor in
policy; both had been supporters of the Triple Alliance, neither
was in the least inclined to throw Italy into 'democratic' war
in a crusade against the authoritarian empires.   In so far as
Sonnino envisaged war at all, it was according to the recipe of
the Nationalists—a war of measured effort at the side of allies
who might in some later war be enemies.   But in the play of
Italian home politics Sonnino was very differently placed from
his predecessor. He was the one Parliamentarian who had
seriously attempted since 1903 to take and hold power as an
opponent of Giolitti.   His nomination caused no public coldness
between Salandra and Giolitti, who throughout 1914 gave no
sign of distrusting the war policy of neutrality proclaimed by
Salandra : nor had Salandra in public pronouncements departed
from that policy.   Shortly before Sonnino joined the Government
Giolitti had, however, begun to show some signs of displeasure
with Salandra, because of a Governmental inquiry into certain
ambiguous statistics of the Ministry of War which concealed the
fact of important deficiencies in the army supplies.   Giolitti could
not obtain from the Government a public statement to clear his
own administration of blame in this connection.

As Premier and (during San Giuliano's illness) acting Foreign
Minister in this catastrophic time Salandra had achieved a sense
of personal power and responsibility which in peace-time no
precariously placed office holder could have indulged.   The
European war also gave renewed prestige and importance to the
royal house.

As a constitutional element in Italian politics, the dynasty
of Savoy had, since Victor Emmanuel II assumed the crown of
United Italy, been relegated to a decorative, symbolic, or at
most a bureaucratic function.   The fundamental statute of the

realm accorded to the King the right to nominate his own ministers. But Victor Emmanuel III, following his father, had entirely acquiesced in the effective limiting of the royal functions to the task of summoning to the Palace the leader who could show that he commanded the support of a majority in the Chamber. The completeness of this acquiescence was shown in the failure of a campaign launched by none other than Sonnino, in 1897, in favour of a return to the literal provisions of the Constitution, that is to a genuine selection of ministers by the King. The effective right of the man who enjoyed the confidence of the Chamber to stand at the head of the Government had been only more strongly confirmed. The King's part was simply to give effect to the changeful indications of the will of the Parliamentary majority. It was on this basis that Salandra had been called to office, and it had been assumed that on similar grounds he would in due course be ousted by the master of the majority, Giolitti.

The extreme gravity of events in 1914 insensibly modified this relation between King and Premier. King Victor Emmanuel, with whom Salandra was drawn by the force of overwhelming international events into a singularly intimate contact, ranked as a firm friend of England and was believed to have acted in concert with Edward VII for the support of France against Germany between 1901 and 1909. It was a sphere of affairs which Giolitti inclined to leave to experts: and the King was an expert. Later the King had somewhat withdrawn from this active share in foreign policy. But in the supreme emergency of 1914, when the Italian Foreign Office and its ambassadors became charged with the solution of so many secret and urgent problems, the King's knowledge and judgement loomed large again: all the larger for the precarious nature of his Premier's authority. King Victor Emmanuel was also actively concerned in military organization. Though he had grown up as 'Prince of Naples'—a title which was in itself a programme—he had never forgotten that the 'Italian' army was the Army of Piedmont, the pride of his ancestors in centuries when the rest of Italy was relatively disarmed. Almost from the outbreak of war, then, the King was in intimate association with Salandra, and tacitly the two must have felt themselves in partnership against any outside influences which might be brought to bear on their policy. The entry of Sonnino into the Ministry enhanced this independence from the Parliamentary majority. In more normal times he could hardly have been introduced into a Ministry existing by sufferance of the Giolittians. The Ministry was strengthened by other changes, but Salandra introduced no close friend or trusted lieutenant of Giolitti.

The management of the Italian Foreign Office at this juncture was a perplexing task. The Italian ambassadors in the chief courts pulled strongly for the policy desired where they were accredited: those in Berlin, Vienna and Constantinople, distressed at the bankruptcy of the Triple Alliance as an active partnership, worked hard to keep open, at least, the prospect of Italian neutrality. But the ambassadors in Paris and London (especially Imperiali, the London Ambassador) lost no occasion for representing Italy in the light of a possible and probable ally. There was no doubt which school of diplomatists enjoyed the chief confidence of Rome. Giolitti became convinced that Salandra had made up his mind for war, and, while remaining in touch with him, he felt that his own advice was no longer treated with deferential respect.

Before any of the powers were actually at war, Italy, in refusing to acknowledge a liability to fight with the Triple Alliance, had pressed Austria under the terms of that Alliance for a compensation to readjust the balance which was about to be disturbed by Austria's occupation of Serbia. Austria had demurred and delayed. Sonnino on taking office pressed Austria to enter into discussions in terms which made Jagow, the German Secretary of State, exclaim: 'This is a threat of war, and Italy is stating the price of neutrality.' To this accusation of blackmail the Italian Government could not at that time retort with the defence which is implicit in Salandra's *Memoirs*—that the negotiations were no more than a mask to give time to get the army ready for an intervention with the Allies which he himself had already decided upon. The Italian interventionists, at all events, remained suspicious for several more months that Salandra and Sonnino, with Giolitti in the background, would in the last resort agree to receive from Austria a price for neutrality. It was a plain inference from the prolonged negotiations which they conducted throughout spring 1915 with Prince von Bülow, the German Ambassador Extraordinary, that they were still open to a bargain.

Early in the year Giolitti made the first public manifestation of his desire that the negotiations with Austria should succeed. He wrote in a published letter (February 2, 1915) that 'quite a lot' (*parecchio*) might be obtained for Italy without a war. The use in such a connexion of the conversational word '*parecchio*' (which in his *Memoirs* Giolitti replaces by a conventional '*molto*') was denounced by the interventionists as being in itself the mark of a grotesquely mercantile and unheroic mind. But the Clericals, the Socialists, the Conservatives took heart to withstand the interventionist agitation. Together with the *Stampa*, the chief newspaper of Turin, and the *Mattino*, that of Naples, the Neutralists disposed of the local Catholic and Socialist papers throughout Italy, to which were added moreover numerous new publications, which had been helped into existence by German advertisement orders dispensed throughout the peninsula more clumsily, and perhaps more lavishly, than the corresponding cheques from Paris which facilitated the birth of papers like Mussolini's *Popolo d'Italia*. The small but numerous organs of the Neutralists withstood the pro-war agitation of the big-circulation dailies. Still, however, Giolitti and Salandra remained on speaking terms. Salandra had given no public notification that he had decided upon war. Giolitti, in Parliament, expressed full accord with what the Government was doing. As late as March the Giolittians voted solidly for the Government, on the ground (Giolitti explains in his *Memoirs*) that any alternative Italian Government must either be a Government of interventionists or else so definitely neutralist that Austria would no longer think it necessary to pay a price for peace. Giolitti stood for peace at a price, and he supported Salandra as long as he supposed him to be bargaining for it.

But Salandra and Sonnino, behind the scenes, were by this time in detailed negotiation with the Entente regarding the terms of Italy's participation on their side. They were, of course, at the same time discussing with the Austro-Germans their terms for neutrality. To gain Italy's neutrality Austria had begun by offering Valona (Albania), which Italy was already occupying. Italy had insisted upon the direct cession of Italian-speaking territories in the Austrian Empire. At this stage Prince Bülow, as German Ambassador Extraordinary, took over the negotiations, and tentatively offered the Trentino without Trieste. Austria entered the way of concessions more than reluctantly, under continual German pressure, and even by February, after two months of negotiations, had not clearly accepted the German proposals, let alone Italy's far greater demands. After a deadlock in the talks with the Austro-Germans, on March 4th Italy took the initiative of offering to the Entente an alliance in arms against Austria at a price. There could, of course, be no equivalence between the price in terms of actual cession of effective Austrian possessions which was asked of Austria in return for neutrality, and the price in terms of territories still having to be conquered which was asked of the Entente in return for war. Italy's minimum price for neutrality was a demand to Austria for the Trentino and Dalmatian Islands in outright cession, Trieste to be a self-governing free city, and the permanent Italian occupation of Valona to be recognized. The minimum price for war was a demand addressed to the Entente of approval for the annexation of the Trentino and Southern Tyrol, of Trieste and Istria, of a great part of the Dalmatian coast, with a share in any territories conquered from Turkey, and compensation in Africa for any gains made there by the Entente.

The bargaining with Germany and Austria was less secret than the bargaining with the Entente, for Prince Bülow was in Rome making no secret of his mission, and the neutralist Press was praying for its success. No one could doubt however that Salandra and Sonnino were at the same time prospecting terms for entry into the war at the side of England and France. But besides these two ministers and their closest colleagues, and the Sovereign, there were few who enjoyed any knowledge of the process of the two sets of negotiations. The facts are still in dispute. Giolitti for ever after denied having known that on April 26th Salandra and Sonnino definitely committed the country to go to war on the Entente side exactly a month later. His testimony clashes with that of Salandra.

But there was another and an even obscurer question. Was the official Italian Government the only power in Rome which was negotiating, in Italy's name, with Prince Bülow? Giolitti defends himself against the charge of having negotiated secretly with Prince Bülow or with any other envoy of the Central Powers, and in particular of having had personal knowledge, in advance of the Italian Government, of certain final Austro-German proposals, much nearer to the Italian minimum demands than any which had previously been forthcoming. These final demands were ultimately submitted to Sonnino only on May 10th, after he had taken the notable step of denouncing the Triple Alliance—that is, after he had plainly intimated to Germany and Austria that Italy was preparing to fight.

Exactly how much Giolitti had been told by Salandra of the
secret negotiations with the Entente—exactly how much he had
been told by Bülow of the ultimate concessions which Austria
would pay as a price for peace—are important perhaps for a
final judgement on the man Giolitti: but Giolitti in his ten
years of Parliamentary dictatorship had made for himself the
reputation by which, at that time, he was judged. When he
returned from his Easter holiday to Rome early in May 1915
he still held the ultimate power by which Italy had come to
be ruled, the power in virtue of which deputies, prefects,
bureaucrats depended for their positions, the Government itself,
therefore, for its continuance in office. He came to Rome,
moreover, intending to bring that power to bear so as to keep
Italy from immediately entering the war. When he arrived,
three hundred and twenty of the Deputies of the Chamber—an
absolute majority—left their visiting cards on him to signify that
they would follow his lead. This intention was clear. As soon
as Parliament assembled, before Salandra could obtain powers
to declare war in accordance with his secret pledges, Giolitti
would provoke a Parliamentary condemnation of the Government, and installed anew in the Premiership he would negotiate.
with Prince Bülow a deal on Austria's final terms. Without
striking a blow Italy would have obtained 'quite a lot'—*parecchio*
—the Italian Tyrol and Valona in outright possession, freedom
for Trieste to govern itself as an Italian autonomous city, negotiations about other strips of territory and islands, a German
guarantee for the execution of the terms. The Giolittian
majority, the Vatican and the Socialists were ready to applaud
and support the policy, and with their backing Giolitti would
have entered more than ever omnipotently into his own.

How had Salandra come to expose himself to such humiliation
at home, and Italy to the extreme discredit of going back on
solemn pledges to three great powers at the very moment of
their execution? Did he believe that Giolitti, for all the
appearances, could not really press Parliament to overthrow
him and that these were merely imaginary risks? Six months
before Salandra had regarded himself as little more than a tenant
of power by sufferance of Giolitti. In the first five months of
the European conflict he had conducted policy in substantial
agreement with this ultimate master of the Parliament, maker
and breaker of ministries. But the battles of Europe raging in a
distant semicircle around Italy, from Belgium to Constantinople,

had thrown Italy, like the belligerents themselves, into a fever of ardours and agitations. The political usages and constitutional inhibitions of 1914 were breaking down in a mood which, as has been argued, had its springs not merely in politics, but in thought, art and fashion. To this change Giolitti remained sublimely insensitive.

II. D'ANNUNZIO AND 'RADIANT MAY'

For many decades prudent and disillusioned men, worldly wise realists, plain and honest plodders had contributed positively to Italy's consolidation and prosperity, attaining their ends by the bargains and compromises of which Giolitti had in the last decade made himself the central broker and negotiator. The closed system worked as though the storms of conviction and passion, of ambition and aspiration, were by some enchantment excluded from the sphere of the ultimate naked reality. Power and interest had divorced themselves from the drama of the nation's destiny. Rebellious movements agitated the intellectual, religious and artistic fringes of the nation: they touched politics only to expire after much noise to small effect. So might a prudent Italian have reasoned in summer 1914. But with war ablaze in Europe images of redemption and catastrophe had penetrated the thoughts of ever wider circles. No longer did revolutionaries, futurists, revivalists of ideas or of faiths seem aliens from reality: crowds flocked to hear Mussolini preach 'a new roseate springtime for Europe, blooming out of the defeat of Germany.' Gabriele d'Annunzio could weave no prophecy of a wondrous Italian future too iridescent for the taste of thousands of readers. The heightened mood characterized the 'interventionist' cause in the great national schism of 1915. It must not be supposed, however, that the 'neutralist' faction was co-terminous with philistinism and the crass pursuit of personal interest. Many men of broad historical and literary culture, forewarned against the meretricious element which accompanies all outbreaks of public enthusiasm, clung to Giolitti as the guarantor of a sane and reasonable management of affairs. They might have judged him harshly as a corrupter of Parliament, but at all events Giolitti's predominance had left the forms of government intact and available for more honest use when the Italian people came to display readiness for the responsibility of true self-government. But such philosophic caution bordered on a cynicism which the younger Liberals and Democrats thought shameful. These continued to assail Giolitti as the arch-corrupter, even when they found themselves side by side with strange and unwelcome allies like Mussolini or d'Annunzio in the great anti-Giolittian front of interventionism. And meanwhile Giolitti and his allies remained unperturbed and maladjusted to the new mood.

Thus Giolitti, who had always been the man of the times, never hesitating to change with them and keep abreast of them, so long as the changes lay within the range of his own observation of human nature, now came to Rome rather as the man of bygone times. So he appeared to the groups, quickly swelling into crowds, which, from the moment of his departure at the railway station at Turin, gathered or were gathered to demonstrate against him. It was certainly not enthusiasm for Salandra and Sonnino which moved them. To a change of mental climate in the country Salandra was not likely to be much more sensitive than Giolitti himself. It was by a coincidence rather than by any quality of his personality that Salandra found himself allied with a vast public agitation against the formerly all-powerful Parliamentarian. The springs of his own rebellion were quite different, and accorded with his character as a dignified and academic Conservative.

Salandra's relations with the King had taken a turn which challenged Giolitti's fundamental assumptions. King Victor Emmanuel had—as has been noticed—long been considered the perfect constitutional monarch. When Parliament voted down a Ministry he took the advice of the outgoing Premier, of all previous Premiers, and of the Presidents of the two houses, and then sent for a politician who could be expected to interpret the will of the Parliamentary majority. For more than a decade Giolitti had been able to limit this will by his own unfailing command of a majority, though not always of quite the same majority. Early in 1914 Giolitti had even improved upon this practice. He brought his long Ministry to an end, and indicated Salandra to the King as his successor, without troubling to go through the motions of suffering a defeat in Parliament. It sufficed him, as a pretext, that a resolution adverse to his policy was passed by the Radical group, and 'in view of the Parliamentary situation' he at once resigned his mandate to the King. 'Parliamentary Dictatorship' thus reached a new degree of perfection: Giolitti claimed the right to bow himself in or out of office without waiting for a direct vote of the Chamber. At the very moment of the discovery of this artifice, however, the prospect of war put a different complexion on the King's office.

By the letter of the Constitution the King declares war and makes treaties of alliance, 'giving the Chamber information as soon as the interest and safety of the State permit it.' He is also Commander-in-Chief of the Forces. In all these capacities, between August 1914 and April 1915, the King had taken a more active part in the highest affairs of the State than his dynasty had done since 1870. He saw Giolitti from a new point of vantage. Particularly must Sonnino, the politician who had tried years before to claim effective powers for the Crown against Parliament in the nomination of ministers, have encouraged Victor Emmanuel and Salandra to take their decisions boldly and to defy the master of Parliament. Parliament had the undoubted right to refuse the Government money for its policy : it had also the right to accept or reject treaties requiring a financial outlay or varying the frontiers of the State. Salandra and Sonnino had no intention of submitting to Parliament the secret Treaty of London by which they had obtained from the Entente the terms of Italy's participation in the war, and had in fact already promised that participation for a particular date. But the Chamber, they believed, would not dare to forbid the Government to declare war when the Government came to it having brought the country to the very brink of war. Either Giolitti would acquiesce, or the Chamber would abandon Giolitti.

But Giolitti determined to withstand this roughshod demolition of his dominance. Like other eminent neutralists (Benedetto Croce, for example) he insisted in after years that he had opposed not Italy's participation in the war, but entry into the war at that precise moment. There were good arguments for dating the entry as late as possible. The Italian army in May 1915, despite all efforts of the precious months to equip it on the scale of the great European armies, was notoriously deficient. 'We entered the war in 1915 with prehistoric armaments' wrote the journalist Prezzolini two years later, seeking to allocate the blame for the Caporetto disaster. 'We had no heavy artillery. Not one of our general staff officers believed in it. . . . For our small guns we had half the ammunition which had been used per piece in France in the winter of 1914. . . . No machine-guns worth speaking of. . . . Hand-grenades unknown. . . . No aviation.' This was no doubt true; just as, on the other

hand, it was true that by delaying the war Italy might fail to
bring utterly essential help to the Allies in due time, or, as the
Nationalists viewed it, might come in too late to satisfy the
appetites of 'sacred egoism' (a phrase dropped rather casually
by Salandra to please them a month or two earlier).

But even if Giolitti meant to resume bargaining with Austria
only in order to gain time: even if he was determined to obtain
by one way or another Italy's military occupation of the
'unredeemed' territories, so as to turn immediately to account
the precarious and reversible Austrian pledges: his return to
office, in the manner which he had confidently planned, would
have been fateful for monarch and people. Giolitti would have
expelled Salandra in virtue of power wielded as the undisputed
leader of the combined neutralists and pacifists, Conservative,
Catholic, Socialist and bureaucratic. The King's right to make
war and treaties would have been shown up as an anachronism.
The triumphant monarchy of 1860 would have finally given way
not to a truly popular republic or to a Catholic federation, but
to a virtually immovable dictatorship based upon a system of
intricate personal bargains, a system which an unchallengeable
master had now under his control. The grand manager of the
electoral system would have stood forth upon the national stage
as the sole heir of the crusades and endeavours of generations of
reformers, prophets and heroes. The prospect was as displeasing
to the King as to the whole miscellany of the enemies of Giolitti.

To forfend that prospect, and to reclaim for the dynasty of
Savoy the military leadership which had been its title to the
throne of Italy, King Victor Emmanuel joined the interventionists. Their campaign of ideals, rhetoric and what was then
accounted 'violence' reached its climax. Gabriele d'Annunzio
put himself at the head of an agitation in the streets into which
the interventionists of every sect and persuasion now poured
their multitudes. On May 5th d'Annunzio delivered near Genoa
a commemorative speech for the inauguration of a great
monument to Garibaldi and his famous thousand companions.
The King and Salandra were expected to attend. At the last
moment they called off their attendance, causing the multitudes
of demonstrators in Genoa, and all over the country, to suspect
that Giolitti had vetoed the ceremony. But they had really
remained absent because at that moment they had finally
committed themselves to war by giving notice to terminate the
Triple Alliance, and were labouring to prepare the opening of

the military campaign a fortnight later. D'Annunzio roused the vast gathering to feverish excitement: elsewhere the minor tribunes, Mussolini, Corridoni and others, took up and expanded the agitation. A crowd of Nationalists filled Rome railway station when Giolitti arrived and received him with threatening yells. Giolitti met Salandra and other members of the Government, and saw the King: he persisted in determining to reverse their policy, and to resume conversations with Prince von Bülow. He was able and ready to defeat the Government in the Chamber and the monarchy would then be left with a choice between calling Giolitti or making a complete breach with the Constitution as it had long come to be interpreted.

From this harrowing dilemma the Salandra Government, and the monarch who had identified himself with it, escaped by the help of the tribunes of the interventionists. Salandra made a show of deferring to the will of Parliament—which was still not in session, but had declared its will in the symbolism of 320 visiting cards left by way of greeting to Giolitti—by offering his resignation to the King (May 11). From May 11th to May 15th the King received Giolitti and the other chief parliamentarians to advise on what sort of government the Chamber would now approve and support.

But meanwhile d'Annunzio had arrived in Rome to focus the agitation of the interventionists. Huge crowds surged through the streets chanting 'Morte a Giolitti!' Some invaded the Chamber of Deputies and broke the windows. Shopkeepers, to be on the right side with the demonstrators, exhibited signs of mourning as for a State funeral. Well-known Giolittian deputies were mobbed in the street. Elsewhere in Italy, in every considerable town, the lesser tribunes fired the motley crowds of interventionists. Nationalist students coursed the highways arm in arm with the semi-anarchists whose disorder, only a year ago, Salandra had so firmly repressed. Now they were his indispensable supporters in the streets.

The Giolittian deputies had known nothing like this in their political lives. D'Annunzio and the lesser tribunes had mobilized against them the hosts of the ardent, the energetic and the reckless, those who had scorned or failed to find satisfaction in the system. The Socialist party and the trade unions who had been so ready to mobilize to prevent the 'other war' (that on the side of Austria and Germany) now remained immobile: the Church feared to put forth any effort to withstand an uproar which could soon have become dangerous to itself. On May 18th the King invited Salandra to remain in office: Salandra convoked the Chamber, declared war, and obtained a favourable vote from all but a score of the Giolittian deputies. These in their hundreds, within a fortnight of their rallying round Giolitti, roared applause to the Government and the monarch which had defied and dismissed their so recently all-powerful dominator.

CHAPTER NINE

WAR; BUT WHAT FOR?

I. WAR TO WHAT END?—Governmental Italy had entered the war on a calculation of rapid territorial gains for Italy, without attributing deeper significance to it, and without any conception of freeing Europe from German militarism and feudalism. The popular agitation of the Left groups viewed the war in this latter light, and demanded that Italy should be drawn closely into the alliance of democratic peoples. A change of Government endeavoured to merge the contrasting war aims in a single effort for victory: but Sonnino retained the direction of official policy.

II. CLARIFYING CATASTROPHE. — The disaster of Caporetto revealed the inefficacy of official Italian policy. Italy's limited war against Austria had culminated in disaster. Italian policy had to reshape itself to gain strength by community with the Allies, and in particular by making common cause with the Slavs to break the Austrian Empire. Allied victory followed suddenly before this process was completed, but not before the doctrine of revolution through defeat, adopted by Lenin in Russia, had fascinated a section of the Italian Socialist party.

III. PERPLEXING PEACE.—Victory came to Italy as a consequence partly of Italian military effort, partly of the break-up of the Austrian Empire by a policy to which Italy had never unequivocally adhered. The obstruction of Italy's territorial claims in the name of 'Wilsonian' principles appeared as Allied trickery, and in Italy the conviction spread that the Peace had been lost. The search for guilty men became the passion of the hour.

I. WAR TO WHAT END?

The domination of Giolitti had succumbed to an agitation of a strangely miscellaneous character. In the tumults of what d'Annunzio called the 'Radiant May' of 1915 the monarchy had made common cause with those political groups which perpetuated a tradition of protest against the 1860 settlement, with Radicals and Republicans who had never, or only precariously, been drawn into the great Parliamentary and Administrative combine built up by Depretis, Crispi and Giolitti, and with those ultra-rebels among the Socialists whose cry it had been to keep the Socialist party pure from entanglement in that combine. By engaging in war against Austria and Germany the Savoy monarchy appeared to have embraced a democratic cause, thus ridding itself at last of those lingering associations with the feudal and the ecclesiastical powers which had ever been suspect to democrats. Yet while profiting by the support of the subversives of the Left the monarchy had found the instrument of its action in a Ministry which was as far as possible from representing the democratic urge. Salandra and Sonnino in declaring war upon the Austrian Empire had no intention whatever of contributing to the liberation of Europe from effete feudal institutions. It was rather their hope that Italy, by acquiring territory and strategic positions from the Empire, might take on some of its character as a strong authoritarian State. The school of Sonnino had no quarrel at all with Germany (and in 1915, when declaring war against Austria, he carefully refrained from declaring war on Austria's allies). On the other hand he viewed Italy's own allies of the Entente with jealous wariness. The Salandra-Sonnino Government had driven a bargain with the Allies over minute details of geographical acquisitions in the Adriatic and elsewhere. Neither the Ministry nor, still less, the High Army Command forgot these limits set to the scope of Italy's war, or ceased to ponder upon the suspicion that allies as well as enemies might frustrate their design of strong Alpine frontiers, dominance in the Adriatic and reinforced importance in the Aegean. Those were the advantages which the terms of the Treaty of London set out to ensure, and the Nationalist wing of the interventionists, the wing with which Salandra and Sonnino were in sympathy, loudly proclaimed that prospect to be the sole reason for the intervention of Italy in a war between the two aggregations of great powers.

It had been anxiously insisted by the Nationalists that Italy must make good her intervention in the spring of 1915 so as to be in time to make a decisive contribution before the Entente either won with its own resources, or was beaten beyond hope of repair. To their mortification the Italian intervention did not swing the scales: it merely stabilized the military equilibrium. Italians claimed that the Entente had been saved from an overwhelming offensive in Flanders by the fixing of fifteen Austrian divisions on the Alps, and by the consequent weakening of Austria's barrier against Russia. But the Italian intervention was not felt in England and France as a decisive factor ensuring victory. Cheated of a quick triumph, the Italian armies settled down on the sun-scorched or ice-bound Alpine frontiers, whence they launched an interminable series of offensives towards Trieste, with only local successes to show occasionally as the recompense for severe hardships and great losses.

While the Government was thus constrained to plan for a long and laborious war effort, the friends of Giolitti, recovering from their recent dismay, took on airs of superior foresight and experience. The motley interventionist bloc had overrun the streets: the Italian and Allied Press had acclaimed this triumph of 'The People' over a Parliamentary clique. If a quick victory in the field had brought tangible advantages to Italy the War Government might have imparted to the country the sense of a new and better internal situation, under virile and vigorous leadership. The slow progress of the war, the anticlimax of repeatedly fruitless offensives on the Isonzo, brought out, on the contrary, all the weaker aspects of the new internal combination of forces. The Salandra-Sonnino Government was not the confident mouthpiece of a great national party. And it was not, as Giolitti in its place would have been, the central headquarters of a system of influence and patronage. In so far as that system still existed it was at loggerheads with the War Government. The overthrow of Giolitti did not automatically oust his henchmen from the command of the prefectures and sub-prefectures where they were responsible for local order and discipline throughout Italy. Many of them administered the war-time decrees with resigned devotion to a distasteful duty. The clergy's cooperation was often not more willing, while the Socialist party circulated to its branches and to its affiliations, and to the elected municipal councils which they controlled in many important cities (notably Milan and Bologna), the instruction '*Nè aderire nè sabotare*'—do not support the war but do not hinder its prosecution.

Discontent prevailed also among the resolute supporters of the war. The democratic groups which had done service in intimidating Parliament and hounding Giolitti from Rome remained suspicious of the Salandra Government, dissatisfied with its limited war programme, and were themselves in turn suspected both by the Government and by General Cadorna's High Command which clung strictly to the conception of the limited war. It was complained that the former Socialists and members of other Left parties who had participated in the interventionist agitations were actually held under special observation, and regarded as dangerous elements when they took their places as volunteers in the army.

The Parliament, which under intimidation had assigned far-reaching emergency powers to the Government, was seldom convoked. Yet no logical inference had been drawn from the fact that Parliament's will had been brutally overridden. The Government which owed its survival to the palace and the piazza still purported to be the instrument of the will of the electorate: and the deputies gradually recovered sufficient courage to make Salandra's own position untenable. This marked the end of a first attempt to govern Italy without the good-will of the Parliamentary and bureaucratic milieu, and without admitting the advocates of popular democracy to participation in power. An attempt was now made to give the country a Government representing everything and everybody. The King summoned an aged and eloquent patriot, Boselli, to head a Ministry in which Sonnino retained the Foreign Office, while certain former neutralists on the one hand and partisans of the cause of democratic war on the other hand took other important offices of state. Although Sonnino at the Foreign Office represented a line of policy in sharp contrast with democratic aspirations, this Government at last declared war on Germany (August 1916), thereby fulfilling the ardent demands of the democratic wing.

Still, however, the war dragged on without approaching a climax. After two years Italy was no nearer a decisive victory than on the first day: on the contrary the desertion of Russia left her at single grips with Austria. As the war now proceeded in unforeseen and incalculable conditions, the credit of Giolitti and his friends recovered. Their plan was not to emerge prematurely from their silence and detachment, but to bide their time till the war fever was spent, then to guide the nation back to the routine of peaceful civilization and economic progress. There were, however, less cautious pacifists who took every opportunity to call for peace negotiations. In the third year of the war their clamour became public and insistent. An august sympathizer gave prestige to their efforts. Pope Benedict XV, following up informal approaches in the two previous years, addressed a note to the heads of the states at war, suggesting an equitable settlement by the restitution of all conquered territories on either side, and the re-creation of Poland, to be followed by disarmament and a universal promise to settle disputes by arbitration (with Sanctions against the aggressor). Friends of the Vatican constituted one wing of the active Peace agitation. The other wing lay in the ranks of the official Italian Socialists. Participating in a Socialist Conference on neutral soil at Zimmerwald, in 1916, the Socialists had enunciated a programme for peace which harmonized closely enough with that of the Sovereign Pontiff.

Faced by much evidence of the unpopularity of the war, the democratic groups threw the blame upon the narrowness and inhumanity of the war aims which had been framed by Salandra and Sonnino, which stood in stark contrast to their own view of the war as Italy's act of adherence to the European cause of democracy. To this narrow vision of the war they ascribed both its unpopularity and the elusiveness of success. They claimed that by fixing Italy's war aims in the Treaty of London (secret, but soon known in outline) Italy had sacrificed the full co-operation of the Allies and had even made an enemy of one of them, Serbia. These democratic interventionists accordingly summoned the Government to restate its war aims in such terms as to make the destruction and partition of the Austrian Empire chief among them. Such a result of the war had been very far from the calculations or desires of the Italian Government in 1915. The terms concocted with the Allies had presupposed that the Austrian Empire would remain a great power, though weakened to Italy's advantage by the cession of Trieste and Dalmatia and by Italian occupation of Albania (Valona).

But if the Austrian Empire were doomed to disappear, then the Adriatic settlement which the Allies had agreed to, for Italy's advantage, would take on a different significance. By virtue of it, a greater Serbia or South Slavia rising from the remains of Austria would be cut off from the sea-coast by the new trans-Adriatic expansion of Italy. The democrats strongly urged that this part of the Italian claims should be abated. From a frank declaration to that effect they expected a change in the whole prospect of the war. Close understanding with the Yugoslavs would bring Italy into co-operation with all the subject peoples of the Austrian Empire, and decomposition of the Austrian Empire would achieve what endless offensives on the Isonzo could not.

It was not only in the entourage of Sonnino that such proposals roused foreboding and bewilderment. Powerful personages in the Italian General Staff had hardly yet ceased thinking in terms of the Triple Alliance. Generals and staff officers regarded the democrats' war aims, with their emphasis upon the need to assist South Slavs and Albanians to full national autonomy, instead of wresting from Austria the dominance over them, as little short of treasonable. The democrats retorted that the generals and the Nationalists were delaying victory, indeed courting defeat, by rendering Italy as odious as Austria itself to the minds of the Balkan peoples. Thus while Italy still remained far from victory those Italian groups which were afterwards dubbed the 'saboteurs of the victory' and 'Rinunciatari' (renouncers of Italy's full claims) were already in sharp conflict with the upholders of the territorial claims which had been embodied in Sonnino's agreement with the Allies. Expressing the views of circles much wider than their own small party, the Nationalist journalists harped constantly upon Italy's claims to Dalmatia and other territorial war aims of the Treaty of London. The Radicals, Freemasons and Reformist Socialists retorted that the war could be won only by understandings with the Balkan peoples, and that such understandings alone gave promise of a fruitful peace. These political groups, however, were in a state of flux which admitted of numerous cross-currents. Temperament, rather than party divisions, drew the line between the rival schools.

The 'Rinunciatari' (as their opponents called them) included such outstanding younger captains of the political revolt against Giolittianism as Gaetano Salvemini, historian, deputy and tireless controversialist, Giovanni Amendola and G. A. Borgese, the chief counsellors of the pre-eminent newspaper of Italy, the *Corriere della Sera*. As a ringleader of pro-war Socialists Benito Mussolini was certainly considered to be in their ranks. In the Boselli Ministry the 'Rinunciatari' had an important spokesman in Leonida Bissolati, the Reformist Socialist leader, but as minister without portfolio he could do little to influence the political conduct of the war, which Sonnino continued to direct from Rome in accord with General Cadorna at the front.

The divergence of outlook was profound, but the pacifists of all parties were too bold and active for the war party to sacrifice the appearance of national unity incarnated in the joint presence of Sonnino and Bissolati in the Boselli Ministry. Giolitti re-emerged from retreat with a speech, in a local government assembly in Piedmont, in which he warned the country of terrible dangers to be expected after the war, and of the necessity of abolishing secret diplomacy. In Piedmont, where Giolitti was strong, anti-war demonstrators were coming into the streets. Giolitti still remained away from Parliament, which, indeed, was convoked only rarely, all legislation being enacted by decree. But the Giolittians had taken their part in turning out Salandra, and men who were considered still to be semi-Giolittians, Nitti and Orlando, were in the Boselli Government. It was a constant consideration, in the minds of the two wings of the war party, that Giolitti might yet return in triumph as the negotiator of a peace of compromise, if their own dissensions as to the method and use of victory went beyond a certain limit.

The official Socialist party, in an attitude of complacent blamelessness for the sufferings which the war had brought to the working population, stood ready to profit by the discredit of the war party, confident that, however the war ended, it would be without a triumph proportionate to the endurances which it had required. The official Socialist attitude stopped short of resolute 'defeatism'. Italy's entry into the war (said the Parliamentary leader of the party, Filippo Turati) had been procured by the Salandra Government for petty motives, and by methods which it would be impossible ever to condemn enough. But by dragging the country into the war the 'bourgeois parties' had exposed Italy to the risk of defeat and disruption. The Socialists would not only refrain from weakening the national resistance by petty party manœuvres (which, said Turati, would be 'idiotic and criminal'); they would actively co-operate to repair the ravages of war and to alleviate sufferings. They would not however agree to shoulder any share in the responsibilities of those who had desired it. Lazzari, Party Secretary, the same to whom Mussolini had owed his political success in 1912, devised the already mentioned formula, '*Nè aderire nè sabotare*', which successive Socialist party assemblies endorsed in the war years.

The Socialist organizations in the country interpreted the formula in a variety of ways. In certain great municipalities which were controlled by the Socialists the local officials cooperated readily with the State and military authorities for all the purposes of the war. Elsewhere the emphasis was upon '*nè aderire*'. There were expulsions from the party of members who took part in public committees for organizing assistance to those deprived of livelihood or otherwise injured by the war. The long-drawn course of the war meanwhile raised the credit of the leaders of the party. The Socialists by 1917 felt themselves much stronger, much more representative of the masses in the country, than two years earlier. When the eminent Socialist parliamentarian Claudio Treves exclaimed in Parliament in July 1917, 'Gentlemen of my Government and of all the Governments of Europe, hear the voice that rises from all the trenches . . . the ultimatum of life to death: Out of the trenches before this winter!' the Socialists greeted him with prolonged applause. Shortly afterwards, in his letter to the belligerent powers, Benedict XV called the war a 'useless massacre'. The smaller Catholic Press commented upon the Pontifical document in language not very different from that of the Socialist orator.

From numberless opponents or lukewarm supporters of the war, who held controlling positions in the country (Giolittian prefects, clergy, Socialist mayors and local councillors, trade union leaders), a stream of indulgence went out towards those who evaded military conscription and towards the deserters from the front who year by year found their way back in increasing numbers to the villages. The peasantry was encouraged to believe that it was only the peasants who were fighting the war, while the 'bourgeois' were ensconced in comfortable offices. Yielding to clamour the authorities sometimes thrust into the trenches men who were performing necessary skilled service in the rear. To avert a gathering resistance of the peasants to war service, the High Command was obliged to spread through the trenches promises signed by the Prime Minister himself that after the war the peasants would by a 'great act of justice' enter into possession of the land. While the Government thus attempted to identify the cause of the war with that of the peasants' ambitions, Mussolini's newspaper and the small syndical organization which followed its lead tried to identify the war with the industrial workers' aspirations. A mountingly emphatic propaganda spread a very different view of the war: it was the crime of the possessing classes, their pretext for abolishing civil liberties and frustrating the advent of Socialism. Giolitti measured his words so as not to offend needlessly those of his former supporters who had joined the war party but who might seek his leadership again when the whole country should cry out for an end to the slaughter. But he too echoed the condemnation of those who had dragged Italy into it. Exasperated at the tolerance with which the Rome Government permitted such manifestations, the generalissimo Cadorna made himself the absolute ruler of a 'war zone' which was extended to cover a large part of northern Italy. Here he disbanded the local authorities and conducted all affairs by overriding military decree. Meanwhile he vainly urged the Rome Government to forbid speeches and writings against the war. The armies at the front knew all about the gathering peace movement in the rear, and long before the climax of the Caporetto disaster, which ended the long phase of stationary and indecisive warfare in November 1917, deserters were making their way to the rear, often with the connivance, when they got there, of the local authorities.

II. CLARIFYING CATASTROPHE

For two years the war bore the character of a bloody, painful and intermittently renewed assault of the Italian armies upon the strong line of the Julian Alps, beyond which lay the prize of Trieste. In the intervals the army lay in dreary and immobile anguish. At last, in the summer of 1917, the Italians shook the balance by the capture of the important town of Gorizia. It was the moment of the collapse of the Russian armies—the Central Powers, triumphant in the East, made ready to hurl their released forces against the West. The German High Command felt able, at last, to respond to the year-long plea of their Austrian allies for assistance in the Alps, rendered all the more needful by the humiliating defeat of Gorizia. The Italian front, as it lay still, after two years, closely hugging the national frontiers, may be visualized as an S lying prone to the right or eastward side. German assistance to Austria took the form of the dispatch of seven picked divisions to launch a sudden attack —supported by massed Austrian forces—upon the eastward semi-circle of the S, round which the Italian lines ran in an extension justified only by the supposedly impregnable character of the chain of Alpine peaks. Once the enemy had forced one of the rare passes, as the Germans did on October 23, 1917, the Italian armies could only precipitately shorten their line, surrendering the whole of the semicircle—that is, half of the entire region of

Venetia.   Such in barest outline was the military event which brought the troubled condition of Italy to a sudden climax. At this point military history irrupts into the political situation, and the event of Caporetto must be explored in a little more detail.

The Germans accomplished their break-through with poison gas, of which the Italians had little experience, under cover of dense mists, launching their detachments forward with the boldest disregard for contacts on the flank or communications with the rear.   None the less, according to the considered verdict of military critics, the Italian front would have held had not General Cadorna and General Capello, who commanded the Second Army, comprising twenty-five out of the forty-four divisions of the whole available forces, remained up to the last moment at cross-purposes, even when fully aware of the enemy's great preparations.   Capello obstinately resisted his chief's order to prepare a defence in depth.   Until three days before the German blow he stuck to dispositions planned with a view to counter-offensive, for which mode of warfare he believed the Italians to be specially suited.   Cadorna, even while issuing his orders for the preparation of the defence in depth, shrank from making it plain to the powerful Capello, until the very last moment, that the general plan of campaign ruled out wholly his plans for the counter-offensive.   The Germans attacked in the very midst of a hurried shifting of Capello's divisions which, in the heavy mists, could not reconnoitre their positions.   It is perhaps only of symbolic significance that Capello was the most prominent Freemason among the high commanders, while Cadorna was a notable Clericalist, and that the great disaster was rendered possible by the confusion of their incompatible strategies, much as the political success of the war was at the same time being compromised by incompatible policies.

Within forty-eight hours of the German penetration the great Second Army was streaming back in a sixty-mile retreat across the northern plains.   About 200,000 surrendered to the enemy. The rebellious element in the ranks broke all discipline, heading for their homes or simply for the interior of Italy, and spreading panic and desertion among the more orderly detachments which they overtook.   Desperate officers strove to rally and reassemble the fugitives at the point of the pistol: many were already accustomed to exacting obedience by making terrible examples. Cadorna himself, in the agony of the moment, encouraged Italy to see in the collapse not a strategic defeat at the hands of the enemy but a 'military strike' on the part of subversive elements in the ranks. On October 28th he issued this *communiqué*:

'Detachments of the Second Army, abandoning resistance, cravenly retiring without giving battle, and ignominiously surrendering to the enemy, have enabled the Austro-Germans to break our Left Wing on the Giulian Alps. . . .'

The Government censored the *communiqué* for the Italian Press, but the Allied news agencies received and transmitted it unchanged. In Rome and the interior, where the military causes of the defeat could only in course of time be unravelled and understood, the anguished attention of all the factions was turned upon its moral and political origins. The country seemed, by the divided purposes of its directors, to have fallen into imminent risk of German-Austrian occupation and of the reversal of the achievement of generations of patriots.

The Caporetto disaster seemed to be the realization of the worst that the Neutralists had prophesied. All those who bore the public responsibility for Italy's entry into the war, whatever their ulterior views and motives, felt themselves to be on trial at the bar of their country. Above all, the partisans of the 'Nationalist' war conceived as a purely Italo-Austrian duel saw their theories ironically belied by events. For it was mainly on their prescription that Italian strategy had concocted its plans. Hopes of an ultimate victory were henceforth patently bound up with the discovery of a new strategy, and with the rousing of the Italian people to a zealous defence of their own soil. The Government was at once re-formed under Orlando, with Nitti as its most powerful member—a combination tilted strongly towards a conciliation of its members with Giolitti. Giolitti himself resumed his attendance in Parliament, and joined with other ex-Premiers in exhorting the nation to steadfastness. Turati, for the Socialists, declared that Monte Grappa, the new bulwark of defence behind the Piave, was as sacred to Socialists as to all other Italians. Thither, in good order, the armies on the flanks of the defeated Second Army were withdrawn and there, in a few weeks, Cadorna's successor succeeded in bringing the enemy advance to a complete stop. Collapse was averted.

The partisans of the democratic war, of victory to be gained by a hearty understanding and co-operation between Italy and her external Allies, could now demonstrate that utter failure had followed on the policy of 'Italy's own war'. In answer to the seven divisions of the Germans Italy at once received six French and five British divisions. Cadorna was relieved of his command after reorganizing the defences at Monte Grappa, and behind the Piave. Not only on the Italian, but also on the British and French side, a closer co-ordination of the war effort of all the Allies was now insistently demanded: a Conference of Allied Premiers and Commanders met on Italian soil and took the first steps towards establishing a single high command, which however —chiefly, it has always been supposed, through the determined opposition of King Victor Emmanuel—stopped short of the subordination of the Italian armies to a French general.

The Italian democrats now had a hearing for their war aims among groups who had hitherto been in sharp contrast against them. Even the Nationalists were drawn into the movement for a close understanding with the subject peoples of Austria-Hungary. In the view of men like Salvemini and Guglielmo Ferrero, the outstanding democratic publicists, the path of Italian policy lay plainly in the direction of that understanding with the South Slavs which had in the nineteenth century been ardently advocated by Giuseppe Mazzini. The Austrian Empire stood for feudal and authoritarian principles, the negation of the right of peoples to express themselves through national institutions. Italy by helping the Slavs to nationhood would herself shake off the remains of feudalism and attain full democracy. The Nationalists could indeed have no sympathies of that sort with the Slavs and they had no desire to destroy an empire as such: but if they had to choose between destroying Austria or possibly being left isolated while the French and British entered into a separate peace with Austria—it was the moment of Emperor Karl's gropings towards such a separate peace—then they needs must opt for destroying Austria.

Playing upon such fears Giovanni Amendola, a leading spirit of the more or less democratic 'Corriere della Sera,' drew the Nationalists themselves into discussions with national leaders of the Czechoslovaks, the Yugoslavs and the Rumanians, assembled in Rome for that purpose. The Italian Government itself was notoriously divided between the policy implied by these approaches—a policy of renouncing large parts of the expected spoils in Dalmatia in favour of a new Yugoslav State— and the policy of the Treaty of London to which Sonnino clung, refusing to renounce any of the Italian claims against Austria in anyone's favour, and by the same token refusing to make a war aim of destroying the Austrian Empire. But the pliant Premier Orlando favoured and patronized the Congress of the oppressed nationalities.

Another notable development had rendered the Sonnino policy obsolete and antiquated. The United States had entered the war, officially 'knowing nothing' about the pledges made by the original Allies to Italy in the secret Treaty of London. President Wilson was proclaiming principles which, on the contrary, fitted in well with the war doctrine of the Italian democrats.

In these circumstances members of the Italian Government saw plainly enough (it is placed on record by the Minister of Supply, Silvio Crespi) that Italy was running the risk of coming to the Peace Conference equipped with two contrasting policies, one laid down in the black and white of the Treaty, insisted upon by Sonnino, the other proclaimed by Bissolati, the most vigorous of the other Cabinet Ministers, and more than half publicly endorsed by the Premier Orlando. An open breach might appear more healthy: yet the war was far from won, the pacifists and defeatists were far from extinct, and the national situation required a sacrifice of all controversial issues to unity in face of the task of getting the invader out of the Italian provinces now occupied by him. The anti-democrats were not entirely pig-headed. As long as an understanding with the Yugoslavs appeared to be plainly necessary for the breaking-up of Austrian morale, even the Nationalists could be relied upon for lip-service to the principle of self-determination of the peoples. They would wave their flags side by side with the democratic and revolutionary wing of the war party, with Bissolati, and also with that arch-enthusiast for Wilson's new and better world, the rebel socialist Benito Mussolini.

But if Parliamentarians were able—under the impact of Caporetto—largely to sink their differences, so that Giolittians and interventionists of either school worked for the common end, the nation in its wider ranges was by no means so quickly drawn into a sacred union. Monte Grappa could not wholly efface Caporetto. The Italian armies, with the stiffening of eleven French and British divisions in their rear, reconstituted themselves indeed solidly enough along the line of the Piave, but they risked no active fighting in 1918 until they had successfully withstood a new offensive in June—the last determined stroke of an Austrian army which was thenceforth progressively distraught by the movement towards internal dissolution of the Empire. Early in 1918 the new Commander-in-Chief General Diaz set out to study the needs and sufferings of the Italian private soldier. He abrogated much of the pedantic or even brutal discipline of which Cadorna bore the blame. But at least until the June enemy offensive the army was on tenterhooks. Large numbers of the deserters from Caporetto were drafted into an army corps that was sent to the French front: but scores of thousands of others were spread through the land as far as Sicily, where they joined and reinforced the stay-at-home elements clamouring for peace.

And the peace clamour now took on, in the light of an earth-shaking event in the East, a new and fascinating appeal. In the very week of the Caporetto disaster Lenin and Trotsky precipitated the rebellion of Petrograd. The Russian Bolsheviks seized power in the conjoint cause of an immediate end to the war and of an immediate end to capitalism. The event seemed rich in portent to the discontented masses of Italian workers, whose political leaders in the mere act of dissociating themselves from the war had also dissociated themselves, not unwillingly, from the idea of social revolution. The Italian Socialist party, when it declared in 1915 for neutrality (and for 'nè aderire nè sabotare'), assumed, willy-nilly, a deepening conservative shade: for its associates in the agitation for neutrality, and in the rejection of responsibility for the war, were the men of Giolitti's system and the clericals. That noted apostle of sudden revolution by insurrection against the constituted powers, Mussolini, had abandoned the conservatizing party in order—as he said—to seek revolution by putting weapons in the hands of the millions. He had perhaps no very clear notion how the regimented millions could be got to exert their armed strength for achieving Socialism. He was not the only politician who in an inscrutable situation simply gambled upon something turning up. The working classes, with insignificant exceptions, left him to his own romantic dreams and realistic ambitions.

But the Russian example fascinated the more temperamental pacifists in the Socialist party. Since Caporetto, the attitude of the party leaders to the war had perceptibly changed. Turati, like Giolitti and many another ex-Neutralist, took occasion from Caporetto to try to heal the national schism of 1915. His pride would be to show to the world an Italy united for defence as it never had been for mere adventure. But the congenital revolutionaries who had remained in the party when Mussolini left it—his former warm patrons and supporters, like Costantino Lazzari and Niccola Bombacci—had now before them the inspiration of Russia. There, in the East, a successful revolution against the constituted powers of feudalism and capitalism had been achieved by deserting them in the battlefield, and yielding to enemy terms, in sure and certain hope that the constituted powers of the enemy too would be sapped in the same way before they could inflict permanent damage on the defeated nation. Lazzari and Bombacci, now Secretary and Vice-Secretary of the party, were arrested early in 1918 and were condemned to three years' imprisonment. They thus gained lustre as the martyrs of Italian Bolshevism, a new and pregnant force among those competing for the Italian people's allegiance.

III. PERPLEXING PEACE

The Italian armies, restored after the Caporetto disaster by the obstinate and successful defence of the Piave line, had only just time to show their mettle in beating off the last desperate Austrian offensive against that river (June 1918) when the Central Powers gave evident signs of an impending collapse. The Italian army, reconstituted by the humane and sagacious Diaz, had redeemed its honour and regained its rank as a formidable fighting force when a final stroke broke the imperial armies of Vienna into hopeless decomposition. It was a victory, at one and the same time, for the Italian army and for the Wilsonian principle of self-determination which had brought to the Allied cause an accession of internal allies inside Austria. Thus the Italian Government found victory on its hands before it had resolved the utter divergence between the war aims of its most powerful members. Orlando's half endorsement of the democratic war aims had already contributed to accelerating the breakdown of Austria. Czechoslovak deserters from the Austrian army made up a fighting division on the Italian front. But meanwhile, indifferent equally to President Wilson's proclamation of a world of self-determining peoples, and to the vague and informal engagements which had been given to the Yugoslavs in the Pact of Rome, Sonnino clung to his no longer secret Treaty of London (the Russian Bolsheviks having naughtily published it), in which Italian occupation of the Dalmatian coast was provided for with the utmost geographical minuteness, while all other territorial objectives (colonial expansion in Africa, advantages in the Eastern Mediterranean) were left vague. Meanwhile of the great economic advantages which Italy might well have asked of her partners (admission of immigrants or Italian goods on favoured terms) there was—in Sonnino's charter of war aims— no mention at all.

Bissolati, at the other extreme wing of the Italian Government, regarded the Treaty of London as having been rendered void by reason of the disappearance of the Austrian Empire, and he, with the partisans of democratic war in general, regarded an Italian occupation of Dalmatia as something which would be most dearly purchased by the enmity of the Balkan peoples which it would bring with it. Meanwhile the question of the minor port of Fiume raised a new and confusing issue. Sonnino had explicitly left this little port, despite its Italian name and character, to the presumptively humbled Austrian Empire from which he had intended to seize Dalmatia. But the Austrian Empire had ceased to exist and Fiume had proclaimed itself part of Italy. The Yugoslavs contended that if they were to be regarded as the successors of Austria in the matter of surrendering Dalmatia to Italy, they must also be successors to the retention of Fiume, which would be their only respectable port in the Mediterranean. Bissolati threatened to resign from the Government sooner than endorse the Sonnino policy: Orlando suspended judgement: Nitti, Minister of the Treasury, never more than a mild supporter of the war at all, manœuvred to displace him.

By the end of the war the assemblage of parties which had procured Italy's entry into it were thus in full discord about Italy's interest in the peace. Those who had dedicated themselves to the democratic war, and who sought to view Italy's needs in the setting of a New Europe of self-governing peoples, were assailed by the Nationalists as traitors, since they were ready to bargain away the 'sacred rights' of the Treaty of London. As England and France showed their determination to impose on Germany a punitive peace, and to distribute unwilling German populations among the new border States, the Italian Nationalists grew bolder. They held up the 'saboteurs of the victory', the 'rinunciatari', to rebuke as specimens of a perversity unique in the world. Had not the democrats everywhere else supported their local imperialism, and was it not only in Italy that ministers were resigning and great newspapers arguing against the national demands of their own country? That President Wilson now personally involved himself in

Italo-Yugoslav issues, trying to exert a direct pressure on the
Italian Government, gave the Nationalists particular opportunities of holding up the democrats to obliquy. In January
1919 Wilson made an official visit to Italy. The Government
and interventionists of all groups had exploited Wilson's name
and promises of a better world to the utmost, in the last months
of the war, among the troops, the munition workers, and the
people at large, as a counter-charm to the name and promises
of Lenin which were exploited by the extremist Socialists.
Wilson visited Rome and Milan as Head of the American State,
but he was received with uproarious acclamations by crowds
which greeted him as the herald of a new world. Mussolini,
whom the democrats still regarded as on their side, greeted
Wilson with the headline in his paper 'Welcome to the Prophet
of the Peoples,' and the comment 'Italy is unanimously Wilsonian.
Italy is the least imperialist of the peoples.' In the very days
of Wilson's visit, however, Bissolati, a truly genuine Wilsonian,
gave up hope of making his views prevail in the Orlando
Government. Bissolati resigned from the Government, and it
was as a notorious opponent of the Sonnino policy that he held
a discussion with Wilson during the visit. A few days later
Bissolati gave an interview to the London *Morning Post* in which
he explicitly opposed the Italian claims on Dalmatia, the South
Tyrol and the East Mediterranean as they were provided for in
the Treaty of London.

Sonnino thus proceeded to Paris with Orlando as the chief
Italian negotiator, to demand enactment of the Treaty of London.
On those terms he had negotiated for Italy's entry into the war;
the Allies with Italy's help had won the war, and he presented
the bill truly signed and accepted. Of its authenticity and
binding character there was no question: all that could be
urged as a counsel against seeking its application was that during
the struggle the Allies had accepted overriding principles, which
were exemplified in the fourteen points, and that Italy had
accepted them too. This would mean that the war, in the
event, had proved to be a struggle for the overthrow of feudal and
militarist empires to make way for freedom-loving democracies.
It was an interpretation of the war which had deeply stirred
the leaders of the young generation of Italians in 1915.
Without it, the interventionist campaign could hardly have
brought Italy into the war in that year, or kept her striding
through the disaster of 1917 to the victory of 1918. But it was

an interpretation which the Italian Government had at best tolerated alongside of the doctrine enshrined in the Treaty of London. Very soon the mode of exploitation of the victory chosen by Great Britain and France reinforced the conviction of the Italian Conservatives that the Wilsonian principles were, in the mouths of their Allies, mere devices. Britain and France had succeeded in making large additions to their empires, out of the wreck of the empires of their opponents. Italy alone found 'Wilsonian' principles standing in the way of an ambition to exploit the victory in the double measure of what firstly her rulers had staked out as her peace claims before the war was won, and what secondly the overwhelmingly complete victory of the Allies seemed to render possible.

Gathering economic distress, on the morrow of the victory, spread a conviction that the peace had been lost, and this single formula covered both the frustration of certain territorial ambitions through opposition of the Allies, and the impoverishment and confusion of the exhausted country. The nation called for an indictment of guilty men. On all sides the passionate elements in the country's politics rose to offer themselves as judges and executioners. There were, however, alternative versions of the bill of indictment. According to one of these, the guilty men were those who had dragged Italy into a fruitless war: according to the other, the guilty were those who, whether by opposing the war or by embracing the Wilsonian principles, had obstructed Italy's exploitation of the victory in a manner that would have been fruitful. One class of persons found themselves in either case in the dock—the adherents of the doctrines of democratic war and of Italy's need to make common cause with the Danubian Slavs. They were odious alike to the 'defeatists' and to the Nationalists. Few paused to inquire whether the major causes of Italy's distresses did not lie in the field of economics, to which the Italian treaty makers had displayed—amid their preoccupation with territorial and strategic ambitions—a complete indifference.

CHAPTER TEN

DEFEAT BY VICTORY

I. FALSE DAWN.—Orlando's Government, torn to the last be-tween rival conceptions of Italy's war—whether it was local and dynastic, or an integral part of a world war of human significance —bungles the Peace negotiations. Nitti, a forward-looking democrat, succeeds to office. He would wish to preside over an era of popular government befitting a people matured by war: but the spirit of democratic victory fails when the Socialists attempt to put Italy's war leaders in the dock, and anti-democrats capture the spokesmanship of the ex-soldiers.

II. PATTERN OF DEADLOCK.—New forces and old forces in post-war Italy—the mass parties: Socialists and Populars; Mussolini; the Nationalists; d'Annunzio. Mussolini, branded by the Socialists, pits himself against all hazards to wrest from them the captaincy of a 'Revolution'.

I. FALSE DAWN

Italian politics from the armistice of October 29, 1918, to the day, just four years later, when Mussolini installed himself as Italy's official saviour, work up into a climax of moral and intellectual disarray from which release is at last sought in the simplicity of an audacious gesture, an orgasm of headstrong improvisation. The period ends with the acceptance by Italy of the most ambitious and least scrupulous of candidates for national leadership, in the name of the most miscellaneous and uncritical programme. This possibility alone remained when the intellectual and moral efforts of a generation of seekers after a stronger and saner liberty in Italy crumbled at the moment of their great opportunity.

During four years of war, and its immediate aftermath, the ultimate authority of the army chiefs, standing between Italy and a German irruption, masked the breakdown of the political structure which had evolved under the semi-dictatorships of Depretis, Crispi and Giolitti. That structure, as has been shown, had for half a century, with gathering irritancy, dis-appointed and offended the eager and imaginative of all schools, Catholic and Democrat, Socialist and Nationalist, in whom the moral and mental impulses of the Risorgimento survived. Its character was dry-as-dust: its method, an interlinking of

interests and apprehensions in a system invisibly controlled by
an arch-sceptic. Like all forms of government it was reviled
by the irresponsible and anarchic of various persuasions, but it
stood condemned with impressive unanimity by the intellect and
the morality of the nation. The collapse of Giolitti in May 1915
had its most visible cause in the whipping-up of mob violence
by d'Annunzio; but men of honour had saluted his downfall
with satisfaction, as a nemesis overtaking a covert tyranny.
They believed that war by the side of the free peoples could be
Italy's way to a fuller freedom, and for them the unruly outburst
of May 1915 was a surface wound accompanying an organic
purification of Italian politics.

This could have been the true diagnosis on one condition:
if the purpose of a free and orderly Italian democracy integrated
in the wider democracy of Europe had fused with the purpose
of an Italian victory, inspiring those to whom victory brought
authority with a determination to use it for the realization of
democracy.

Such a hope had to contend with two negations, that of those
who desired victory but not democracy, and that of those who
desired democracy and not victory.

The shape taken by these two negations in the course of the
war has been traced in a preceding chapter. The school of
Sonnino sought victory for Italy with a view to territorial
conquest in the Adriatic: it sought victory over the Empire of
Vienna in order that Italy might rise from the dominated to the
dominating position in the traditional game of Central European
politics. In a word it sought victory without democracy.

Neither social nor economic aspirations marred the purity of
Sonnino's devotion to this ideal of territorial and strategical
gain at the expense of Austria. Nor did the resort of Salandra,
Orlando and others of his colleagues in the various war cabinets,
to social and democratic appeals distract Sonnino from his
tenacious insistence upon the war aims enshrined in the Treaty
of London. His retention of the control of Italian foreign policy
throughout the war bespoke the strength of the tradition which
he represented in the Court, the army and the circle of politicians
trusted by them. Sonnino, it is true, had been a bitter and an
honourable opponent of the system of Giolitti: but isolation and
personal pride had ended by making him the incarnate negation
of a new democratic Italy.

If no glimmering of a fusion of the democratic ideal with the purpose of victory was to be found in this preserve of Italian politics, correspondingly in other quarters where the social and economic purposes of democracy were loudly embraced, there was indifference to the ideal of victory.

There was serious meditation, in the Socialist party, on the shape of the Italy which should emerge from the war. There was too a ferment of reforming projects in the Catholic organizations which were at that moment shaping themselves into the 'Popular Party'. But neither Socialists nor Populars were identified with the will to victory. True, the disaster of Caporetto stirred many Socialists and Catholic Democrats into a sincere ardour of solidarity with the army which stemmed the invader's advance into Italy (just as it stirred Conservative ministers and generals into fervours of enthusiasm for 'the people'), but the twelve months of doubt which ran from Caporetto to the final victory found their parties keenly currying favour in virtue of their freedom from original lack of responsibility for the war. Sonnino tarred Italy's war with the brush of reaction, the Socialists and the Populars even while they raised the standard of a mature democracy, shaking themselves loose of Giolittian entanglements, tarred the democratic banner with an imputation of defeatism.

To the last war-time Government of Italy, that headed by Orlando, it was reserved to expose to the whole world during the Peace negotiations the chaos of conflicting tendencies which had been amalgamated into the 'sacred union' of Italy's war effort: a union which had never managed to embrace either formally or substantially more than a fraction of the organized Socialism and Catholicism of the country. Victory and sudden peace caught the Orlando Government in sharp intestinal disagreement on the nature of Italy's ambitions: and these dissensions became public at the delicate moment of the Peace Conference.

In disappointment at the Allies' attitude towards Italy's claim to Dalmatia—and the Fiume question here made confusion worse confounded—it was almost forgotten that Italy had won by far the most important factors of the 1915 war programme: the redemption of the Italian lands of Trentino and Trieste, with far more admirable strategic frontiers than strict 'self-determination' as between Italians on the one side, Germans and Slavs on the other, would have admitted.

There was resentment, too, at the absence of attribution to

Italy of shares in the spoils of Turkey and of the German Colonial Empire. What was much less noticed was that Italy had put forward no schedule of economic demands, and was thus almost at her own instance left at the end of the war in an unrelieved situation of economic inferiority which neither her realized nor her unrealized territorial claims could have remedied. Far more than the repudiation by the Allies of conditional territorial pledges which new circumstances had entangled in unforeseen difficulties, what gave general substance to Italian embitterment over the common democratic victory was the lack of any economic reward. Sonnino had not thought in such terms, and the Allies lacked the imagination to pierce to Italy's real needs.

The Orlando Government thus vanished amid a great vociferation about the 'lost peace'. And although the Nationalist wing of the recent war coalition were the chief authors of this cry, profit was sought from it in diametrically opposite quarters, by those who were determined to show that their opposition to the war had been justified. Whatever were the concrete defects for Italy of the peace settlement, the year 1919 saw a deliberate attempt to reinterpret the result of the victorious democratic war of Europe as a defeat for Italy, and it saw a campaign to build upon that defeat an internal political ascendancy like that which the Bolsheviks had attained in defeated Russia. The Italian democracy which had the right to claim equality and prestige for Italy in the society of the victorious democracies was utterly outshadowed by a democracy—that is to say by mass popular movements in Italy—which washed their hands of the war and in the last resort preferred to regard its outcome as a defeat.

The two mass parties which appeared to have the political future of Italy in their hands tended, though not in equal measure, to take this view—the Socialists and the Catholic Populars. General elections, municipal elections and the greatly augmented strength of the affiliated trade unions in 1919 combined to show the Socialist party and movement to be in possession of overwhelming strength, challenged less by the fragile remainders of the old Giolittian clan, and of the offshoot from it represented by men like Salandra, than by the Popular or Catholic Democratic party which the war had suddenly matured from a vague movement into a great political organization, as will shortly be described.

The Premiership passed immediately after the Versailles

Peace Conference from Orlando to Francesco Nitti, a southern economist and administrator of great intellectual brilliance, convinced that the political Italy of the Giolittian clique had passed away for ever. In him victorious Italy acquired for her official leader a politician who foresaw Italy's future in terms of democracy, and who viewed the mass parties as the manifestations and organs of the Italian people's ripeness for self-government. His was a mind well fitted to appreciate how the great mass parties should frame and execute their programmes at the outset of the new era. But it was a politically disembodied intelligence attempting to preside from outside over forces in search of a strong and full-blooded leadership from within. The circumstances of Nitti's assumption of power had brought passions into play amid which his voice sounded helplessly professorial. He had to construct a policy of which the structure, far from being sustained by the scaffolding of military emergency and martial law, must be able to resist the shock of the demolition of that scaffolding. No system of threads comparable to that which had converged in Giolitti's hands gave him an assurance of secret command over great interests and organizations in the country. The convergent threads which for half a century had linked the Chamber of Deputies, the municipalities, the trade unions, and on occasion the parish parsonage to a Premier sitting at the centre of patronage had snapped, leaving these various entities with a sense of buoyant independence.

Nitti had been, if mildly, an interventionist in 1915. He did not retreat from that attitude. His outlook upon affairs was broad, generous and democratic. But when it fell to him to preside at the first efforts of Italy to advance from victory in a democratic war to an era of popular reforms, the baffling circumstance that the reforming parties repudiated the war was one which he did not attempt to alter, but accepted as destiny. The aspect which his Government assumed was one of pocketing national pride in order to appease the repudiators of the national cause, favourites, as they were at that moment, of the war-weary multitudes. Instead of leading a mature Italian democracy forward from the basis of a great victory, it was Nitti's destiny to preside over the nation's relapse into a condition of civil hostilities—not to abuse, by applying to events upon a somewhat petty scale, the solemn word 'war'.

II. THE PATTERN OF DEADLOCK

The Chamber of Deputies which on the fall of the discredited Peace Conference Cabinet accorded its support to Nitti was that same Chamber which had been elected in 1913, the product of manhood suffrage exercised in single constituencies and of the Giolittian system of bargains and patronage. It was the Parliament which had bowed to riot in 1915 and accepted war shamefacedly after the event. In November 1919 Nitti summoned the people to elect a Parliament by the new method of proportional representation. No hidden hand predetermined the result. The method itself rendered much traditional parliamentary scheming obsolete, and Nitti made no attempt to build up a substitute for Giolitti's manœuvres. The electors returned 156 Socialist Deputies, all but 100 Catholic Populars and 256 representatives of eight other groups, representing in part the old Giolittian caucus and the cluster of Conservatives around Salandra (some 60 in number), in part the various shades of semi-Socialist radicalism. The new Chamber of Deputies was thus for old-fashioned Parliamentarians a horrifyingly transformed assembly. There was little confidence, in such circles, of being able to stand up directly against the novelties it would bring forward.

Fed by the forced growth of a great new urban industrialism in the northern centres, Italian Socialism had in the war period registered the most outstanding progress in its whole career towards a dominating position in the nation. The prophecy of Mussolini that war would be the matrix of Socialist achievements appeared on the way to being realized—but not to the advantage of Mussolini's own sect of dissident Socialists, which scorned by the electors seemed practically to disappear. It was to the official Socialist party that by far the largest coherent block of electors—1,840,000—gave their confidence. Two-thirds of all the electors indeed voted for other than official Socialist candidates, of whom 1,175,000 for the Populars and 2,500,000 for the non-mass parties. The votes accorded to these last parties—a medley of Liberal and Conservative remnants, with a fair proportion of progressive radicals—were however to a great extent cast in the conviction that the future lead must be socialistic: a point of view to which even wealthy landowners in the first months after the war resigned themselves. An expectation—welcome faith in some, fatalism in others—prevailed almost throughout the country that the next stage in Italy would be socialistic. A great demolition of the privileges of wealth and property would be the chief characteristic: on this basic assumption the Popular party differed little from the Socialists: the survivors of the older groups disputed the tempo and method rather than the purposes of the Socialists.

It was the situation which men like Filippo Turati and Claudio Treves had aspired after for half a century. Strictly limited first-fruits had been won under their leadership by Socialism in the Giolitti period; a much fuller harvest now lay ready for the reaping of a Socialist party which had become the biggest political force in the country, courted by all others. It was necessary only for the Socialists to assume the authority belonging to such power, and to observe the limits set by the need of the co-operation of the Populars and of the progressive and democratic groups, or at least, in all circumstances, of one or the other. If these precautions were observed, a triumphant realization of Socialist purposes might be effected almost without encountering resistance.

The mentality of the Socialist party as expressed in its pronouncements of 1917 would have adequately met the situation. In a programme published in March of that year the party's main demands were formulated as follows: Republican constitution, government by single chamber elected by universal suffrage, full civil liberties, election of magistrates and high officials, social insurance, public works and big land reclamations.

With these internal postulates the Italian Socialist party coupled the international principles of free trade and the reign of law between nations.

The proposals were full of controversy but in their general scope not more sweeping than what, in the vast political lobby of the armies at the front, the nation had come to expect. A spirit of continuity with the previous history of United Italy was not wholly wanting: what the Socialists undertook to do was to give greater speed, clearer outline and more definite directions to the development in Italy which had been in course since the beginning of the century. Few Italian patriots trembled at this.

Unfortunately for these prospects, however, the party of 1919 had moved far from its positions of 1917. Crucial facts had interposed themselves: the Leninist coup in Russia, Caporetto and Vittorio Veneto in Italy and the Peace of Versailles. Passions and recriminations had flared up: catastrophic situations had given scope to unmeasured ambitions. Frustrated prophecies had filled the prophets with rancour. Late in 1917 the Caporetto disaster found Filippo Turati among the national leaders of the state who summoned the Italians to close their ranks and restore the integrity of the nation. He made no profession of conversion to the cause of the Italian war as it had been launched by Salandra, but his words breathed an unqualified Italian patriotism in the face of the supreme external danger. It sufficed to reconcile a great body of the war party to Turati as a national leader and potential Head of a Government. Very different was the attitude of others of the Socialist chiefs. The peril of Italy at Caporetto roused them not to solidarity but to an embittered repudiation of the whole armed effort of Italy as the result of a gigantic 'bourgeois' crime. The accusation had rung through the trenches before the great disaster, of which it was a contributory cause, though military history can adequately account for the defeat at Caporetto apart from that factor. Socialists were not the only politicians to give currency to this active and wilful defeatism: there were Catholics and 1915-neutralists from the old Giolittian camp who viewed the process with much complacency. It was, however, in the Socialist leadership that defeatism in 1917 placed its germs of infection: germs which were to incapacitate the Socialist party in 1919 from entering into its heritage, leaving it as a vast unmanageable and enigmatic entity to decompose from within and to crack under the blows dealt at it from without.

The overthrow in Russia of Kerensky's democratic war Government by a small group of men bold enough to promise immediate peace fired the remnants of the insurrectionary school of Italian Socialists with ambition to achieve something similar— remnants, because in the person of Mussolini the most formidable of the insurrectionists had left them to pit his personal future upon the promise of revolution on the other side of victory.

Pre-eminent figures among the insurrectionists were Nicola Bombacci, a Romagnole of Mussolini's region and generation of romantically prophetic appearance and language, and Mussolini's old patron Costantino Lazzari. The two agitators were arrested in the Caporetto period. Events for a while then held their propaganda in check. Their ambitions required an Italy as distraught and hopeless as Russia had been a few months earlier. But in the presence of extreme national peril numbers of previously indifferent Italian citizens had given support to the cause of the war: the authorities made a serious effort to improve army morale by providing recreation facilities for the troops, in which they were assisted by American and British friends in Italy, and by abating disciplinary vexations. Officers were instructed to form educational circles in the battalions, and were provided with suitable points for discussion with the soldiers. Desertions from the front had continued, it is true—on so great a scale that at the end of the war 150,000 fugitives were reckoned to be in hiding and a million cases (a great many of them, it is true, merely technical) were awaiting judgement by court martial. But the Italian armies had stood firm on the Piave: the final Austrian offensive broke down in June in the face of an Italian army now increasingly fortified by the flow of American and British munitions and supplies. The prospects of a catastrophic defeat grew dim: and for victorious Italy the ideals of victorious America, enshrined in the principles of President Wilson, took on a realistic appearance at the expense of the ideals of defeated Russia. The change was assiduously promoted by Government agencies which did not weigh the promises which they made of social justice for the people after the war in a world to be liberated by the principle of self-determination from the fears and burdens of competitive nationalism.

The war had not yet ended, however, when the defeatist wing of the Socialists raised its standard with fresh truculence, and on the morrow of the armistice the effect was shown in programmes and manifestos which were showered by Socialist quarters on the country. A bewildering number of organs, with more or less genuine authority, made themselves the mouthpiece of the Socialist masses—the National Congress of the Party, the Party Executive Committee, the Socialist Parliamentary Committee, the Executive Committee of the General Confederation of Labour. The seeds of the civil war to come lay not in the general demands for constitutional and social renovation which were common to all the official Socialist organs, and appeared equally in the manifestos of the Mussolinian faction, and, far more important, in that of the Popular party. They lay in the new 'Bolshevik' dogma of proletarian vengeance for the war.

There was, for example, a difference only in degree and emphasis between a programme of the General Confederation of Labour calling for the convoking of a 'Constituent Assembly', the establishment of syndical commissions to take over from Parliament the tasks of social legislation, gradual socialization of the land and its cultivation under the direction of peasants' co-operatives, right of workers' control over factories: and the full fruit of labour for those who have produced it—and a simultaneous programme of the Populars: 'universal suffrage for men and women, proportional representation, an elective senate with direct participation of national, intellectual, administrative and single organisms, fiscal reform, social aid and insurance, support for small owners, systematic exploitation of idle landed estates.'

Demands put forward by Mussolini in his first post-war manifesto on behalf of the pro-war ex-Socialists—that of March 23, 1919, which first officially named them 'Fascists'—were, as regards the new constitution which they advocated, on still more closely similar lines to those of the official Socialists. They asked for universal suffrage for both sexes, a constituent assembly, national technical councils, workers' participation in the management of industry, capital levy and expropriation of large estates, confiscation of 85 per cent. of war profits. The Fascists also demanded the replacement of the army by a purely defensive force, and the seizure of ecclesiastical wealth by the State.

It was no sharp disagreement about the social and economic future which ruled out the prospect of an era of administrative and social reform under Socialist leadership with the support of the great new reforming Catholic party. Nor was there much essential conflict between these reforming projects and the principles professed at this immediate post-war juncture by independent politicians like Nitti and Orlando, or by the small Liberal and democratic groups in Parliament which represented a vague continuity with pre-war Parliamentarism. The offence lay not in the aspirations but in two categorical demands which from this time onwards echoed more and more sonorously, and in ever closer combination with each other, in the language of the loudest-mouthed Socialists: the demands of 'Bolshevik' dogma.

Both demands rang out in the version of the Socialist programme issued by the Executive Committee of the party in December 1918. The first urged the working class to turn deaf ears to any profession of Socialist principles by 'those responsible for the present situation, now seeking to renew their lost political prestige'. This could mean only an anathema against all politicians who had advocated and supported the war. The second was a call for 'Dictatorship of the Proletariat' as the means for bringing about the realization of Socialist principles. These demands sounded the note of an absolute intransigence against all who had formed part of the war coalition of May 1915: against ex-Socialists like Mussolini, and against radical, republican and similar groups who in the name of Italy's victory claimed a creative part in the constitution of the wider post-war world. Socialist homage to the Russian model at the same time played into the hands of every Catholic authority who desired to see the new Popular party develop along lines of sharp hostility to Socialism, fearing the evolution of the Catholic Left.

The bewilderingly confused political proceedings in Italy in the ensuing four years, which end (for the purposes of this narrative) with Mussolini's march on Rome, group themselves around the imposition upon the Socialist party of the doctrines of necessary vengeance against war leaders and of necessary dictatorship of the proletariat. Their acceptance marked the Socialist party's simultaneous decomposition as a democratic movement for furtherance of the social good of the Italians by the methods of education, persuasion and tactical alliances for the attainment of limited ends: and its crude negation of national ideals consecrated on the battlefield.

This transformation of Italian Socialism was not, however, the unaided achievement of those Italian Socialists who between 1919 and 1921 purged the party of its humane and liberal leaders in order to hoist the banners of anti-patriotism and dictatorial Communism over the proletarian legions. The Communistic assault on the controls of the Socialist movement followed at four years' distance upon an earlier grand assault upon Socialist unity. The defection of Benito Mussolini was already four years old. The rancours produced by it were not yet abated. It had brought to the aid of a cause of Italian intervention a highly vital contingent of young Socialists, severing them from the law-abiding and laborious mass of the Socialist party, in order, as Mussolini flamingly announced, to realize revolution through war—a preposterous pretext for the pursuit of ambition in the atmosphere of war, said Mussolini's detached critics: mere venal treachery, said his personal sworn foes.

In regarding their enemy as a mere hired renegade, they underestimated him. Mussolini did really cherish the ambition of becoming a 'revolutionary' leader through war though his ideas about revolution were free-and-easy. It was therefore in bitterness and almost desperation Mussolini found, at the end of the war, another sect of Socialists proclaiming, with far more immediate effectiveness, revolution through the impeachment of all the war-makers and the dictatorship of the proletariat, that is, of themselves, the defeatists. Jealousy and contempt possessed him as he watched the loud-mouthed Bombacci, and similar old cronies whom he knew through and through, claiming the revolutionary mantle which he himself had not relinquished.

It was not to be outclassed by a new clique of revolutionaries that Mussolini had cut away from the main body of Socialism proclaiming himself the sole resolute revolutionary of the party. At thirty-five years of age (1918) his temperament had calmed and he had now learned the uses of compromise and the tendency, in politics, for opposites to embrace. But as revolutionary or as counter-revolutionary his purpose was clearly set—to regain the captaincy, or rather to assume the generalship, of the Italian labour movement. It was obvious that he would not be re-admitted, unrepentant of his war crusade, into the Socialist party, and he was not of the repenting kind. His position in 1919 seemed desperate, and a mock announcement of his death printed in the *Avanti* after his personal fiasco in the elections of that year seemed to hit the mark. He awaited his opportunity from the break-up of the Socialist party which for his part he helped on with the greatest tenacity and a clarity of mind sharpened by hatred: also from any other chance alliances and combinations which in so much confusion might come his way. Here there was no lack of opportunity.

The embracing of opposites in the interventionist campaign of 1915, and in the subsequent three years of warfare not merely against Austria and Germany but particularly against the 'internal' foe on the home front, had brought Mussolini many previously undreamed-of associations. As one who had left his own party on the sole issue of war, and with only a handful of individuals loosely following in his wake, Mussolini floated from 1915 to 1918 in indiscriminate association with other inter-ventionist leaders. His natural attachment on one side went to the radical, republican and reformist groups who, weak in numbers and parliamentary representation, none the less dominated the major organs of the Press and powerfully affected the official complexion of Italy. It was these groups, as has been shown, which in the months between Caporetto and the too sudden victory procured a marked shift in the emphasis of Italy's war policy, aligning it far more closely than in 1915 and 1916 with that of the Allies, and of the United States, and giving it the provisional and as it turned out the illusory aspect of an

Italian participation in a universal crusade for democratic and humanitarian values.

Much phraseology common to radicalism and socialism of all schools prior to 1918 permitted Mussolini to participate in the war rhetoric of this school, and to be cited in 1916 and 1917 as a paladin of the 'democratic' theory of the war. Advocate as he is, in those years, of ruthless and total war it is still in the name of a coming 'revolution' and not of national aggrandizement that he whips up the readers of the *Popolo d'Italia* to rage against the defeatists, the pacifists and the half-hearted. The theory of Italy's isolated and quasi-dynastic war against Austria, Sonnino's theory, is for him antiquated nonsense. 'It is in Berlin that the enemies of the human race are gathered. . . . We stand together with France, with England, with the United States. That is the true International, deep and lasting, even if it lacks the dogmas and the sacraments of official Socialism,' he says still in February and May 1918. At the beginning of 1919 he figures among the most enthusiastic adherents, in Italy, of President Wilson and of the League of Nations, calling the former 'the Prophet of the peoples' and publishing the League Covenant with the headline: 'Now begins the new history of the peoples.' These are words of one who hopes to save his future by collaboration with the radical left and to effect a conciliation with the democratically inclined elements in Socialism.

But an all-devouring ambition drives him simultaneously along opposite courses, and temperamental sympathy, becoming increasingly evident in the course of the war, approximates Mussolini to those elements in the war front for whom the ethical ideals of the democratic school are meaningless. In the sphere of politics and journalism these men are represented by the small Nationalist party, with a handful of deputies, a competent Press, some influence in the universities, and a considerable backing from the heavy and armament industry. Also the landowners and the high bourgeoisie already see in these eccentrics the germ of a reaction against the vast wave of equalitarianism incarnated in the mass parties. Their outlook expresses itself in a hard dogma presenting as the sole aim of Italian existence the building-up of a formidable Italian national power under the leadership of a resolute *élite*. Projects of social betterment, at home, international attachments and solidarities have meaning only as moves in a game: and as was seen, a few days in 1914 sufficed for the Nationalists to switch from demanding to be the war ally of Germany to demanding war against Germany. They remained faithful only to their scorn and rancour against democratic ideals, and against those who would sacrifice anything of Italy's 'sacred egoism' to wider purposes in war or peace. Shy sympathies had sprung up between the Nationalists and the syndicalist wing of Socialism as far back as in the Tripoli war; the passions of 1917 and 1918 brought about a marked approximation between Nationalists and Mussolinians. The 'democracy' spoken about by Mussolini was redeemed, for the Nationalists, by Mussolini's implacable feud against the leaders of the Socialist party. Nationalistically flavoured phrases about Italy's Roman mission—with already a hint of animosity against Italy's Allies—turn up in Mussolini's speeches of 1918 alongside of phrases of the fullest democratic, internationalist and 'Wilsonian' flavour. Mussolini was not a personage of sufficient importance in the war—editor though he remained of a daily paper which made its way—to have to work painfully for consistency.

A figure of far greater national prominence floated between, or rather above, the competing fractions in Italy's internal front at the bewildering moment of victory, and to some extent carried Mussolini in his wake. This was Gabriele d'Annunzio, who had followed up the rhetoric of words, so powerful in bringing about Italy's intervention in the war, with a rhetoric of picturesque exploits in the air and at sea. Master of the most diverse attitudes to human affairs, equally ready to exalt the pride of empire or the dignity of labour, the one firm fact about d'Annunzio in 1918 was his share of responsibility for bringing Italy into the war and of glory for keeping up the national morale by a type of dramatic activity which encouraged imitation and emulation. He was idolized by a type never absent from Italian history which, as the war progressed, came more and more into prominence. In other circumstances his admirers would have been (and frequently had been) brigands and bravi in the country, heroes of the *demi-monde* and the underworld in the towns. Incurable rebels against drill and the trenches, they were ready for any adventures that war might offer; and a large number of them attained special status as *Arditi* ('Daredevils') attached to army units for special raids and ventures and excused all part in humdrum soldiery. What distinguished them was their lack of roots in any society organized for peace. It was by the light not of a programme, but of nature, that these warriors sought an immediate home front to replace the suddenly vanished war front as a field for their talents and a stage for their glorification.

The 'Ardito' temperament flourished in many breasts besides those of the recognized and official *Arditi*, and naturally above all in those of the schoolboys and students for whom the call to arms came just too late for the sobering experiences of real warfare.

All observers of the early post-war crowds which flocked to salute d'Annunzio, and on a much more modest scale formed Mussolini's audiences in Milan, agree on the importance of these 'too late for the war' youths, so numerous in prolific Italy.

The young Italians due for call to the colours in the first year of peace numbered some 50,000 more than those due in France. Adolescents formed a much higher proportion of an average crowd in Italy. The numbers and exuberance of these youths who had come to precocious adolescence in the decay of old political loyalties and improvisation of new enthusiasms in the war period made of them an estate of the realm, rendering a fascinator like d'Annunzio more formidable than any reckoning of the strengths of political parties could suggest.

At the moment of the armistice these elements of Italian political life appeared inscrutably confused behind a veil of wondering hopefulness evoked by a victory and a peace which supervened with a sort of ironical prematureness on the threat of defeat and collapse.

The pause was short-lived. Events in Paris, in Fiume and not least in Moscow produced in Italy a multiple cacophony. Firm and sagacious democracy might have drawn strength from honest conflict. Instead, insoluble hatreds between groups and parties often advocating closely similar programmes set into a fatal pattern. Far-flung events frustrated the hope of a strengthened and purified Italian democracy to take the place of the Parliamentarian régime of 1860–1915 whose frail and insincere character was delineated in the middle chapters of this book. Our remaining chapters recount the process of frustration.

CHAPTER ELEVEN

STILLBIRTH OF A DEMOCRACY

I. FIUME, D'ANNUNZIO AND FASCISM.—Mussolini boxes the political compass, turning to denounce the democrats with whom he had made common cause in the war. D'Annunzio's military revolt against Versailles and Rome gives a rallying centre for anti-democratic nationalism and inaugurates an atmosphere of civil war, with Parliamentary Rome as Fiume's enemy. D'Annunzio as the forerunner and teacher of the Duce.

II. NITTI AND THE SOCIALISTS.—In Rome, a Parliament in which manhood suffrage had brought in the Socialists and Populars as dominating parties drifts into impotence. The Premier Nitti cannot command the co-operation of the Socialists whom a small clique fascinate into an extreme verbal bellicosity unaccompanied by practical effects.

III. THE POPULARS.—Their part as a mass party: their position towards Nitti: their rivalry with the Socialists. How Nitti could not and did not make of them the Party of State for the attainment of an authoritative democracy. Nitti's vulnerability, and eclipse.

IV. THE REIGN OF A GHOST.—Giolitti re-emerges as 'national saviour'. High tide and ebb of revolutionary Socialism. Occupation of the factories. Giolitti liquidates d'Annunzio. The attempted restoration of his 'system' fails. A year of Government chaos.

I. FIUME, D'ANNUNZIO AND FASCISM

When the armistice bells rang out in Europe Italy stood high in the favour of the liberal and progressive world. Italy's triumph over Austria warmed the heart of millions who saw in it the final act in the long-drawn struggle of the Italians for the freedom denied them by Viennese despotism. Of a sudden, the Italian liberals sharing the vision of a humane and co-operative Europe cease to weigh in the counsels of their country. The name and notion of Italy take on a new connotation. Doubtless it is the superficial observers who are chiefly surprised: the reader of this narrative knows something of the harsher reality of Italian circumstances long before 1919 or 1922. But the chance opening of an Italian newspaper, even be it Mussolini's own newspaper, of any anterior date does in fact confirm the impression of a sudden and portentous change in the moral aspect of the nation.

An event in Milan in January 1919, recorded by an eye-witness in a brilliant critique of Fascism, symbolizes the eclipse of that force in Italian international policy which in 1917 and 1918 brought about the 'Pact of Rome' against imperial Vienna, and which represented impulses derived from the purest spirits of the Risorgimento, in particular from Mazzini; the eclipse of a belief that Italy might gain high rank among the nations as the champion not merely of Italian ambitions, but of national liberties in the whole family of European nations.

The scene described by Borgese consisted merely in Mussolini joining a crowd of rowdies to shout down a lecture by Bissolati in support of the League of Nations. The sight of Mussolini among his shameless hecklers was too much for Bissolati—says Borgese—and the veteran soldier-statesman abandoned his attempt to dominate the audience. Bissolati, it may be remembered, had behind him a career with some outward resemblance to Mussolini's own. He had been the first editor of the *Avanti*: he had been thrown out of the Socialist party for supporting a war—in his case the Tripoli war of 1911 when the ringleader of his expulsors had been none other than Mussolini. The Great War found Bissolati a veteran independent Socialist. He joined ardently in promoting Italy's intervention, and insisted upon serving as a front-line volunteer, though sixty years old. No sentimentalist, at the moment of Caporetto he had shouted to the pacifists in Parliament: 'I want to see you shot.'

His ruthlessness, however, was in the service of humane ideals. He appears thitherto to have given Mussolini credit for a similar idealism: and when he saw the independent Socialist of the younger generation engaged in hooliganism against the democratic war aims for which, as he believed, they had both contended, this—we learn from Borgese—was a shattering revelation to Bissolati. Mussolini had now boxed the political compass, and advertised the fact without scruple.

Embittered by the hostility of the official Socialists and finding an escape from isolation in the support of groups of *Arditi* and in the patronage of d'Annunzio, he joined in the campaign to shout and stamp down the advocates of that policy which took its inspiration from the democratic interpretation of the war. His personal position was not important enough to make his

attitude a decisive political event: but his acumen showed him
that Bissolati's was a lost cause.   Wedged between the denouncers
of the war and the champions of a ruthless expansionism, railed
upon by both, the supporters of a peace settlement in harmony
with democratic professions were already doomed to neglect and
contempt.   Their authority henceforth waned steadily.

Their frustration in foreign policy struck deeply into the
Italian internal situation.   The democratic outlook on Italy's
share in the war was closely bound up with the ambition to see
a strong, free and orderly democracy, based on a working
arrangement between the new mass parties which had arisen
out of the irreparable ruin of the shadow democracy of the
Giolittian era.   Those who aspired to put Italy's international
policy on a basis of understanding and collaboration with other
peoples—first and foremost with the new neighbour state of the
South Slavs—were the same men who designed to base the
government of the country upon a new and robust representation
of the people in Parliament.   Such had been the sense of their
whole policy since 1915.   The latter design, scarcely less than
the former aspiration, fell upon disaster, from which it never
recovered, with the March of Gabriele d'Annunzio on Fiume on
September 12, 1919, which must now be drawn into our tale.

On that day Gabriele d'Annunzio marched a corps of some
thousands of demobilized or mutineering officers, *Arditi*, and
adolescents cheated of the war adventures they had been brought
up to expect, into the small Adriatic port which was then
occupied by French and British troops, the Italian garrison
having recently been cut down to put a stop to brawling between
them and their French comrades.   The status of the city—as of
the East Adriatic littoral in general—had received no definition
from the peacemakers in Paris: it awaited a later settlement
between the Rome and Belgrade governments.   In this situation
it easily became symbolic of Italian indignation against the war
Allies, America, Britain and France—a ewe lamb denied to Italy
by these plump profiteers of the victory.   The privateer's seizure
of Fiume crowned the discredit of the Italian Government in
the eyes of all who were striving for a resettlement of Europe on
the basis of a new order among the nations.   The news was
received by Nitti—as the responsible agent for Italy's participation in that new order—with an open show of consternation.
Instantly the fury of Fiume turned against him, and against the
embryonic post-war democracy which he represented.   The inter-

national significance almost paled beside the internal significance, for Italy, of what had happened. Fiume was claimed to be the true Italy, the moral capital of the nation, the mirror held up to the face of decadent Rome.

In the relaxed state of Europe, exemplified in a prompt decision to withdraw the Franco-British garrison from the scene of these proceedings, a small but unencumbered field was suddenly offered for the conduct of an Italian experiment in the politics not of politicians, burdened by precedent and sobered by the vigilance of their rivals, but of a poet, a number of journalists, and a great many more or less authentic war heroes at their wits' end to conceive how to uphold their dignity in the unresponsive theatre of civil life. Not merely was the field unencumbered, but its local economic problems were for the moment miraculously solved by seizure of war stores and of a number of loaded cargo vessels, whose captains yielded from enthusiasm or sheer bewilderment or under constraint. For d'Annunzio did not lack some units of the Italian navy which put themselves at the service of his adventure.

The companions and followers of d'Annunzio comprised persons who, though having property or privileges to lose, felt no hesitation about falling under the ban of the official Italian State, so low did they estimate the prospects of an orderly evolution in Rome which would brand them as senseless rebels; and largely admixed with these were persons who had nothing to lose at all. Those whose presence in Fiume constituted military desertion and rebellion felt well covered by the obvious connivance of high officers in d'Annunzio's proceedings. There was a complexion of nationalist and anti-plebeian military revolt about the whole affair, yet d'Annunzio's personality incarnating a spirit of audacious innovation, in contest against the whole political system centring around the Rome Parliament, attracted the most miscellaneous support. It was not five years since the poet had given voice to that insurrection of the streets which overthrew Giolitti and took Italy into the war—an insurrection far from anti-plebeian and inspired in the main by democratic ideals, however much astute men in the background might be ready to exploit them for other ends. And *motifs* echoing these ideals, transposed into a key of magical rather than prophetic enthusiasm, breathed forth from the speeches, edicts and declarations of rights which d'Annunzio, having installed himself as the 'Commandant' of Fiume, proceeded to turn out in exuberant quantity. Democratic phraseology poured forth from Fiume, unaccompanied, however, by any suggestion that the elected representatives of the people ranged in political parties in the Rome Parliament might by deliberation and orderly procedure give effect to those aspirations: and d'Annunzio's action was, in Europe at large, deemed deadly for the liberal mission of Italy.

The episode of Fiume, which remained as an open sore throughout the remaining nine months of Nitti's premiership, consummated the loss, by the men of evolutionary and parliamentary mentality, of the moral representation of Italy's combatant generation. There had been room, in the street insurrection of 1915, for a wide variety of temperaments and schools of political method. The revolt against Giolitti had been directed against what the active intelligence of the country condemned as a stunted and distorted democracy: whether the distortion or the underlying pattern of democracy was the object of dislike did not signify greatly in the line-up for the war and against the master of Parliament. War policy, as has been shown, came only at one moment of crisis, after Caporetto, under the strong influence of the democratic groups. At least, however, until the parting of the ways in 1919, the champions of a full democracy could raise their voice as authoritative, forward-looking interpreters of the intervention, the war and the victory. Neither argument nor energy failed them for rebutting the accusations of 'war guilt' hurled at them openly by the official Socialists and covertly by Giolittians and clericals. But 1919, and the Fiume episode in particular, faced them with the accusation from their own recent associates of being the 'saboteurs of the victory'. To have desired and fought the war for Italy in the spirit of the Mazzinian gospel—which is to say in the hope of an integration of Italy in a democratic Europe, raised by international benevolence above the conflicts of petty territorial cupidities—this, after 1919, was to receive blame for the war from the mouth of the pacifists, and blame for the peace, with all its disorders and disappointments, from the mouth of those who now arrogated to themselves the sole title to national patriotism.

It was also to receive, from either extreme, a battery of ridicule for the theories of representative government, and for the ideal of a supersession of the boss-rule of a Giolitti by a Parliament of parties drawing their strength from a sincere appeal to the electorate.

The breach between the democratic partisans of the war on the one hand, and those rallying to d'Annunzio's flag on the other hand, widened until it exceeded that between d'Annunzio and the Socialists of the extreme wing. Among d'Annunzio's acts at Fiume was the address of a fraternal telegram to Communist Moscow, and Lenin appears to have expressed a favourable opinion of the poet. The lines of communication were never wholly cut between d'Annunzio and certain Socialists who saw in him a just conceivable figurehead for a revolution in which they might bear their part. Later, indeed, as he found himself ousted by Mussolini from the position of chief idol of the *Arditi* and of the imperialist school in general, d'Annunzio's name, in a last flight of his fanciful political destiny, became attached to shadowy projects of a Socialist race to Rome ahead of the Fascist march which was clearly being planned.

For the moment, Mussolini remained a minor figure, and Fascismo, the new form and name given by him to his small movement of pro-war Socialists in Milan, appeared but as one among a plethora of new political groupings. Its association with the Unione Italiana di Lavoro, the trade-union nucleus which had defied the great Confederazione General to support the war, was loose. Fascismo at this stage was little more than a tendency of prejudice and sentiment in a small local circle: a tendency determined above all by personal rivalries and rancours.

For a year Mussolini had been in sharp controversy with the democratic war groups: this had culminated, in the first postwar January, in the crude demonstration against Bissolati. There was no doubt where he stood in the split of the former war front which the Fiume affair dragged into the fullest glare of publicity. In the invective which they now addressed against Italy's recent Allies, the Peace Treaties, and Geneva, the poet and the Fascist leader were wholly at one. But on the manœuvring ground of practical affairs collaboration was, from the outset, fragmentary and fractious. Mussolini's paper, the *Popolo d'Italia*, exhorted young men to go and give their services to d'Annunzio at Fiume. It opened a subscription for the city. But there were angry controversies about the use to which the money was put, and not long after, when Giolitti made his reappearance and proceeded to clear up the Fiume tangle by expelling d'Annunzio and negotiating a compromise settlement with Belgrade, Mussolini gave to this his endorsement to the tune of resentful comment by the poet's 'legionaries'.

Mussolini had in him, after all, the experience and instinct of a mass party movement. As a Socialist his Marxism had been suspect, and the sociologists of the party regarded him as a romantic actor. But it had not been within his scope to float like a magician over the surface of national life conjuring up combinations by sheer heat of rhetoric. The road of ambition, for Mussolini, lay through party and syndical organizations to be conquered. It was as leader of the Socialist revolution that he had first dreamed of reaching supreme power in Italy: if some time after his expulsion from the party he dropped the appellation of 'Socialist', he was far from meaning to resign to those he left behind him the control of the great organizations of the working class. He would not be d'Annunzio's deputy in a flashy pronunciamento which might gain the support of those organizations for a mere tactical victory. To annex and to absorb the forces of the working classes after rupturing their existing political unity was the end pursued by Mussolini in his feverish, and at times desperate, activity through the periods of the Nitti Government, the Giolitti restoration and the year of political incoherence which issued in the March on Rome.

He would not be d'Annunzio's deputy; yet the d'Annunzian escapade in Fiume enriched Mussolini's mental formation with elements new to his experience.

The style of Mussolini in dress and language, until this time, had fluctuated between that of the petty bourgeois intellectual and that of the workman-apache. Inflammatory rhetoric he wielded familiarly: but ceremonial language and gesture and the application of pageantry to politics had been outside his ken. These were the instruments of d'Annunzio's virtuosity: and in Fiume the poet enjoyed unexampled facilities for putting them into practice. During fifteen months of his rule there filtered back to Italy, and largely to Mussolini's own organization, youths to whom d'Annunzio had taught the 'Roman salute', the intonation of ritual slogans in chorus and the use of a semi-uniform attire combining weapons, badges and accoutrements, with an easy-going variety of basic garment.

It was not only as *régisseur* of political ceremonial, but also as legislator, that d'Annunzio applied startlingly novel colours to the stuff of Italian politics. A number of moral and political principles and of organizational fantasies were issued under d'Annunzio's name as the Statute of the Province of Fiume. The mirth shown by the outside world, both in Italy and elsewhere, was premature: d'Annunzio had divined the rhetoric which the new generation wanted.

A sample may be given from the provisions of this extraordinary document:

IV. The province recognizes and confirms the sovereignty of all citizens without distinction of sex, race, language, class, or religion.

But above all, and beyond every other right, she maintains the right of the producer. . . .

And subdivides offices and powers so that by their harmonious interplay communal life may grow more vigorous and abundant.

XVIII. The State represents the aspiration and the effort of the people, as a community, towards material and spiritual advancement.

Those only are full citizens who give their best endeavour. . . .

Whatever be the kind of work a man does, whether of hand or brain, art or industry . . . he must be a member of one of the ten corporations.

[Here follows a list of the corporations: No. 1—industrial and agricultural labourers, etc.; No. 2—technicians and managers; No. 3—shopkeepers, etc.]

The tenth has no special trade or register or title. It is reserved for the mysterious forces of progress and adventure.

XLIII. When the province is in extreme peril the National Council may nominate a Commandant.

During the period of his rule the Commandant holds all the powers—political and military, legislative and executive.

On the expiration of the period the Council may confirm him in office, change him, or banish him.

The Statute of Fiume in brief promised the completest liberties to all citizens, together with a maximum of hieratic organization and authority. Every provision was invested with the sanctity of an element in a mystic whole; and the document ended with a dedication of the municipal orchestra to heaven:

'In the pauses of music is heard the silence of the tenth corporation.'

From this constitution of a not quite imaginary but astonishingly idealized Fiume, a compost of the poet's own paganizing cult, and of hints culled from the proclamations of French and Italian nationalists and syndicalists, Mussolini had nothing to learn about politics: but something, which he did not fail quickly to utilize, about his countrymen's psychology.

II. NITTI AND THE SOCIALISTS

In the fourth month of d'Annunzio's occupation of Fiume King Victor Emmanuel proceeded to the Palazzo Montecitorio to open the Parliament in which Socialists and Populars, elected under Nitti's new law of proportional representation, occupied half the seats, supported by sympathizers in many of the remainder. This was the assembly where Italy's enlarged and purified democracy proposed to shape the laws of a new historic epoch in the unfolding of Italian democracy.

As the King entered, the hundred and fifty-six Socialist deputies, each with a red flower in his buttonhole, rose and left the Chamber chanting the *Red Flag*. It was an intimation, to any who doubted it, that the prevailing spirits of the most numerous party intended to shine by truculence.

In fact, from the rostra of the Socialist party in their own 'Chambers of Labour' and other meeting-places, Socialist orators impugned the Parliament in Rome with as much vehemence as d'Annunzio, if with less distinction of style. They too pointed away from Rome to a mystic city where the future was in incubation: to Moscow, whence the Third International was issuing bitter condemnations of social democracy coupled with a verdict of total guilt against all who had promoted, accepted, or compromised with the national war policies of their countries.

Following upon one of these Moscow pronouncements, the Executive Committee of the Italian Socialist party early in 1919 disaffiliated the party from the International Socialist Bureau (Second International), declaring that this had 'yielded itself into the hands of the imperialist bourgeoisie of the Entente.' It fulminated against the 'social-patriots of the imperialism of the Entente, betrayers of the people', and declared for the constitution of a revolutionary Socialist international on the basis of the principles laid down by 'our Russian communist comrades'.

Brawls between *Arditi* or other soldiers, in uniform or semi-uniform, and red-rosetted partisans now became frequent in the streets. There were some insults to officers. In Milan, the rancour of Mussolini against the Socialist headquarters fused with the quarrelsome inclinations of the *Arditi* and grave incidents ensued. The office of the Socialist daily *Avanti* was burned down early in April, 1919.

The stormy encounters between red rosettes and black shirts —these were originally the insignia of the *Arditi*, soon to be adopted by Mussolini's political as well as his free-booting associates—intercrossed confusedly with the manifestations of sheer economic unrest. To millions of the Italian working classes the war had brought a hitherto unknown prosperity;

indeed one acute analyst of the times, Mario Missiroli, declared that the problem of the living wage in Italy was now solved. Prices, however, raced up in competition with wages: and fixed monetary incomes lost value disastrously—a consequence of the sudden stoppage of the large Anglo-American war supplies and subsidies. There were sporadic riots in protest against the high cost of living. The margin above sheer want is, in Italy, small at the best of times, and the new 'prosperity' had nothing to spare for a sudden fall in the value of money.

The Premier's political aspiration stretched out towards the enlistment of the authority of the two mass parties for a programme of sweeping but orderly social and economic reform. He was, however, hopelessly lacking in the capacity to dominate the assembly which his electoral reform had brought into being. More and more he endeavoured to meet the disorders in the country behind the back of Parliament, by the use of special powers, the legacy of war-time usage.

While Parliament debated unceasingly on the first principles of human society, the Government, formed mainly of isolated politicians since the Socialists declined to participate and Nitti put strict limits on the extent of his collaboration with the Populars, ruled by decree. In the country at large his name became identified chiefly with the institution of a new armed police corps for the maintenance of order, the Royal Guard, which achieved a tremendous unpopularity on all sides. He abolished, but subsequently reimposed, the war-time censorship of the Press. The Parliament, upon whose election such emphasis had been placed as of the creative organ through which the country was to renew itself, remained as distant from the conduct of practical affairs as the previous Parliament which the war-time Government had frankly ignored.

Outside Parliament, in counterblast to the rhetoric of d'Annunzio, the Socialist party in its official pronouncements hastily endorsed the anathemas of Moscow against the principle of peaceful constitutional and social progress. Nicola Bombacci, principal protagonist of defeatist conspiracy in the war, became the party secretary. Having taken his seat as a deputy he declared: 'I will not remain in Parliament—to do so is not compatible with my temperament.' By a huge majority the National Council of the party carried a proposal for the immediate constitution in the country of Workmen's Councils, modelled upon the Soviets.

The course of policy indicated by this resolution (but followed up by no practical attempts to realize it) ran clean counter to the advice of the older leaders of the party, Turati, Treves and others. It was reluctantly followed, at a distance, by the General Confederation of Labour, the central organ of the Socialist trade unions. The fascination exercised at that juncture by a clique over the party, and by the party—thus dominated—over the trade unions, placed a complexion upon Italian Socialism which within a short time all were to condemn as disastrous. At the moment, though the veteran leaders both of the party and of the Confederation did not conceal their distaste and apprehension, they took the unity of the Socialist movement, and not the efficacy of a Parliament which manhood suffrage had placed at the disposal of the people, for their guiding star. A great inflow into the party of young workmen uprooted from their families to work in the suddenly expanded industries of the north; a mass inflow, also, of Slav workers in the newly annexed province of Trieste, sufficed, in the comparatively small active membership of the party (at the beginning of the 'peace' a mere 100,000 persons), to hoist into the high places of the party bureaucracy the spokesmen of a doctrine which menaced the national society with a gigantic and inscrutable upheaval.

What in actual practice these preachings came to mean was not 'revolution' but an abstention or desertion from the conduct of public affairs—the whole existing organization of the State being classified as untouchable and all civic loyalty as reaction. In this spirit, when in the next year elections took place for the councils of the 8000 Italian communes, the National Council of the party called upon voters to put Socialists into office in order that the communes might be made centres for disrupting the bourgeois State. With such a programme on their books, though certainly not in all of their electors' hearts, the party did in fact obtain a majority on some 2000 of the councils. It was as though neither d'Annunzio's faction nor the controlling group of the Socialist party could adjust their minds to the end of the war. The former transferred their combative instincts, and the latter their itch for mutiny and desertion, on to the field of civil affairs.

The Socialist party, despite its huge electoral strength, and its still unsnapped links with the major trade union organization, being in so equivocal a situation, much hope and sympathy, even from those not hitherto well disposed to the Church as a political power, were attracted to the party which, though not officially a Church party, and not requiring religious orthodoxy from its members, was obviously in practice the fruit of an earnest and ambitious attempt to acquire power in the State for the realization of Church ideals. This too was a mass party: and it had attached to itself, in a rival nation-wide organization of trade unions, a large party of the working class.

III. THE POPOLARI

Early in November 1919 a high dignitary at the Vatican confirmed that all ecclesiastical bans upon the participation of practising Catholics in the politics of the Kingdom of Italy had been withdrawn. It was the final stage in a series of acts by which the Popes had renounced their nineteenth-century claims against the 'Piedmontese usurper' of their sovereignty, and it opened the way to a wholly unembarrassed competition at the polls of the new Catholic Popular Party, in the name of a programme which had been issued to the nation some months earlier.

As has been seen in the account of Giolitti's system of government, this was by no means the first case of a 'Catholic vote', or even of an organized Catholic electoral participation in the affairs of the Kingdom of Italy. Giolitti's deals with clericalists were powerful instruments in adjusting the composition of the Chamber to his requirements. The Papal bans had, however, restrained clerics and devoted laity from putting their efforts into forming a political party or parties with a definite intention to gain political control through the Chamber of Deputies. Catholic congresses and associations meanwhile brought Catholic thought to bear on the problems of society and the State. Pope Leo XIII, author of the famous encyclical 'Rerum Novarum', pressed problems of industrial organization and social structure into the forefront of their attention before the old century was out. A network of ecclesiastical friendly societies and banks spread across the country in the prosperous first decade of the new century, rivalling the organizations of the Socialists. At moments of political crisis Catholics revealed their division into a high conservative class, inheritor of Neapolitan and Austrian traditions of local paternalism, sullenly disposed to the Italian State in itself; a realistic class deeply enmeshed in things as they were, and keen to influence the State in the Church's own material interests—of this class Giolitti made an astute use; and finally a class approximating in their bold advocacy of unsettling changes to the syndicalists, the revolutionary Socialists, and the other groups who gave a character of impatient aspiration to the young generation of Giolitti's Italy. The intellectual complexion of these Catholic 'modernists' at the height of Giolitti's domination has already been considered.

The initiative in the creation of the Popular party in 1919 sprang from the last-named class after, however, it had shed that fringe of theological Modernists who attempted, during the Pontificate of Pius XII, to reinterpret the Church creeds as venerable symbols of social mysticism. The leader of these luckless Modernists, Don Romolo Murri, became, significantly, an early adherent of the Fascist movement. It was left to Don Luigi Sturzo, a brilliant but level-headed Sicilian priest of sure theological orthodoxy, to create, from elements matured in a great variety of local and specialized Catholic organizations, a party which simultaneously with Socialism's apparent triumph stood as the stoutest barrier against the sort of social upheaval which the fanatics of the Left contemplated. At the same time the Popular party, in the moment of national expectation of a far-reaching social readjustment, issued its own challenge to property and privilege: a limited and concrete challenge in the name of landless or smallholding peasants crying out for the additional acres of which, in the trenches, they had received a promise from the most conservative of premiers, Salandra, and in the name of industrial workers who demanded not a total transformation, but an amelioration by orderly stages, of the productive organization of Italy.

If the 156 Socialist deputies, intimidated by the small extremist bureaucracy of their party, refused to give Nitti the moderate measure of support which would have given a solid background to his Government, Nitti on his part would not meet the odd hundred of Populars on their own ground. The Populars immediately set about promoting a land reform on a grand scale to satisfy their own rural followers, grouped mainly in Venetia and in the rich agricultural regions of the Po Valley and North Central Italy.

The Popular party legislative programme differed from the Socialist, in 1919, by the important fact that it sought to catch up with, and to regularize, a revolution which was already taking place.

Accepting literally the promises held out by Salandra and other statesmen during the war, peasants took possession of derelict or under-worked land, sometimes consecrating the act with a religious procession led by the clergy. The Nitti Government legitimized these seizures by decree: but an organic land reform law, for which proposals were put forward by the Popular party, was not placed on the statute book.

The Socialists fiercely combated the Popular party even where the agrarian agitations of the latter took a form which the landowners termed 'White Bolshevism'. Its activities, however closely parallel in practice with those of the Socialists, were denounced by the latter as a breaking of the unity of the working-class front. In this view Nitti appeared to concur. Though the Socialists gave him such short shrift, and treated his Government as though it were set upon demolishing the ambitions of their movement, Nitti behaved towards them with the respect due to the predestined masters of to-morrow. He eschewed any confidences with the Populars which would have brought them into a position of superior authority, and so further antagonized the Socialists.

Nor, indeed, as a party of State upon which to build a demo-cratic Government of national complexion were the Populars exempt from the defect of the Socialists. They too, though quite unaggressively, forswore the cause of the war and claimed credit for their innocence of what Pope Benedict XV, to the deep disappointment of all those Italians who attributed a moral meaning to the world conflict, had called, in an encyclical of 1917, 'this useless slaughter'. Against the 'black crows', too, the devotees of Fiume vented irritation, and never wholly extinct phobias about the rule of the cassock lived a new life in the scurrilous journalism of 1920.

It was none the less in sharp rivalry with the Socialists, whom they held to be enjoying undue favour and indulgence from Nitti, that the Popular party finally resolved to deliver an attack on the Premier—not before he had twice attempted to readjust matters by reshuffling the offices of his Cabinet to their advantage. Nitti was now highly vulnerable in and outside Parliament. At Fiume, thousands of Italian combatants defied the legal Government. The Royal Guard, associated with his name, were viewed with bitter dislike by the people at large. Ex-combatants, egged on by d'Annunzio, regarded him as the author of all disrespect for their rights, and an amnesty for war deserters, though in reality those gaining by it had been in the vast majority of cases little worse than passive participants in military disorganization, was made the subject of ferocious insults. In Parliament the Populars easily found allies among the nondescript deputies of the old groups, and forced Nitti out of office shortly before midsummer of the second post-war year. The feeling that an experiment had been tried and had failed was widespread, and it was in an anguish of search for political capacity that the call went up for Giolitti to forget the past and to exercise once again the arts which had for so long kept conflicts and contradictions within bounds.

IV. THE REIGN OF A GHOST

Nitti's year of government concluded under forbidding auspices. Fiume's lawless carnival still mocked official Rome and compromised Italy in the eyes of Europe; harvest failure, coinciding with cessation of Allied economic aid, had caused the resort to huge public subsidies for wheat imports, throwing back the Budget into a deficitary condition as serious as in war-time; self-help brigades were springing up in the countryside among the landowners to resist the 'squatting' of returned soldiers and landless peasants; the large new heavy industry, born of the war, was clamouring for State aid as an alternative to a collapse which would involve powerful banking interests; and in face of all this the Socialist party, 'rising sun of the future', refused to diagnose a gathering economic crisis in any other terms than those of a just retribution for the folly of the war, which capitalists and their minion-politicians must expiate.

A year after the Peace Conference, what remained of hope or trust in an era of progress about to inaugurate itself almost automatically as the natural consequence of Italy's national maturity gained during the war? The fact of the constitution of great mass parties, commanding many millions of votes, though the chief of these spurned or feared the attainment of power through Parliament: the fact of men in all the parties, of high public prestige and renown, still pointing towards a policy of democratic understanding at home and abroad—these remained. But the threat from Socialist absenteeism on the one hand, from counter-revolutionary anarchy on the other, had now altogether overshadowed the hope of democratic development. In 1919 the search had been for a Government which could make the best of the new democratic forces: in 1920 the search was for one which could solve day-to-day problems by any means at all. In these circumstances a call went up for the return of the greatest equilibrist of modern Italian history—for Giovanni Giolitti: and the Piedmontese veteran, who had confidently awaited this day since his pitiable departure from Rome just seven years earlier, stepped back, erect and cheerful, into the scene. He was seventy-eight years old and ready to regard what had happened since his seventieth year as an unusually long interruption in his trusteeship.

He faced with composure the transformation of the balance of groups and parties in the elective chamber for which he had himself prepared the way by the extension of the suffrage in 1912. He had expected and desired a large Socialist representation, and in the Catholic Popular party he saw but a larger edition of the clericalist groups with which he had brought off many a deal. He summed up with frigid calculation the political standing and resources of the man who had incited crowds to assassinate him five years earlier—of Gabriele d'Annunzio, 'Commandant' of Fiume—and made plans to propitiate the ex-interventionists by a retrospective approval of the war. A programme of indulgence and appeasement framed itself with natural ease in his experienced mind. The serious breach in continuity which he had to repair lay not on the surface of politics, where principles and aspirations are openly proclaimed, but in the offices where the threads of administrative control converge. Here the Prefects and the Ministerial Directors willingly sought once more the touch of the hand which before the last turbulent quinquennium had used them as the instruments of its concealed and easy-going but in the last resort efficacious control of national affairs. The problems were grave, but the mechanism for solving them seemed in one sense actually to have been simplified, since Giolitti last held office. Parliament, for all its turbulence, was interfering less in the actual conduct of affairs than ever before. 'Look back to 1920, or to 1915,' wrote Amendola, a , scrupulous judge of parliamentary affairs, in a retrospect composed a year or two later. 'You will notice that Parliament has been engaged exclusively on political discussions in the narrowest sense— discussions which tested out the ability of the Government to command a majority. The work of legislation in detail has been relegated wholly to Ministers and Civil Servants.' During the war, in fact, the Governmental decree had been the sole method of legislation: and that practice was continued by Nitti in the impossibility of gaining the attention of the excited

Parliament of 1919 for law-making. The task facing Giolitti in 1920 was that of holding together a majority in Parliament to legitimize his Government by expressions of confidence. As long as votes of no-confidence could be staved off, the Government's administrative innovations could proceed unchallenged. The bureaucratic resolution of current problems would have to provide sufficient satisfactions to purchase the support of an adequate proportion of the members of Parliament, and Government stability could thus be won afresh from day to day.

It could be won in that way providing only that satisfactions commensurate with the demands of the parties could be provided without unleashing a more intense civil struggle than Giolitti's methods would enable him to handle. In fact, each problem had its explosive implications. The minimum satisfactions demanded of him from various sides included the elimination of the unprecedented breach of national discipline at Fiume—a matter which touched the ex-combatants and in particular the *Arditi* on the raw; a financial restoration to stave off incipient inflationary panic—and this meant coping with the bread-subsidy question; and some arbitrament to remove the incubus of an impending collapse of the war-engendered mushroom industries of the north. The last-named of these critical issues was the first to face Giolitti with grim difficulties. The European post-war boom was now giving way to a general trade crisis: the North Italian heavy industry denounced its wage agreements, and there opened, in September, the brief but dramatic episode of the major 'occupation of the factories'—major in distinction to similar events on a smaller scale the year before.

Ignoring a lock-out proclaimed by the engineering employers' unions, factory workers under direction of their own union, hesitatingly supported by the Socialist party organs, forced access to 280 engineering works in Milan in August 1920, and proceeded to carry on production as far as the limitation of supplies and the non-co-operation of the higher technical staff admitted. The movement extended to other localities and to affiliated industries until it affected about half a million workers. Giolitti regarded this formidable organized defiance of property rights as the recurrence of a situation well known to him. In his *Memoirs* he wrote: 'I saw in the occupation of the factories merely the repetition, in other forms and circumstances, of the general strike of 1904 which had caused such terrors but

soon manifested its impotence.' The diagnosis, on the strength
of which Giolitti held the public forces entirely aloof from the
dispute, was correct in one respect. The Socialist trade unions
looked to their political party to back up this first major revolutionary initiative in the industrial sphere with a bold political
advance. In the first flush of the impression made by the
occupation there were, it seems, overtures to Filippo Turati and
to the trade union leaders, from persons of high authority in
the world of 'bourgeois' politics, promising them an orderly
acquiescence on the part of liberal and industrialist circles if a
Socialist Government were to take office to clear up the deadlock.
But the prevailing faction of the party repelled all such suggestions
with reaffirmations of their contempt for democratic method.
The trade unions, accordingly, reached an agreement to evacuate
the factories at the end of the eighth week, after gaining from
Giolitti a promise of legislation to give labour a share in the
financial control of the engineering concerns.

So far Giolitti was justified : but the easy evaporation of the
one and only great revolutionary step attempted under Socialist
auspices had repercussions which sapped his system at its basis.
The surmounting of this crisis in such undramatic fashion—
though some episodes of violence committed against managerial
staffs were exploited in lurid style by the nationalist Press—gave
a great fillip to what now, for the first time, became a perceptible
element in Italian politics : a movement of confident anti-
Socialist resistance and reaction on the part of the industrialists
and their financial backers.

If Giolitti viewed the occupation of the factories as a variation
upon the events of 1904, the Socialists, he must have expected,
would review their affairs in chastened mood, and perceive the
wisdom and necessity of seeking workaday advantages in collaboration with the Government. The propertied classes,
recovering from their fright, should also prove amenable to
management and to bargaining.

On neither side did events take this pattern.

Elections for the local councils of Italy's 8000 communes took
place during the closing stages of the factory crisis. The National
Council of the Socialist party framed the party's policy in the
following terms :

'General tactical reasons must persuade the party, as a means
towards ensuring the triumph of the revolution of expropriation,
to capture the greatest number of the existing organs of power,

with a view to replacing them, when the moment comes, by communistic organs.

'The control of local bodies will be a means for the party to prosecute its struggle against the State (*la lotta anti-statale*) by conducting administration upon exclusively proletarian lines including the imposition of taxes without regard to the limits set by the State on the powers of local bodies.'

The admonition was treated with scorn by many of the local Socialist groups who approached their town and village problems in a sober and realistic spirit. In fact, the local elections marked a high tide of support for the party in the country at large: Socialist control was established in over 2000 of the communes, and in nearly half of the Provincial Councils (superior regional bodies of less real importance than the former). There were however communes in which the Socialist administrations proceeded to break off relations with the State. What was in the light of events even more important, there were communes where influential property-owners, now beginning to see their way beyond recent counsels of resignation, defied the Socialist communes.

It was not only against the Socialists, but also against the Catholic Populars, in the regions where these last were the spearhead of the peasant land-hunger movement, that the land-owners felt the moment to be ripe for resistance and counter-offensive against revolutionary forces which familiarity, and the inconclusiveness of their agitations, had begun to render contemptible.

This agrarian reaction was as yet something quite distinct from the Fascism of Mussolini, nor, at this stage, was there a common field of activity for them. The slender following of Mussolini was an amalgam of old Socialist revolutionaries and of *Arditi* without roots in either the industrialist or the landowning classes. As to the menace of Socialist lawlessness, Mussolini's followers had been the instigators of one of the minor factory 'occupations' (in 1919): and in the later and major occupations his paper, the *Popolo d'Italia*, gave to the workmen a support tempered, or spiced, by bitter girding against the Socialist party leaders. Even so, this girding was on the level of personal polemics, harking back perpetually to the feuds of the war; not on the level of social and economic policy. The agrarian reaction, which in Italy as in other countries equipped itself with 'white guards' in 1920 to withstand the threat of socialism and of peasant-pietism against the security of land property, grew up unhelped by the Mussolinian Fascism whose quarrel with the Socialists still bore the strong mark of an internal rivalry between factions of social revolutionaries. The white guards of the agrarians coincided, on the other hand, in great degree with the upper elements in d'Annunzio's 'legions' at Fiume: it was the eclipse of d'Annunzio and the profit which Mussolini drew from the emotional vacancy so created which drew together these distinct currents into the common stream of the Fascism of 1922. In the autumn of 1920, however, d'Annunzio was still basking in glory at Fiume, a standing insult to official Rome. To wind up this overt scandal was the next problem which Giolitti had perforce to cope with.

He first propitiated the army and the ex-combatants by a patriotic demonstration in Rome such as had not been seen since the close of the war. On the second anniversary of the armistice, barely five and a half years after his departure from Rome in the character of arch-appeaser of the Central Powers, and principal villain in the eyes of the whole conglomerate war party—indeed less than one year since he himself had inveighed against the 'witless, soulless and impudent minority which dragged Italy into war against her will'—Giolitti, side by side with King Victor Emmanuel and surrounded by the high commanders of the war services, proceeded amid military pageantry to the 'Altar of the Fatherland' in Rome, for the first great celebration of the victory. So strongly, after the confusions and disappointments of 1920, did Giolitti's figure impose itself as that of the one possible pilot, that the old rancours in the political world sent no ripple of protest to disturb the scene. What rankled more with the nationalistic groups than Giolitti's war record was a decision taken by him, shortly after resuming power, to withdraw Italian troops from Albania following a mutiny of regiments indignant at being ordered for garrison work in that scene of vaguely defined Italian aspirations.

In Giolitti, d'Annunzio was confronted by a very different measure of prestige and confidence from that of Nitti a year earlier. Nitti had appeared as the presiding genius of a popular Italy forming itself around two great mass parties which forswore the war, and one of which called for the outlawry of those responsible for bringing it about. The retort from Fiume was insult and ridicule. Giolitti appeared with an aura of irresistible achievement derived from the past, now solely intent upon keeping the

existing forces running in some sort of system of mutual accommodation and supported in that character by the conservative
forces in society and the State.

A fruitless series of parleys, and then a small naval and military
expedition which opened fire upon Fiume and killed a handful
of legionaries, procured the evacuation of the problem-city by
its unique 'Commandant' with ease and rapidity. The clearance
enabled the Italian Foreign Office, in charge of which Giolitti
placed the active and cultured Count Carlo Sforza, to implement
terms which had just been reached with the new neighbour
state of Yugoslavia. The drawing of the frontiers was on the
broad lines long since advocated by Bissolati. The Italian claim
to the Dalmatian coast, based upon Sonnino's Treaty of London,
was dropped in recognition of the changed historical circumstances : Fiume, save for a Slav suburb, became a 'free city'.

There hung over these negotiations, however, the uneasy sense
that it was not the willing policy of a victorious Italy which
reached these terms with its neighbour, but an Italy gasping to
release itself at all costs of all embarrassments at a moment when
its internal cohesion was only just being maintained. The truth
of this impression was shown by the refusal of successive Italian
governments to give effect to the promised neutralization of
Fiume.

An instability such as Italy had experienced in 1920 does not
prolong itself indefinitely : either its causes are overcome, or
their threats take concrete and destructive form.

By the spring of 1921 Italy was no longer in the fever of
expectation which had pervaded her in 1919 as hope tinged
with perplexity, in 1920 as perplexity turning to despair.

The Socialist movement with its aspirations and its phobias
had been the dominant character in the political drama of these
years, felt as such both by its friends and by its enemies. From
the moment of the abortive factory occupations its prestige sank
perceptibly. Rhetoric which had been pardoned as mere
exuberance, and internal divisions which had seemed a product
of vitality, came to be viewed as symptoms of serious degeneration and of ineradicable contradictions in the premisses of the
movement.

In two years of loud Socialist boasts, not a step on the path
towards a political and a social reformation had been taken by
Socialist initiative or under the inspiration of plans shaped by
the mind of Socialism. Yet the political party's influence on

organized labour had been exerted to encourage unlimited wage demands on the theory that an infinite reserve wage fund lay ready to be tapped, were not a great social reformation being obstructed by a reactionary Government. Participation in the Government, on however flattering terms, the party, swayed by its loudest-mouthed wing, had perpetually rejected.

The image of Communist Moscow, of what Lenin had achieved by a ruthless exploitation of the sickness and despair of war, bursting the bonds which the belligerent State had clamped on the suffering people, haunted the Italian Socialist movement. But its deep roots in a purely Italian past, its association with a trade-union movement of cautious disposition, and with a great system of co-operative enterprise well integrated in the existing state of society, inhibited the Socialists from assuming the totally insurrectionary character which Moscow demanded. The contradictions within the party became so intolerable that in January 1921 the 'pure' Communists split away to form their own organization. Even this brought no coherence to the main block which inherited the continuity of the party. For within it an anti-democratic and theoretically violent section still prevailed over the democratic and constitutional wing, until after many agonies the latter, in 1922, in turn broke away to form that 'Unitary Socialist Party' of which Matteotti became the secretary, and to which, when the Fascists were at the very threshold of power, the trade unions, sick of an association which had led them through three years of misadventures and frustrations, too late transferred their allegiance.

The Popular party, though no obedient chorus of unanimous democrats, had stood the wear of two years' peace much better, and its trade-union organization had enrolled a million workers, bidding fair to rival the numbers of the socialistic confederation.

It aroused, however, fierce antipathies. It was not merely that in certain regions this party's authority stood behind the claim of peasants to lands from which the agrarians were with increasing aggressiveness now driving them: nor that, on the other side, it defended the huge economic interests of the Church and of a well-known complex of Catholic banking organizations. Its relations to indispensable allies and colleagues of radical and liberal tendency were habitually strained. In the narrowly political field its alert and brilliant political secretary, Don Sturzo, who could be neither deputy nor minister on account of his clerical cloth, took the fullest advantage of the party's situation as the most numerous coherent group in the Chamber. The existence of Don Sturzo, who had strong views on policy and a large measure of power to threaten the Government with adverse combinations in the Chamber, revealed with painful clearness that the basis of Giolitti's power, his command of the confidence of Parliament, was not in the least secure.

In these circumstances Giolitti prepared for general elections.

With the change to proportional representation the methods of electoral preparation which Giolitti had brought to such perfection in the first decade of the twentieth century had necessarily to be revised, but within the new limitations they were elaborately conceived and executed.

Giolitti presented himself at the head of an electoral 'block' in which were ranged the greater part of the 'liberal' groups, the Nationalists, the 'agrarians' (who had now formed a party to defend property rights)—and finally, their first serious approach to electoral politics, Mussolini's Fascists. This block, the model for which had already been formed in the municipal elections a year earlier, was to stand against the Socialist and the Communist party, and against the Populars. Careful bargains preceded the acceptance of candidates for the block, and as in Giolitti's palmiest pre-war days the prefects' offices were headquarters for the arrangements.

It had always been Giolitti's practice to make an economical use of violence and chicanery in the conduct of the elections. He desired no more than an adequate measure of support in his parliaments, which therefore consisted of those friendly to him who could be won without resort to such methods; a necessary supplement of those supporters for whose return the dubious arts had to be called into play; and finally his opponents whose exclusion had been unnecessary, and would have entailed at least a disproportionate deployment of force.

The prevention of free speech, the breaking up of meetings, the physical removal of voters from the booths, the disappearance of voting papers were no novelty in the remote south of Italy where the necessary supplement for Giolitti's majorities had always to be found. The process was, on the contrary, new to the north, and it was by way of an experiment in its possibilities in the populous regions of Socialist and Catholic democratic prevalence that Giolitti accepted, in 1921, the collaboration of Mussolini's Fascists in his national block. 'They are our black-

and-tans,' he complacently told a high British official who
questioned him on these new political allies.

The mass terrorism of the subsequent elections, those held in
1924 under the aegis of Mussolini himself, greatly outclassed the
rehearsal played out in 1921. These last Giolittian elections,
however, were considered memorable at the time. 'They will
remain an unparalleled example of organized violence and
scoundrelism,' wrote Mario Missiroli, a brilliant observer—
untruthfully as regards the prophecy.

The result, however, cheated Giolitti of his hopes and proved
that his return to office could bear no character—in the new
circumstances—but that of a temporary expedient. All the
intrigue and the force that the Governmental block brought to
bear did not avail to bring back into the Chamber a Giolittian
majority. The Popular group returned notably reinforced, with
106 deputies: the Socialist party (despite the defection of the
Communists who gained 13 seats) again returned with much
the largest representation—122 members. Five groups of forty
to a dozen members each represented the shades of support—
from Nationalists at one end to Social Reformers at the other
end—among which the Premier must play for his Ministry and
his support if, as was to be presumed, the Socialists refused to
share in responsibility, and the Populars made their help conditional upon a share in initiative which would have ruined
Giolitti's conception of government.

In fact, Giolitti had no choice but to attempt an accommodation with the latter. Representatives of the Catholic party once
more entered his Government. An educational reform, taking
serious account of their religious aspirations, had already been
accepted by the Government in the form of a Bill proposed by
the illustrious philosopher Benedetto Croce, as Minister of
Education—no orthodox Catholic, but a fervent Italian who,
from a renewal of the imprint of Christian tradition upon the
teaching office of the State, hoped to see a healing of the deep
wound inherited from the generation which constructed the
Italian State against the anathemas of the Church. This
concession had already strained to the uttermost the patience of
indispensable supporters of Giolitti among the secular-minded
groups. But the Populars also opposed elements in Giolitti's
programme of financial reform which would have affected the
material interests of the Church. Giolitti renounced the struggle
in July 1921. His methods had failed, and his prestige with them.

The Governmental situation in the following year was of an intricacy eluding detailed description. In brief, its character was that of an attempt by Giolittian lieutenants, one of them a man of courage and character, Bonomi, the other a cheerful and ingenuous drifter, Facta, to hold together Parliamentary majorities from elements purchased by *ad hoc* concessions: the greatest of all the concessions insisted upon by the Populars being the permanent withdrawal of Giolitti himself from the Prime Minister's post.

The Governmental situation bore a progressively diminishing resemblance to the situation in the nation at large. Here there was a marked economic improvement, a financial recovery symbolized by the cessation of State-subsidized grain supplies, a decline in labour disputes, a regularization of Italy's diplomatic relations to the wider world. It might seem that the affairs of a nation in this condition of recuperation no longer called, as in 1919 they so obviously did, for energetic and inspiring leadership.

But the vacuum set up by the failure of democratic leadership in 1919 had sounded an alarm which did not stop ringing merely because the immediate problems had become simplified. A space had been opened which no emanation from the discredited Parliament was now going to fill.

The system of government culminating in Giolitti's régime had given way in 1915 before the sudden combination of many forces each of which from its own standpoint proclaimed: 'This dingy engine is not the expression of the Italian nation united, in the Risorgimento, for the revival of ancient dignities'—or, as others preferred to put it, 'for the exemplification of a new ideal of humanity.'

The promise of a dawn had failed to come down to earth in the cause of a strong democracy; a return to Giolittianism had proved impossible. But something 'new' was going to happen, and our concluding chapter briefly outlines the answer, ironically ambiguous, given by history to Italy's prayer.

CHAPTER TWELVE

MUSSOLINI FINDS HIS WAY

MUSSOLINI'S FASCISM.—The man. The movement. The circumstances.

His alternative paths to power: Parliamentary manœuvre, or armed insurrection?

His ambition for leadership above party: and how his party set limits upon the ambition.

The Fascist *coup*: a political solution helped out by violence.

Italy and the Liberal Conscience of Europe.

A study of Mussolini's character shows him to possess, harnessed to an insatiable lust for power, a rare variety of potential attitudes. Looking beyond the scope of this book, he is found comfortably at home in the position of a Catholic Conservative reconstructor of Europe (1930) or a proletarian anarchist in international relations (1935). In Italy itself, as head of the Government, he has played the part of the dignified exponent of senatorial prudence (1924): and, without transition, that of the savage instigator of sectarian violence (1925).

From the effective end of the war in 1919 until he became Governor of Italy in 1922 Mussolini explored the possibilities of various attitudes. 'Class collaboration, class struggle, class expropriation,' he said frankly in an election programme for 1919, were methods to be used as and when expedient. His positive programme consisted of little more than the demand for a Republic, and for war to the death, by the men of the Left who had supported the war, against the Socialist party which, in a spirit of reaction, had opposed it. 'A party which was reactionary from 1914 to 1918 cannot have become revolutionary in 1919.' In another utterance of the same time the foes of his aspirations are designated as 'Giolittians, Party Socialists, Clericals.'

A few months later his call is for 'a pact of solidarity between all working men who revolt against the tyranny of the P.U.S.' (United Socialist Party: the initials, bearing an obvious double sense, are an endless stand-by in all Mussolini's polemics of the period).

Here is his declared attitude before the 1921 elections: 'The Socialists had constituted a State within the State. No matter, had it been more liberal, more modern, more genuinely traditional' (*più vicino all'antico* are the words: perhaps a hint of developing admiration for ancient Roman models). 'But as you know it has been even more tyrannical, more illiberal, more conspiratorial than the old state. Our revolution is one which sweeps away the Bolshevik state in the expectation of a later reckoning with the liberal state which will remain.' There is a complaint in this speech of the misunderstanding of Fascist motives by the 'democrats': and an indignant remonstrance against the small Republican party (little more than a local middle-class party in his own region of the Romagna) for opposing a movement so clearly republican as the Fascist.

January 1919 may be taken as the starting-point for Mussolini's post-war adventure in quest of supreme power in Italy. From it dates the breach between Mussolini and the adherents of a democratic peace. Previously his writings and speeches echoed, though not without notes of truculent impatience, the enthusiasm of the democratic groups for the principles of President Wilson. With the sharp repudiation induced by the crisis which arose out of Wilson's mishandling of his appeal to the Italian nation, Mussolini then ranged himself by the side of d'Annunzio in bitter hostility to the 'peace of renunciation': and, by association of sympathies, in a categorical condemnation of the official Rome of Nitti. All the while, his ambition grew.

The moment coincided with an enrichment of Mussolini's following by elements alien from his past. He had been until this a leader of dissident Socialists, including a small but active nucleus of trade unionists, applauded by military and nationalist elements for the contrast of his soundness on the war with the pacifism of the official Socialists. Now he became the journalistic mouthpiece of d'Annunzio and of the demobilized officers, war-hungry adolescents and *Arditi* who made up the conquering legions of Fiume. He rode astride upon the double back of dissident Socialism and of d'Annunzian national paganism, if such a term can cover the spirit of Fiume. 'Here an association of *Arditi*, there an anti-German league: next a Fascio of patriotic action: a popular anti-Bolshevik union: a league of Latin youth: a pro-Fiume or pro-Dalmatian society'—so Gioiacchino Volpe, approved Fascist historian of Fascism, describes the medley of existing groups drawn by Mussolini into his movement in the Fiume period.

The movement was, in its two sides, urban, and to a very

great extent Milanese.   It was as such that Giolitti, when forming his electoral block of 1921, considered its possibilities as
an Italian black-and-tan brigade and adapted it to fulfil in the
northern urban constituencies a function which less sophisticated
mazzieri (clubbed men) had long performed in the obscure
corners of the south.   It does not seem that Giolitti ever attributed
to these henchmen a possible political importance in the future.

The approaches of Giolitti, however, opened a new world of
possibilities to Mussolini.   The rôle of captain of roughs for a
senile semi-dictator, the object of his own lifelong scorn and
invective, was one which he could fulfil for a month or two to
help himself forward to new openings.   Here the turn of events
at Fiume greatly helped him.   In coming to his electoral agreement with Giolitti, Mussolini had deserted d'Annunzio, and
become the object of bitter gibes by the faithful adherents of the
poet.   It was, however, obvious that Mussolini stood in the
stream of national affairs, while d'Annunzio had but grazed
politics as an astounding meteor.   The political heritage of
d'Annunzio reverted to Mussolini, and in the elections in which
Mussolini's movement played the gunmen and clubmen for
Giolitti, the sole serious measure of Governmental success was won
by the Fascists, who entered Parliament, under Mussolini, some
thirty members strong.

It was a wholly new situation for Mussolini, and the exploitation of the contacts into which he could now enter as leader of
a Parliamentary group absorbed his attention.

He approached them as one unburdened by past commitments
or by static prejudices.

In the welter of perplexed intrigue filling the corridors of
Montecitorio at the end of Giolitti's ghost-reign, Mussolini is
found quite at home as a busy parliamentarian.   In Rome,
where the monarchy pursued its unobtrusive routine, enjoying
the unmistakable support of the hierarchy of the army; where
the Vatican calmly calculated for future centuries; where the
proverbial scepticism of the population regarded all revolutionary
talk as politicians' patter, the idea of the syndicalist Republic
tended to wither in the mouth of the speaker.   The soil favoured
other growths.   In the exploitation of coalitions, compromises
and accommodations in which Mussolini exercised himself a
limit was in the first place set only by his own abiding rancours.
Nothing shook his determination that those who had driven him
from the Socialist party in 1915 should incur a recompense of

public humiliation. There were other limits, however, set by the mood and circumstances of his own followers upon whom his future depended. The year and a half of Mussolini's political activity between his election to Parliament and his assumption of the Premiership were spent largely in discovering how far he could go, and where he must stop short, in bargaining with the established Parliamentary leaders, having regard to his dependence upon the 'revolutionaries' of his own movement.

These were not the orderly and homogeneous Fascist militia of later days, but a factious and turbulent miscellany.

It was not by Giolitti alone, and not solely for electoral purposes, that punitive squadrons of Fascists had been engaged to teach discretion to the Socialists, and in lesser degree to the Popular party's organizers and spokesmen. Discovering, with some surprise, that their days were not numbered, that the huge Socialist movement had procured no drastic change in economic organization either by the democratic machinery of Parliament, or by revolutionary methods, the owners of industry and trade had vowed to ensure themselves against such an alarm ever taking serious shape again. Fascism served their politics.

They went further—and in doing so discovered the usefulness of the blackshirts far outside the strictly political field. The trade unions, not merely as repositories of the working-classes' ambition to own the means of production, but as the seed-places of a perennially inconvenient pressure for a more generous deal to those classes, would be better reduced and disarmed. The ambition to wipe out the syndical organizations of the workers was widespread though certainly not universal among employers. It was veiled or modified by a desire to see the workers' interests represented not exclusively by the Socialist and Catholic unions but also by those small dissident unions which represented the syndical side of Fascism, and to which others, of recent and independent origin, had attached themselves. Great industrialists like Agnelli, the creator of the 'Fiat', it should be said, took no such simple view of such a short cut, through violence, to a capitalist paradise. The shopkeepers' animosity was directed against a different branch of Socialist and Catholic activity— against the great co-operative enterprises which, as regards those in Socialist hands, the pre-war régime of Giolitti had financed and encouraged diligently in a successful endeavour to attenuate the revolutionary impulse of the party.

As the menace of a proletarian offensive against property

evaporated, the counter-offensive of the property-owners developed, finding ready instruments in the tens of thousands of
unemployed adventurers left high and dry by demobilization,
and gravitating in a growing mass into the Fascist organization.
The reaction reached its climax in the middle of 1921, and flamed
or flickered on into the next year, while the defending Socialists
and Communists occasionally, but with steadily diminishing spirit
and success, took the counter-offensive. With a totally ineffective
general strike in August 1922 the last shot of militant Socialism
in the towns had been vainly fired.

This urban civil war, however, paled beside the simultaneous
civil war in the most fertile agricultural regions of Italy and in
those cities which flourished as their rural centres. The origins
of this were altogether older and deeper than that in the
towns, with which Mussolinian Fascism was more authentically
connected. Rural reaction too now assumed a Fascist style.

Half of the whole Italian population is directly employed upon
agriculture. All varieties of land tenure are found prevalent in
its different regions, from vast absentee-owners' properties,
adjacent each to each, in the south, to close-packed small holdings
in the north-east and mixed systems in Tuscany.

In some regions of North and Central Italy highly bellicose
situations existed, between owners and peasants, before the war
of 1915. A three-cornered struggle in the Romagna, between
landowners, leasehold farmers and wage-earning farm hands,
found the first and the last at times closely united to subdue the
second. Primitive hatreds found their outlet in these contests
and the economic struggle often overflowed into physical conflicts.
Something has been said, in an earlier chapter, of the celebrated
'Red Week' of Romagna in 1915.

The big landowners had not waited long, in the immediate
post-armistice period, before employing their own means of
violence to withstand the squatting of peasants upon portions of
their estate.

In Sicily, where the large estates were biggest and most
neglected, and where lands were solemnly taken over by villagers
led by their priests and church banners, the reaction did not
need to dub itself 'Fascist'. Except in the single region of
Apulia—a small southern counterpart to the Po Valley in many
respects—Fascism remained a distant report until long after the
March on Rome. Elsewhere the reaction was merely 'agrarian'.

It was among the small holders, some of them ex-combatants

in the war who had profited by State financial support to acquire or to extend their holdings, that the example of 'Fascist' punitive expeditions against the local Socialist organizations, spreading from the towns, caught on as the national power of Socialism visibly declined. There was by early 1921, in the region of Italy between the Po and the Arno, a vast system of organized aggression against these Socialist leagues and co-operatives which —favoured and assisted by Giolitti—had for years dominated the labour market and the produce market. The relation of this agrarian 'Fascism' to Mussolini's earlier following lay partly in the *Arditi* and similar elements, ready to be hired for any enterprise : partly in the common enmity against the Socialist party, though Mussolini's foes were primarily the political leaders, while the agrarians' foes were the bureaucracy of Socialist economic institutions functioning within the laws of the State.

As head of the Fascist parliamentary group, Mussolini suffered no small embarrassment from the agrarian extension of Fascism. His own influence was based upon Milan : the language best known to him was that of the urban factory dispute. The agrarian wing of Fascism, moreover, though its muscular energy lay in small property and its cause was sufficiently popular and proletarian to be drawing whole leagues of Socialist and Catholic peasants into its well-armed orbit, shaded off into landowning conservatism and army tradition, to which the symbol of the monarchy was sacred. For if the big landlords' agrarian defence was prior to and independent of Fascism, yet they too soon welcomed the reinforcements of the blackshirts. Between Mussolini's programme of political advancement as a republican revolutionary, and the leadership of the agrarian movement by wealthy bruisers of the nobility, a sharp tension developed. Thus began an internal struggle within Fascism in which Mussolini was hard put to it to affirm and maintain command over his swollen creation.

The civil war, urban and rural, though not grave enough to impede a perceptible economic recovery, and in general confined to the regions of the Po and the Arno, caused great scandal and discredited the authority of the State in a manner pregnant with infinite dangers, not the less because the officers of the State, still obsessed with the verbal threats of Communism, by the turn of 1921–22 almost everywhere favoured the Fascists. Prefects and mayors in whole regions of northern Italy were soon notoriously trembling before the Fascist gang leaders or were the mere instruments of these. Hundreds of local councils, of Socialist or Popular complexion, had ceased to function. The tolerant official policy of the State towards its subjects of alien race in Trieste, and soon afterwards in the Upper Adige province (South Tyrol), was flouted and reversed by insurrectionary elements who had become the real masters. And yet huge regions of Italy, practically the whole of the southern half of the peninsula, remained untouched by Fascism. Its manifestations barely touched Rome. And the working men of the north, especially of Piedmont, clung stoutly to their trade unions and their Socialist sentiments.

A great chance for national leadership evidently lay open to whoever could promise a pacification. It was in such a conjuncture of opportunities that Mussolini framed plans to ride to power as a national conciliator in case the avenue of fortune should open to him in that way. This avenue, leading through the complexities of political negotiations, seemed altogether more hopeful than the avenue of an armed assault upon the Parliamentary citadel. And yet it was the command of armed legions which gave importance to this otherwise minor Parliamentary chieftain. This dilemma gives a key to the nature of Mussolini's manœuvres precedent to his attainment of power in October 1922. It suggests also the answer to the riddle 'Was it a Revolution?' which long provided Italian controversalists with a subtle theme. The answer can only be an evasive 'Yes and No.' Meanwhile it was to the method of political negotiation that Mussolini addressed himself as his ambitions waxed.

The first stage was to be a treaty of peace between Fascists and Socialists. The next was to be the elimination from Socialism of the political leaders against whom his personal feud ran high: the final deal, in fact, he intended to make with the General Confederation of Labour, separated from its association with the Socialist party. An understanding with the Populars was to complete the triangular basis for an arrangement by which Mussolini would assume something to outward appearance not unlike the mantle of Nitti, with beneath it, however, a coat of mail and an array of daggers and bludgeons, and in his breast a faculty of command unknown to Nitti.

The formalities of the first step were actually accomplished. On August 3, 1921, Mussolini put his name to a document by which the Fascist and Socialist parties pledged themselves to call a halt to violence. At once, however, Mussolini began to feel the limits set to his approaches to supreme power along that avenue. Fascism was not yet his instrument.

A great outcry among the agrarian Fascists ensued, led by tough youngsters whose names stood now for important centres of the Fascist movement in agricultural North Central Italy— Balbo (Ferrara), Grandi (Bologna), Farinacci (Cremona). Mussolini, however, was inflexible on his line of policy. Only by dissociating himself from civil violence carried to ultimate extremes could he hope to attain the national position which a Fascism overrun by recklessly vindictive landowners would not give him. It mattered little to him that the strife flamed up inextinguishably a few weeks later: he had shifted the main responsibility from himself: the wider circles of the nation distinguished him from his bloodthirsty associates.

While Mussolini sought to free himself for an accommodation with the parties of the Left, the new elements of his party had meanwhile drawn exceedingly close to the old Nationalist party, represented in Parliament by a dozen deputies, but with an important dual root in the country: in the heavy industry, and in the universities.

Fascism had grown as a combative organization step by step with the circumstances which have been described. But its programmes and literature did not get far beyond the changeable expressions of doctrine found in Mussolini's own speeches and leading articles until there occurred, with extraordinary speed, a grafting into the Fascist organization, that rapid growth without intelligible design, of the doctrine formulated long since by the Nationalist party, a schematic design which had failed in long years to assemble around itself a body of supporters. Each time that Mussolini veered towards pacification and conciliation with the parties of the Left the Nationalists gave expression to disappointment and dismay. They warmly supported the agrarian and Conservative Fascists in their protest against Mussolini's truce of August 1921.

Modelled upon the '*Action Française*' of Charles Maurras, the Italian Nationalist doctrine had not, of course, been a wholly self-contained phenomenon: correspondences between the doctrine and temperament of the Nationalists and the syndicalist wing of the Socialist party in the pre-1914 period were remarked upon earlier in this book. They then formed an interesting feature of the gathering of political forces from every political quarter against the Giolittian *status quo*.

Basically, Nationalism taught the divinity of the nation as incarnated in the State: the subordination to this divinity of every ethical or economic concept: the natural vocation for leadership of those who embraced this faith. It had also, daringly—in the light of past history—canonized the Savoy monarchy as an incarnation of the Italian nation.

Not only in respect of this last tenet, the formulae of Nationalism represented in many ways the extremest antithesis to those sentiments which were most natural to Mussolini: and if in the course of 1922 Mussolini himself came to adopt them for his own, this was a price paid by him for the cohesion of his party, not without some personal humiliation.

To that wing of Fascism which was strong in muscle, vehemence and emotional rhetoric, the Nationalist doctrine, raising the conduct of the elect above all criticism from human, ethical and economic standpoints, appeared an incomparable revelation of truth. Soon Mussolini was its ardent prophet.

The 'truth' was this: what advantaged Italy was cosmically justified: and the elect, they only, were Italy, whether (as not infrequently happened) they were working hard upon some service to their fellow-men, or (as also happened frequently) indulging their personal instincts under cover of patriotism.

The further struggles of Mussolini with his party; his momentary abandonment of its leadership, in a last show of repugnance against swallowing that ancient bugbear, the monarchy: his obscure and tortuous negotiations in 1922 with Salandra, with Giolitti even, and even with Nitti, cannot be followed up here: nor yet the semi-military episode of the March on Rome with its necessary precedent, a secret agreement with King Victor Emmanuel, and perhaps a still more secret agreement with another prince of the House of Savoy who guaranteed that the army would prefer to follow him if King Victor Emmanuel sought to withstand the 'nation'—that is, Fascism.

These events belong to the story of the seizure and tenure of power by Mussolini's Fascists, a story which has been far more amply illuminated in a great number of English as well as Italian narratives than the rise and fall of the democratic movement which we have attempted to illustrate in broad outline in this book.

Luigi Facta, the last Premier called to office by King Victor Emmanuel as the trustee of the will of the elected Italian Chamber, resigned office on October 27, 1922. It was by this time clear that Mussolini and the Fascists, who had already 'marched on' a large proportion of the towns of Northern Italy, and held whole rural provinces in their sway, would form the backbone of a new rule.

It was not, however, clear to what extent this new rule would violently overthrow Parliament, and repudiate the forms as well as the substance of democracy. There was a precedent, that of May 1915, for merely intimidating Parliament into transferring its allegiance to the favourites of the streets.

The Fascists were themselves racked by dissension as to whether insurrection or intimidation was their purpose. In the event, the proceedings of October 1922 were much nearer to insurrection than those of 1915, but the element of mere intimidation, leading up to a compromise between Mussolini and certain of the Parliamentary cliques, including those of Salandra and Giolitti, still bulked large.

It is enough to emphasize here how Mussolini's conduct in the whole period leading up to the March on Rome ran to the last on parallel lines in two fields. There was the field of leadership of the new squirearchized and nationalistically indoctrinated Fascism with its large unofficial army of hot-blooded youths: and there was the field of political accommodation with the parties represented in Parliamentary Rome and inspiring the great trade unions. From these parties, the representatives of the people, no new and strong democracy had yet sprung: for no leader had been equal to interpreting the balance of forces in terms of a forward-looking programme. But what if a leader disposing of the extraordinary stimulus of a huge armed movement behind him should sting and goad the popular forces of the country into activity? Might he not atone for much brutality by administering an ultimate salutary shock to the overwrought and lethargized parties? That hope alone could account for the support given to Fascism by such a mouthpiece of the aspirations of liberal Italy as Albertini, owner-editor of the *Corriere della Sera.*

Or was that hope a cowardly illusion? Was there necessarily in the nature of the extraordinary powers wielded by the Fascist leader—as simultaneously a politician competing politically with other politicians, and the leader of an armed faction—a poison which must corrupt whatever he touched? Would the taste of arbitrary power, conceded by the nation to the Fascist leader, in sheer weariness of waiting for leadership from the authentic chosen of the people, set up a craving for ever stronger doses of autocratic might?

The tens of thousands of enthusiastic Romans whom the writer saw acclaiming Mussolini as he led the armed blackshirts up the Corso to the Altar of the Italian fatherland on a fine October afternoon in 1922—the ceremonial conclusion of the March on Rome—had for the most part no opinion about the affair beyond: '*E una bella festa.*' The almost unanimous middle classes in shops, banks, churches, universities and newspapers throughout Italy took the optimistic view, and so did the ministers of the various Parliamentary parties to the 'Right' of the official Socialists, who formed almost the whole of the Duce's first Government. For this, just like the post-war governments of the other premiers, was composed of members of the various Parliamentary parties, excluding only the Socialists who had up to that moment always voluntarily excluded themselves.

The contrary and pessimistic view was taken by a small remnant of severe doctrinaires in the political parties: by certain sparse and solitary—though sometimes famous—intellectuals: by cowed factory-workers: and by the liberal conscience of Europe. Liberal Europe watched with all the more dismay the evolution of Italy, in the ensuing twenty years, because great Italians had taught her to see in the unification of Italy, three-quarters of a century earlier, the promise of a great nation vowed to virtue and gentleness.

After the dulled and tarnished epoch of Italian politics which followed upon the unification, Italy emerging as a victorious power by the side of the democratic nations appeared to be ripe for the humanizing and liberalizing function in Europe which the prophets of Italian nationhood, casting their minds forward, had always assigned to her.

But it was necessary first for certain ancient poisons to work themselves out in adventures, internal and external, which were to bring the new great nation, favoured offspring of liberal Europe, to the edge of moral and physical disaster.

TABLEAU OF FASCISM'S CAREER IN POWER

1922–24. Coalition Government headed by Mussolini conducts affairs with the co-operation of the *Popolari* and of democratic groups till 1923. Full powers to govern by decree accorded by Parliament by 306 to 106 votes. Opposition parties and Press, Socialist and Popular trade unions, tolerated in theory; in practice, subject to sporadic violence. Strikes forbidden. Economic individualism proclaimed by Mussolini: buoyant business recovery.

Non-Fascist elements in coalition supported by Conservative Fascists demand disbandment of Fascist armed bands and abolition of all Fascist usurpations of powers of the State. But Mussolini embodies Militia as State force and reinforces organization of Fascist party as 'State within the State'. Extensive illegalities continue.

1923. Corfu. Mussolini bombards Greeks in Corfu, defying League of Nations, till warned off by British fleet.

1924. Mussolini imposes electoral reform giving two-thirds Parliamentary majority automatically to any electoral list getting the relatively largest number of votes throughout the country. Mussolini's coalition qualifies for this.

Murder of constitutional Socialist M.P. Matteotti with complicity of high Fascist leader. Anti-Fascist members boycott Parliament and agitate throughout the country, forming '*Aventine*' (extra-parliamentary) opposition. Non-Fascist members of Mussolini's coalition withdraw and form new Parliamentary opposition.

1925. Italy joins Britain as guarantor of Locarno Treaty.

1925–26. January 3. Mussolini proclaims end of tolerance of anti-Fascism. Within a few months anti-Fascist Press disappears, parties dissolved, Freemasons forbidden, professional and soldiers' organizations taken over by the State, Fascist trade unions given the exclusive right of negotiating with employers on wages and conditions. 'Totalitarian State' theory proclaimed. Repeated attempts on Mussolini's life. Blood-bath in Florence. Special tribunal instituted for trial of political offenders by Fascist officers. Liberal leader Amendola dies from club injuries.

1926–29. Mussolini orders deflation to stop lira depreciation. Severe business crisis, ending with State control of banks and concentration of private industries under State direction. Individualist economics give way to State control. General wage-cuts repeatedly ordered by Mussolini over whole industrial field.

1929. Lateran Treaty: Mussolini cedes Vatican sovereignty and financial compensations to Pope. Pope abandons protests against 'usurpations' of House of Savoy. He rejects Pope's claim that Church is the educator of youth, forcing dissolution of Catholic boy scouts and withdrawal of 'Catholic Action' from secular educational field.

1932. Mussolini supports Dolfuss Catholic dictatorship in Austria. In rivalry with France seeks to group Danubian countries behind Italy.

1934. After frigid meeting with Hitler, unleashes Press against Nazis for their Austrian policy. Sends army corps to Brenner following Dolfuss murder.

1935. (January) Agreement with Laval for Italo-French *entente*. (April) Anglo-Franco-Italian agreement at Stresa. (September) Mussolini launches war in Abyssinia. Promises Italians that Sanctions will never be forgotten. Gives watchword 'Proletarian Italy, arise!'

1936. He takes title 'Founder of the Empire'.

1936–39. Italian 'volunteers' fight in Spain. Rosselli brothers, leading anti-Fascist *émigrés*, murdered in France.

1937. Mussolini fêted in Germany.

1938. Fascism proclaims conversion to anti-Semitism.

1939. (May) 'Pact of Steel' between Italy and Germany. Mussolini announces 'non-belligerence'. Ciano reveals that Germany had promised there would be no war till 1942–44.

1940. Mussolini declares war against Britain and France. (October) Invades Greece. Graziani's Egyptian invasion army routed.

1941. Loss of the East African Empire.

1942. Italy occupies French Riviera, Savoy and Corsica.

1943. Loss of Libya.

Mussolini dismisses his whole Cabinet, the Fascist party secretary and vice-secretaries, many leading prefects. He hands over the police for the first time to a Fascist chief, and announces that it will be rearmed.

Changes in the military and naval commands.

1943. Special civil commissions appointed in Sicily and Sardinia. With fall of Tunis and Bizerta all North Africa is an invasion base against Italy.

July 10. Allies invade Sicily.

July 25. MUSSOLINI OVERTHROWN.

POSTSCRIPT

SOME practical inferences from the interpretation of the Fascist episode in Italian history which underlies the narrative of this book have been drawn in the introductory chapter on 'Britain and the Italian Prospect.' A word will be added here to link our examination of the past with our glimpse into the future.

The union of Italy, the joint result of many currents of endeavour, ambition, and imagination, assumed in 1859, and thereafter retained, the form of a tightly centralized monarchy of which the laws and institutions, as well as the dynasty and the army, were a derivation from the small state of Piedmont, rapidly and rudely thrust upon Italy as a whole. The motives of discontent which kept this kingdom in ferment through several generations were inherited from those regional forces and those ethical and social movements which played a necessary part in producing the union, but were hastily overborne at the moment when the union took shape. The deeper content of the urge towards a democratic renovation and reformation, of which the frustration opened the way to the Fascist despotism, was a claim by those forces and movements to a rightful place in the state which they had jointly created.

The Fascist despotism, of which few of the original Fascists foresaw or would have welcomed the ultimate shape, may now appear as an extreme development of the centralized power which from the beginning the bolder and freer intelligences of Italy had striven to place under the restraint of organized public opinion.

Little of the sober and realistic spirit which was the justification of the hegemony of Piedmont had survived in the governing class between the two world wars, and the Savoy monarchy itself had lapsed into impotence. The centralized power, intensified almost out of recognition, had been grasped by other hands, though with the complicity of the Savoy dynasty. For the disaster which has overtaken Italy through the irresponsible adventures of the new despotism some Italians seek a remedy in a return to the earlier and milder forms of the centralized monarchy. But if the diagnosis of this book is a just one, the regional and social forces of Italy will now clamour and agitate for a much more radical reform. They will not recognize in a return to the outworn forms of 1915 a remedy for the exasperation of those forms in the following three decades.

The Englishman's task is not to interfere with future Italian developments, but to judge them realistically and, by making clear to the Italian nation our own standpoint in regard to matters of necessary joint import to the two nations, to stimulate the Italians to clear their own minds.

NOTES ON SOURCES AND LITERATURE

As indicated in the introduction this book arises primarily out of discussions with Italians during the two decades between the wars on the origins of the Fascist 'Revolution'. Discretion forbids the mention of individual Italians to whom I am beholden. They include victims of Mussolini's police rule, political exiles, and personages of the Fascist régime, including Cabinet ministers. Over many years I obtained much help from the views of other British journalists of long experience in Italy, including the late Sir William McClure, Mr V. Cunard and Mr P. Cremona, all of *The Times*, Mr William Miller and Mr Ion Munro of the *Morning Post*, Miss B. Baskerville of the *Daily Telegraph* and Sylvia Saunders (now Sprigge) of the *Manchester Guardian*. The following is not a bibliography but a brief record of the books, almost wholly Italian, which have assisted my inquiries. Each book is mentioned once only under the heading of the first chapter to which its subject has relevance.

CHAPTER ONE

For the general history of Italy a reliable compendium is the *Sommario* of L. Salvatorelli (Turin, 1938).

The same author's *Pensiero Politico Italiano dal 1700 al 1870* (Turin, 1935) gives a good purview of the intellectual origins of the nineteenth-century movements in Italy. The general background for these movements lies in the works and correspondence of Mazzini, Gioberti, Cavour, Garibaldi and Cattaneo.

Some interpretative modern volumes:

G. Salvemini, *Mazzini* (Rome, 1920).

Alessandro Levi, *Il Positivismo Politico di Carlo Cattaneo* (Bari, 1928).

P. Gobetti, *Risorgimento senza Eroi* (Turin, 1923).

G. de Ruggero, *Storia del Liberalismo Europeo* (Bari, 1925).

G. F. H. Berkeley, *Italy in the Making* (3 vols. Cambridge, 1932–40).

G. Gigli, *Il Congresso di Vienna* (Florence, 1938).

F. Quintavalle, *Storia dell' Unità Italiana* (Milan, 1925).

CHAPTER TWO

For general Italian conditions in the eighteen-seventies I have found a main background in the *Inchiesta agraria e sulle condizioni delle classe agricole*, the celebrated State inquiry into the land presided over by Count Jacini, Rome, 1881.

The standard, and rival, modern political interpretations of the whole period from 1860 to 1915 are Benedetto Croce, *Storia d'Italia* (Bari, 1928); G. Volpe, *L'Italia in Cammino* (Milan, 1928).

E. Tagliacozzo, *Voci di realismo politico dopo il 1870* (Bari, 1937), recalls forgotten contemporary criticisms of the Cavourian settlement of Italy.

Comparison of Depretis, Crispi and Giolitti: L. Giusso, *Le dittature democratiche in Italia* (Rome, 1928); M. Hentze, *Pre-Fascist Italy* (London, 1939).

On economic development: R. Morandi, *Storia della Grande Industria in Italia* (Bari, 1931); G. Fraenkel, *Storia di una Nazione Proletaria* (Florence, 1938).

CHAPTER THREE

For the problems of the south in the Crispi period: G. Fortunato, *Il Mezzogiorno e lo Stato Italiano* (2 vols. Florence, 1921).

A contemporary British view of Crispi's Italy: C. Martel, *Military Italy* (London, 1884).

A recent interpretation of Crispi: G. Ardau, *Francesco Crispi* (Milan, 1938).

The Adua disaster recalled by a survivor: C. G. Parini, *Adua* (Turin, 1926).

CHAPTER FOUR

Giovanni Giolitti, *Memorie della mia Vita* (2 vols. Milan, 1922).
Luigi Lodi, *25 Anni di Vita Parlamentare* (Florence, 1923).
A classical English survey of Giolitti's Italy: B. King and T.
Okey, *Italy To-day* (London, 1901; 2nd enlarged edition, 1909).
Gaetano Salvemini, *Il Governo della Mala Vita* (Reprint, Florence,
1920). (The classical exposure of Giolitti's methods.)

CHAPTER FIVE

For social analysis and history of Italian Socialism: Robert
Michels, *Sozialismus in Italien* (Munich, 1925); Arturo Salacci,
Il Crespucolo del Socialismo (Milan, 1929).
For the Nationalist movement: E. Corradini, *Discorsi Politici*
(Florence, 1924); G. Papini and G. Prezzolini, *Il Nazionalismo*
(Rome, 1911).
For Catholic Modernism: G. Prezzolini, *Il Cattolicismo Rosso*
(Naples, 1908).
For the Idealist movement: Benedetto Croce, *Coltura e Vita
Morale* (Bari, 1926), also *La Letteratura della Nuova Italia* (Bari,
5 vols.) and other works; G. Gentile, *Educazione e Scuola Laica*
(Florence), also *Discorsi di Religione* (Florence, 1920).
On d'Annunzio: G. Borgese *Gabriele d'Annunzio* (1909, re-
printed, Milan, 1932), also B. Croce *G. d'Annunzio* (1904).

CHAPTER SIX

For Mussolini before 1914: G. Megaro, *Mussolini in the Making*
(London, 1938)—a probing inquiry with abundant documenta-
tion; M. Sarfatti, *Dux* (Milan, 1927); I. de Begnac, *Vita di
Mussolini* (Milan 1936-40. 3 vols.).
Italy's economics in 1914: F. Nitti, *Il Capitale Straniero in
Italia* (Bari, 1915).
British views of Italy in 1912: R. Bagot, *The Italians of To-day*
(Tauchnitz, 1912); F. McCullagh, *Italy's War for the Desert*
(London, 1912).

CHAPTERS SEVEN AND EIGHT

A Salandra, *La Neutralità Italiana* (Milan, 1928).
For the intellectual atmosphere: G. A. Borgese, *Italia e Germania*
(Milan, 1915).
Italy's military rôle: H. Wendt, *Der Italienische Kriegschauplatz
in Europäischen Konflikten* (Berlin, 1936).

CHAPTER NINE

Descriptions of Italy at war:

A. Tosti, *La Guerra Italo Austriaca* (Milan, 1938).
G. M. Trevelyan, *Scenes from Italy's War* (London, 1919).
H. Charriaut and Amici Grossi, *L'Italie en guerre* (Paris, 1916).
Jacques Bainville, *Italy and the War* (London, 916).

Caporetto and after:

Colonel G. Conquet, *Caporetto* (Paris, 1936).
N. Papafava, *Da Caporetto a Vittorio Veneto* (Turin, 1925).
G. Prezzolini, *Caporetto* (Rome, 1919) and *Vittorio Veneto* (Rome, 1920).

The war of ideas:

B. Croce, *Pagine sulla Guerra* (Bari).

The democratic doctrine of war:

G. Salvemini, *Dal Patto di Londra alla Pace di Roma* (Turin, 1925).
A. de Viti de Marco, *La Guerra Europea* (Rome, 1918).
I. Bonomi, *Dieci Anni di Politica Italiana* (Milan, 1924).
F. Rubbiani, *Il Pensiero Politico di L. Bissolati* (Florence, 1921).
La Voce dei Popoli, edited by U. Zanotti-Bianco (Rome, 1919).

CHAPTERS TEN AND ELEVEN

A. Malatesta, *La Crisi Socialista* (Milan, 1923).
B. Mussolini, *Discorsi Politici* (Milan, 1921).

Early Fascism through friendly eyes:

A. Lanzillo, *Le rivoluzioni del dopo guerra* (Città di Castello, 1922).
A. Zerboglio and Dino Grandi, *Il Fascismo* (Bologna, 1921).
C. Pelizzi, *Problemi e Realtà del Fascismo* (Florence, 1924).
Odon Por, *Fascism* (London, 1923).

Early Fascism through critical eyes:

M. Vinciguerra, *Il Fascismo visto da un Solitario* (Turin, 1923).
L. Salvatorelli, *Nazionalfascismo* (Turin, 1923).
Three deputies, *Il Fascismo visto da Repubblicani e Socialisti* (Bologna, 1922).
P. Gobetti, *La Rivoluzione Liberale* (Bologna, 1922). Articles from Gobetti's famous periodical of the same title.

Catholic and Popular Party views:
V. G. Galati, *Religione e Politica* (Turin, 1925).
L. Sturzo, *La Libertà in Italia* (Turin, 1925) and *L'Italie et le Fascisme* (Paris, 1927).
F. L. Ferrari, *Lé Regime Fasciste Italien* (Brussels, 1928).
Marxist view:
Ignazio Silone, *Der Faschismus* (Zurich, 1934).
Liberal apologetic for Fascism:
C. Licitra, *Dal Liberalismo al Fascismo* (Rome, 1925).

CHAPTER TWELVE

The triumph of Fascism:
(Pro-Fascist)
G. Volpe, *Storia del Movimento Fascista* (Rome).
C. Giacchetti, *Fascismo Liberatore* (Florence, 1922).
P. Bolzon, *Le verghe e le scure* (Florence, 1923).
Curzio Suckert, *L'Italia Barbara* (Turin, 1924).
(Anti-Fascist)
M. Missiroli, *Il Colpo di Stato* (Turin, 1924).
C. A. D. Gualtieri, *Il Fascismo* (Turin, 1925).
E. Lussu, *Marcia su Roma e Dintorni* (Paris, 1931).
G. Ferrero, *Da Fiume a Roma* (Milan, 1923) and *La Democrazia in Italia* (Milan, 1925).
G. Amendola, *La Democrazia* (Rome, 1924).
G. Borgese, *Goliath, the March of Fascism* (London, 1938).
M. Ascoli, *Fascism—for whom?* (London, 1938).
A. Rossi, *The Rise of Italian Fascism* (London, 1938).

Non-Italian viewpoints:
Edgar Mowrer, *Immortal Italy* (New York, 1922).
Carleton Beals, *Rome or Death* (London, 1923).
M. Pernot, *L'Experience Italienne* (Paris, 1923).
J. W. Mannhardt, *Der Faschismus* (Munich, 1925).

The Rise of Fascism, in Fiction:
Ugo Ojetti, *Mio Figlio Ferroviere* (Milan, 1922).
G. A. Borgese, *Rube* (Milan, 1923).
P. Albatrelli, *I Conquistatori* (Rome, 1925).
I. Silone, *Fontamara* (London).

Newspapers and Periodicals:
It may be recalled that up to 1925 the newspaper Press of Italy was notable for literary brilliance and breadth of discussion,

especially the *Corriere della Sera* and *Secolo* (Milan), the *Stampa* (Turin) and the *Resto del Carlino* (Bologna).

La Critica, founded by B. Croce in 1903, gave a continuous record of Italian culture. *La Critica Sociale*, controlled by F. Turati and C. Treves, was the chief intellectual organ of the Socialists. *La Politica* was a solid quarterly devoted to the nationalist cause. *La Civiltà Cattolica*, organ of the Jesuits, interpreted the strict Catholic outlook. A weekly publication which immediately after the war won a central position in Italian politics, ending only with its suppression, and the death of its editor, P. Gobetti, was *La Rivoluzione Liberale* (Turin).

INDEX

AGNELLI, SENATOR: Head of Fiat firm, 196.

ALBERTINI, LUIGI: Owner of *Corriere della Sera*, starts by supporting Fascism, 202.

ALFIERI, VITTORIO: Restiveness against Piedmont, 21.

AMENDOLA, GIOVANNI: A counsellor of the *Corriere della Sera*, 140. Promotes Rome Congress of oppressed nationalities, 146.

ANTONELLI, Cardinal: Denounces occupation of Rome, 45.

ARDIGO, ROBERTO: Spiritual leader of the Positivists, 74. Assailed by Croce and Gentile, 96.

BALBO, ITALO: Fascist leader at Ferrara, 200.

BARATIERI, GENERAL ORESTE: Campaign on Red Sea, 67. Disaster at Adua, 68.

BENEDICT XV, Pope: Peace proposals, 1917, 138.

BISSOLATI, LEONIDA: Socialist leader; youthful influences on him, 74. Stands with Giolitti in Libyan War. Congratulates Victor Emmanuel on escaping from attempt on his life and, attacked by Mussolini, withdraws from Socialist party, 105. Minister in 1916, opposed to Sonnino's policy, 140, 150. During Wilson's visit resigns from Government and openly attacks Italian expansion programme, 151. Reviled by Mussolini, January 1919, 169.

BOMBACCI, NICOLO: Vice-Secretary of Socialist Party, arrested after Caporetto, 149. Insurrectionist agitation, 160. Elected deputy he reviles Parliament, 177.

BONOMI, IVANOE: Socialist politician, favours Libyan War, 104. Attacked by Mussolini withdraws from Socialist party, 105.

BORGESE, G. A.: A counsellor of the *Corriere della Sera*, 140. Quoted on Mussolini's breach with Bissolati, 168.

BOSELLI, PAOLO: Forms National Government, 1916, 138.

CADORNA, LUIGI: Chief of Italian Army, 138. Ruler of the 'war zone' of Northern Italy, 143. Disastrous disagreements with General Capello, 144. Issues communiqué notifying 'ignominious surrender' at Caporetto, 145.

CAIROLI, BENEDETTO: Lombard conspirator, 53. Forms Government, 1878, 54.

CALDARA: Socialist Mayor of Milan, war-time associate of Mussolini, 122.

CAPELLO, General: Commander of Second Army. Misunderstandings with Cadorna a cause of Caporetto disaster, 145.

CARLO ALBERTO: Heir to throne of Piedmont. His French upbringing, 22. Stakes claim of dynasty for throne of Italy, 24. Calls Gioberti to office, 30. Defeat and abdication, 30.

CAVALOTTI, FELICE: Politician and literary man, enemy of Crispi, 65. Raises 'the moral question,' 66, 69. Anti-Crispi demonstrations at his funeral, 69.

CAVOUR, CAMILLO: Encourages railway construction and concludes Anglo-Piedmontese Trade Treaty, 25. Champion of Free Trade, 26. Contempt for Mazzini, 35. Severity against Mazzinians and quarrel with Garibaldi, 40. Early death, 40.

CORRADINI, ENRICO: Initiator of Nationalist movement, 92.

CORRIDONI, FILIPPO: Syndicalist intellectual and organizer, founds first Fasci with Mussolini, 1915, 122.

CRESPI, SILVIO: Orlando's Minister of Supply, describes split in Cabinet on Peace Aims, 147.

CRISPI, FRANCESCO: Assists Garibaldi in Sicily, 38. Accepting the monarchy, breaks with Mazzini, 42. Joins Depretis Government, 1887, 61. Early career and character, 62-63. Oscillating Church policy, 64. Rage against France, 65. Detested by Extreme Left, 65. Assailed by Cavalotti, 65. 'The moral question,' 66. His repression of Sicily, 66. Claims Protectorate of Abyssinia, 67. Hectic policy in Africa, 68. Overthrown and execrated for Adua defeat, 1896, 69. Horror of Socialism, 70.

CROCE, BENEDETTO: Philosopher and public man. Embraces Socialism, 75. Repudiates Marxist doctrine, 95. Influence of his idealism, 95. Difference with Gentile, 96. As Giolitti's Minister of Education prepares School Reform, 191.

D'ANNUNZIO, GABRIELE: Poet. Elected Deputy of the Right, turns Socialist,

75. Condemned by Croce, 96. Tries out all doctrines in turn, 97. Background and influence, 98. Applauds Tripoli War, 100. His 'Radiant May' agitation, 131. Stage-managed overthrow of Giolitti, 134. Idolized by *Arditi*, is the most spectacular war hero, 166. Carries Mussolini in his wake, 167. Marches on Fiume, 170. Resumes flirting with Extreme Left, 173. Half-heartedly supported by Mussolini, 173. Influence of his Fiume régime on Fascism, 175.

DE MAISTRE, JOSEPH: Distrusted by Savoys, 21.

DEPRETIS, AGOSTINO: Piedmontese politician, 53. With Garibaldi in Sicily, 53. Head of Italian Government, 1876, 53. Dissatisfies the Left, 54. Back in office, 1877, 56. Inaugurates system of '*Trasformismo*,' 57. Promotes Triple Alliance, 59. Denounced by the Left for foreign and home policy, 59. Disgraced by Dogali tragedy, 61.

DE VITI DE MARCO, MARCHESE: Anti-Giolittian radical, 94.

DIAZ, GENERAL: Replaces Cadorna in Supreme Command, and remedies soldiers' grievances, 148.

FACTA, LUIGI: Last pre-Fascist Premier, 201.

FARINACCI, ROBERTO: Fascist leader at Cremona, 200.

FERRERO, GUGLIELMO: Author and political writer, implicated in student unrest, 75. After Caporetto demands policy of collaboration with South Slavs, 146.

FERRI, ENRICO: Positivist criminologist and Socialist leader, 74.

FORTIS, ALESSANDRO: Stopgap Premier for Giolitti, 79. Discredited by mishandling railway problem, 81.

FORTUNATO, GIUSEPPE: Southern deputy, attempts to clarify political principles of the Left, 58.

GARIBALDI, GIUSEPPE: Early adventures, 36. Co-operates with Cavour in 1856, 36. Expedition to Sicily and March on Naples, 38. Meets Victor Emmanuel II at Naples, 39. Imprisoned by Royal Italian Government, 43. Salutes Socialism as 'Sun of the Future,' 51. Dies, 1881, 56.

GENTILE, GIOVANNI: Philosopher and politician, 94. Association and breach with Croce, 96.

GIOBERTI, VINCENZO: His Turin background, 27. Adheres to *Giovine Italia*,

27. Exile and development of his ideas, 28. Return to Turin and rise to power, 29. Later federal theory, 31. Attitude to Cavour, 31.

GIOLITTI, GIOVANNI: Significance of his return to power in 1920, 12. Forms first Government in 1892 and 'makes' the elections, 65. Quarrel with Crispi and flight to Germany, 66. Early life and background, 77. Described as 'greatest statesman since Caesar,' 78. Second Premiership inaugurating his national ascendancy, 79. Refuses to interfere with 1903 general strike, 80. First electoral deal with Clericals, 80. Delegates Government to Fortis, 80. His 'long Ministry' of 1906-9, 81. Declares for universal manhood suffrage, 1911, 81. Forms fourth Government, 82. Working of his political machine, 84. Balancing foreign policy, 84. Electoral methods, 85. Mussolini on his system, 92. Giolitti's outlook on Tripoli (Libyan) War. New pact with Clericals in first manhood suffrage election, 1913, 108. Admits Salandra to office, 108. Giolitti's '*Parecchio*' letter against war, 127. Strained relations with Salandra, 127. Negotiations with Bülow, 128. Plans to resume power, 130. Final perfection of his Parliamentary technique, 131. Succumbs to violence and retreats to Piedmont, May 1915, 135. Regains prestige as war drags on, 138. Manœuvres against war party, 141. Regains office in 1920, 183. Tolerates occupation of factories, 184. Presides over victory celebrations, 1920, 187. Withdraws troops from Albania, 187. Winds up Fiume affair, 188. His last general elections, 191. Fails to re-establish his ascendancy and resigns, 1921, 191.

GRANDI, DINO: In 1915 foretells Second World War with Italy at Germany's side, 118. Fascist leader at Bologna in 1921, 200.

HUMBERT (UMBERTO I): King of Italy, 57.

JACINI, COUNT STEFANO (Milanese patriot): Opposes centralization, 48-49. Report on state of Italian agriculture (1881), 60, 208.

LABRIOLA, ARTURO: Leading Syndicalist, favours war as means to revolution, 101.

LAZZARI COSTANTINO: Founder of working men's Socialist group, 91. Patron of Mussolini in 1912, 105. Fired by example of Soviet Revolution, 149. Secretary of Socialist Party, 149. Arrested after Caporetto, 149.

LOMBROSO, CESARE: Positivist leader, 74.

LUZZATTI, LUIGI: Stopgap Premier for Giolitti, 79.

MAGLIANI, AGOSTINO: Disastrous conduct of Italian finance, 59–61.

MANCINI, PASQUALE: Foreign Minister with Depretis; utterance on Italy's Red Sea venture, 61.

MARINETTI, F. T.: Head man of the Italian Futurists, 97.

MAURRAS, CHARLES: Influence of his *Action Française* on Italian nationalists, 200.

MAZZINI, GIUSEPPE: Relation to Gioberti, 27. Genoa background, 32. View of Papacy, Empire, and Rome, 33. Hatred of Cavour, 34. Breach with Crispi, 47. Scorn for Cavour's successors, 50.

MENELIK (Emperor of Abyssinia): Subtle bargaining with Italy, 67.

MISSIROLI, MARIO: Says living-wage problem solved in Italy by 1919, 177. On Giolitti's last elections, 191.

MURRI, ROMOLO: Leader of Catholic Modernists, 91. Becomes a Fascist, 180.

MUSSOLINI, ALESSANDRO: Father of Benito, 51. His definition of Socialism, 69.

MUSSOLINI, BENITO: Nemesis of his Fascismo in 1943 and British attitude towards it, 10. His complex rôle, 15. Militant pacifist agitator in Libyan War, 101. Background in his native Romagna, 102. Early journalism and adventures, 103. Arrested as anti-war saboteur, 103. Spokesman for Socialist extremists 1912, 105. Editor of the *Avanti*, 106. Approach to Syndicalists, coldness between him and Marxists, 106. Associated with Turati in warning to warmongers, September 1914, 117. Sudden conversion to war cause, 120. Resigns from *Avanti* and is expelled by Socialists, 121. Founds *Popolo d'Italia* and swears vengeance, 121. Joins Corridoni to form first *Fasci*, 122. Regarded, in 1916–17, as being on the anti-nationalist side in the conflict over Italy's war policy, 141. Ardent support of President Wilson in January 1919, 151. Programme of revolution through war, 163. His position and ambitions after the war, 164–165. Reviles Bissolati, 169. Tricky relations with D'Annunzio in Fiume affair, 173. Their characters contrasted, 174. His debt to D'Annunzio's rhetoric, 175. How his post-war outlook developed,

193. Embarks upon parliamentary intrigue, 195. Embarrassed by Agrarian influx into Fascism, 198. Signs truce with Socialists, August 1921, 199. Negotiations with Salandra, Giolitti, and Nitti, in 1922, 201.

NAPOLEON BONAPARTE: Makes Milan capital of 'Kingdom of Italy,' 24.

NAPOLEON III (LOUIS NAPOLEON): Alliance with Cavour against Austria, 35. Strikes at Austria, 1859, 36. Alarm at Italian Unity, compounds with Austria, 37. Napoleonic dynasty in Naples, 38.

NATHAN: Mayor of Rome, 91.

NICOTERA, GIOVANNI (of Calabria): Mazzinian insurrectionary, 53.

NITTI, FRANCESCO: Regarded as a semi-Giolittian in Boselli Government, 141. Most powerful member of Orlando Government, 145. Background and character: becomes first post-war Premier, 157. Fair conduct of general elections, 158. Bugbear of ex-combatants, 181. Ousted by Giolitti, 183.

ORLANDO, V. E.: Member of Boselli Government, 141. Forms Government after Caporetto, 145. Patronizes Rome Congress of oppressed nationalities, 147. Holds scales between Sonnino and Bissolati, 150. Superseded by Nitti, 157.

PELLOUX, GENERAL: Premier, 1898, his repressive conduct, 70. Persecutes Socialist students, 74. Overthrown, 75.

PIUS IX, POPE: Admires Gioberti, 30. Flees from Rome, and takes refuge with King of Naples, 31. Dies, 1878, 56.

PIUS X, POPE: Hunts down the Catholic Modernists, 93.

POLLIO, GENERAL: Chief of Italian Staff, discusses Italian aid to Germany in case of European War, 113.

SALANDRA, ANTONIO: Admitted to Premiership by Giolitti, 1913, 108. Uses strong hand against Romagna disorders, 109. Growth of his authority due to war, 124. Negotiations with both sides preceding entry into war, 128.

SALVEMINI, GAETANO: Historian and polemist. His exposure of Giolitti's method of rule, 85. Advocate of collaboration with South Slavs, 146.

SAN GIULIANO, MARCHESE DI: Giolitti's Foreign Minister, stays on with Salandra, 110. Death, October 1914, 124.

SARFATTI, MARGHERITA: Intimate of Mussolini, 104, 106.

SFORZA, COUNT CARLO: Giolitti's Foreign Minister in 1921, makes settlement with Yugoslavia, 188.

SONNINO, SIDNEY: Interest in Sicilian peasants, 70. Urges exercise of power by monarchy, 71. His stopgap Premierships, 79, 81. Becomes Foreign Minister, October 1914. Negotiates with Central Powers and with Entente, 128. His policy of 'Italy's Own War' against Austria, 137. Finally declares war on Germany, August 1916, 138. Clings to Treaty of London in 1918, 149. Conflict with Bissolati, 150. Peace negotiator in Paris, 151. Obstinate maintenance of London programme, 155.

STURZO, DON LUIGI: Priest and politician, quoted on Italian party politics, 76. Mayor of Caltagirone. Pioneer of Italian Catholic political organization, 94. Welds Catholic bodies into new Popular Party, 180. His existence a menace to Giolitti, 190.

TOSTI, MONSIGNOR: Discusses Church-State question with Crispi, 64.

TREVES, CLAUDIO: Socialist leader, attitude to Giolitti, 104. Forced out of editorship of Avanti, 1912, and replaced after an interval by Mussolini, 106. Proclaims, July 1917, 'Out of the trenches!', 142.

TURATI, FILIPPO: Socialist Leader. His beginnings, 74. Difference with Giolitti over Libyan War, 104. Joins Mussolini, September 1914, in warning Italian 'warmongers,' 117. Defines

Socialist war aims as to repair ravages and alleviate sufferings, 141. Declares defence of Monte Grappa is sacred to Socialists, 145. Works for national unity, 148. Approached by 'bourgeois' leaders in 1920, 185.

VICTOR EMMANUEL II. Accedes to throne of Piedmont, 22. Choice of Ministers, 52. Dies, 1878, 56.

VICTOR EMMANUEL III. Calls Zanardelli to office, showing sensitiveness to democratic currents, 75. His authority enlarged by outbreak of European War, 125. Emancipation from omnipotence of Giolitti 132. Overriding Parliament confirms Salandra in office, 135. Prevents subordination of Italian Army to French command, 146. Insulted by Socialist Parliamentarians, 176. Agreement with Fascists preceding March on Rome, 201. Threatened with deposition, 201.

VILLARI, PASQUALE: Neapolitan patriot, 52.

VOLPE, GIOIACCHINO: Approved historian of Fascism, describes composition of first Fasci, 194.

WILSON, PRESIDENT: His doctrines applauded by Italian democrats, and particularly by Benito Mussolini, 147. Visits Italy, January 1919, 151.

ZANARDELLI, GIUSEPPE: Leader of rebels at Brescia, 1848 and 1859, 53. Minister of Interior, 54. Passion for liberty, 55, 76. Contrasted with Giolitti, 88. Divorce law proposal, 76, 88.